W9-AQE-364

The Myth of
the Middle Class

*notes
on
affluence
and
equality*

The Myth
of the
Middle Class

Foreword by
G. William
Domhoff

RICHARD
PARKER

LIVERIGHT

New York

ST. PHILIPS COLLEGE LIBRARY

301.44
P242m

Copyright © 1972 by Richard Parker.

All rights reserved.
No part of this book may be reproduced
in any form without permission
in writing
from the publisher.

1.987654321

ISBN: 0-87140-539-3
LC Number: 76-167291

Manufactured in the United States of America
Designed by Madeline Caldiero

to my parents,
for the reasons those who
love them know

27015

Acknowledgements

The thanks I need to offer can only begin here. First, I must thank Gilbert Harrison, publisher of *The New Republic*, who approached me solely on the basis of an article I had done and asked me to write this book. Second are my tutors at Oxford, whose helpful comments (including disagreements) have made this a much better book than it would have been. Then there are my friends: William Domhoff, Andreas Papandreou, Grant Crandall, Mike Hathaway, Stan and Betty Sheinbaum, David Olsen, and Nell Wheeler, all of whom by their advice and concern deeply shaped the character and argument of this book. And there is Jill, who knows best why I thank her.

Contents

Foreword by G. William Domhoff *ix*

Introduction *xv*

1. America the Beautiful *3*
2. The Affluent Fifties: Approaching the Gates of Heaven *18*
3. The Sixties: The New Class Comes of Age *35*
4. Looking Backward I: America Before the Fifties *51*
5. Looking Backward II: The Prosperity Decade *74*
6. Contemporary America: The Poverty of New Beginnings *92*
7. The Rich *115*
8. The Lower Middle Class *134*
9. The Upper Middle Class *153*
10. The New Class and the Seventies *167*
11. Equality and Affluent America *186*

Appendix *209*

Notes *217*

Index *227*

Foreword

There is no more myth-shrouded aspect of our society than the pyramid of income and wealth. Throughout the fifties and sixties we were told again and again by social scientists and public relations men that the poor were no longer with us—or that they were about to be elevated into affluence by benevolent government programs. Conversely, we heard incessantly that the big rich were being eliminated, after all these years, by confiscatory taxes. We were asked to believe, in short, that we are part of one big happy middle class society which is on the march to equality in income and wealth.

Richard Parker's *The Myth of the Middle Class* deals effectively with these—and many other—myths. His book is extremely timely, for it comes in a period when some people may be interested in a few facts and figures to help them make sense out of the harsh socioeconomic realities that continue to exist all around them—ineradicable poverty, a loop-hole-riddled tax system that favors the few truly wealthy, subsidies for large corporations, and wage controls for everyone but big executives and independent professionals while prices continue to rise.

It should be stressed that Parker's grim statistics are on the conservative side. This is because every study he has had to rely on has made the most cautious possible estimates at the many junctures where judgments must be made in order to construct what *seem* to be very precise statistics. There is no better way to make this point than to note that a careful interview-study of rich people in one large midwestern city concluded that the findings of even the best previous studies tend to seriously underestimate the amount of wealth held by the super-rich.[1]

Not only is the wealth of the very wealthy underestimated, but so is their income. This is shown in an excellent but little-known study by economist James D. Smith. Using government statistics as the basis for his estimates, and including the income from capital gains that is left out in many surveys, Smith concludes that in 1958 the 1.5% who own 30.2% of all privately held wealth (including 75.9% of all privately held corporate stock) also received 24% (!) of the total national income for that year.[2]

These are stunning statistics, highlighting by contrast that what most Americans have underneath their middle-class affluence are car payments, house payments, furniture payments, and a job. If the job goes, so too the material goods. The "new" middle class, unlike the middle class of small farmers and small businessmen that used to exist in the United

1. George Katona and John B. Lansing, "The Wealth of the Wealthy," *Review of Economics and Statistics,* February, 1964.

2. James D. Smith, "An Estimate of the Income of the Very Rich," *Papers in Quantitative Economics* (University of Kansas Press, 1968). There is every reason to believe that the wealth distribution has continued to concentrate since that time.

States, is a class of propertyless paper pushers and people manipulators who must go along to get along. No wonder most Americans dutifully toe the line drawn for them by their corporate masters.

Reading *The Myth of the Middle Class* reminded me once again that there is one other basic problem that is fogged in by confusion in our society. That is the problem of power: who has it and what is it used for? The reasons for the confusion are similar. The mythmakers would have it that no one group, such as the big rich, has an undue amount of power in America. All the talk about a ruling class or a power elite refers, at best, to a bygone era that was ended forever by Franklin D. Roosevelt and the New Deal. We are assured, as in the case of income and wealth, that the United States is a middle class society with a benign dispersal of power among competing middle class groups who check and balance each other.

The mythmakers cited by Richard Parker in this book once again play a role in perpetuating this incredible notion. And one of the ways they do it is to ignore the fact that wealth and power are closely connected. Indeed, the wealth and income distributions are rarely mentioned when power is discussed. Most American inquiries adopt instead an individualistic view of power in which the concern is with the ability of an individual to induce others to do his bidding. This way of thinking about power turns attention to studies of specific "issues" in an effort to see who initiated, vetoed, or supported a given proposal, and it has no place for the wealth or income of social groups as important power indicators.

An individualistic approach to social power is a dead end. While a few social scientists are waking up to this fact, even they pull back from using the income and wealth distributions as power indicators. Typical of this backing and filling is an essay by political scientist William C. Mitchell which announces a "new" approach to political power studies. Mit-

chell acknowledges the problems of the individualistic approach by suggesting that "perhaps it is more useful and easier
to determine power structures by who gets what and how
much of the output than to identify power by who governs." [3]
He then goes on to state a method of studying power which
in principle gives proper attention to such indicators as wealth
and income: "Let us try defining power not as one who makes
decisions but as who gets how much from the system. Those
who acquire the largest share of the goods, services, and opportunities are those who have the most power." [4]

Mitchell is thus on the verge of conceding the importance
of the wealth and income distributions in inferring the locus
of power, but he soon retreats into the kind of myopia that
The Myth of the Middle Class relentlessly exposes. That is,
Mitchell points to a narrowly-conceived study which suggests that poor people get more from the government than
they put in, and that the rich pay more to government than
they receive back. He sees this as a refutation of the view that
a small power elite dominates our government: "One might
additionally speculate that it is an interesting political situation when the "power elites" permit the lower income groups
to have more favorable or net balances with the government,
while they incur deficits." [5]

In light of the income and wealth distributions that *The
Myth of the Middle Class* reveals in American society, Mitchell's statement is amazingly shortsighted. However, it is
not atypical. Too many people not only mythologize the
disparities of wealth and income, they mystify and muddle
power relationships by detaching them from wealth and
well-being statistics. They cannot accept the implications

3. William C. Mitchell, "The Shape of Political Theory To Come: From
Political Sociology to Political Economy." In Seymour M. Lipset, editor,
Politics and the Social Sciences (Oxford University Press, 1969), page 114.
4. *Ibid.*
5. *Ibid.*, page 119.

of a finding such as that of James D. Smith, cited earlier, which conservatively estimates that 1.5% of the people own at least 30.2% of all privately held wealth and receive at least 24% of the yearly national income.

Richard Parker's fine book, I am here contending, is not only about wealth and income. It is also about power.

G. WILLIAM DOMHOFF

University of California
Santa Cruz, California
May 9, 1972

Introduction

After World War II it became popular to describe America as the Affluent Society and to believe that the unprecedented level of material abundance enjoyed by the middle class had made many traditional problems irrelevant. Poverty was declared an afterthought, and politics was said to be facing an "end of ideology." Gains in education and technology and the growth of a new class of managers and professionals were supposed to be the first steps toward an automated society where leisure, not work, would be a burden.

All of this was a distortion of reality. The trends that were identified influenced a part, but not all of society. The negative aspects of the Affluent Society were downplayed or ignored. When poverty was "rediscovered" and malnutrition was shown to affect millions, they were treated as temporary paradoxes or oversights, rather than as possibly endemic features of American society. This myth of the Affluent Society still enjoys wide popularity.

The effect has been a myopia which ignores or distorts serious issues of social justice. Today the combined wealth of the country's 200 richest citizens is greater than the Gross National Product of any nation in black Africa, yet the average factory worker takes home $100 a week. The richest ten percent of Americans enjoy more income each year than the poorest half. Two percent of the nation's populace controls one-third of the nation's wealth, while nearly half of American families have less than $500 in savings, and a fifth of American families have none.

This situation is shocking because it defies not only the myth of the Affluent Society, but the more fundamental conception of America as a middle-class nation. America's image is of tree-lined suburbs and two-car garages. Yet one-third of the country still lives in poverty, and one-half lives below a budget that the government calls only "modestly comfortable." Somewhere there has been a profound distortion of reality.

The Myth of the Middle Class argues that this distortion stems from the very notion of the middle class, from the traditional American rejection of class terminology, and from the insistence upon equality as a prominent characteristic of American society.

But more important is the further distortion by members of what John Kenneth Galbraith once called the New Class. Building on their own very special affluence after World War II, the members of this class have generalized their experience into the myth of an equalitarian, middle-class Affluent Society. Relieved by the end of the depression and the war, anxious to find good in an America they thought menaced by Communism, they made predictions about this country that have since proved drastically wrong.

For example, they predicted a lessening inequality of income and wealth as the economy grew; instead the distribution of income and wealth has remained virtually unchanged, and may even be worsening. They predicted the disappearance of poverty; instead the poor, despite misleading government statistics, are as numerous as ever and show little likelihood of disappearing in our lifetime. They predicted growing educational and work opportunities for all; instead, as late as 1985 only one in eight Americans will have graduated from college, although education is increasingly the sole means of achieving enjoyable, well-paying work.

All this leads to a fundamental reappraisal of our images of American life. Postwar American society was much more a continuation of older trends than a radical break with the past. The belief that America has only recently emerged from a long period of majority poverty is false; rather America seems to have been a nation of the middle class since prerevolutionary times. *But* the term "middle class" is used here to mean not a hypothetical majority of prosperous and secure individuals, but the two separate groups within it: the upper and lower middle classes. The awareness of these two distinct classes between rich and poor gives a much more realistic picture of America than does the notion of a single homogeneous middle class.

This reappraisal of economic classes should make the reader aware that traditional arguments about poverty, deprivation, opportunity, and equality all remain as critical as they were a hundred years ago. By carefully examining the present state of poverty and deprivation, and its permanence since pre-Revolutionary times, it becomes obvious that reform measures have hardly begun to scratch the surface of needed social change. And by examining the two means of economic reform open to a privately-owned industrial society—taxation and growth—the likelihood of some future incremental reform is discounted.

The Myth of the Middle Class also examines the rich and

the upper middle class as well as the poor and the deprived. There *is* affluence in America, but it is sharply limited to the upper two groups, and not available to the vast majority. Surveying the extent and level of wealth in this country lends credence to Fitzgerald's famous claim that the very rich are different from you and me. And scrutinizing the unique well-being of the upper middle class, one can see why many of its New Class members believe that the Affluent Society is now being transcended by the Opulent Society. What one cannot see, however, is how this new opulence will ever reach those below.

The book concludes with a chapter that discusses the issue around which all the preceding chapters turn—equality. Tracing usage of the term from the American Revolution to the present reveals a clear process of dilution at work. Originally meant by many of the Founding Fathers to encompass not only the procedural equality of due process and equal access to the law, but also a broad economic equality that would abolish both rich and poor, equality gradually became "equality of opportunity," and was used to justify many of the Social Darwinist policies of the nineteenth and early twentieth centuries. Since World War II, however, even that limited sense of equality has been lost in a broad silence, and subordinated to standards of efficiency and technological rationality. After all, as many writers in the fifties seemed to say: What is the relevance of economic equality in a society where all are affluent?

Set against the actual conditions, however, that question becomes absurd. Since America is not simply the Affluent Society, since malnutrition and poverty coexist with enormous wealth, and since the middle class is a term which may describe a family that is only one step ahead of poverty or a family one step short of riches, the issue of economic equality remains as crucial as it was to Jefferson and Paine. Ultimately, the book does not show how we may achieve that equality, but it does show what stands in its way. The solution is absent only because it requires not new ideas, but new will, and that will must come from the majority itself. Returning equality to the vocabulary of Americans is only the first step; whatever further steps are taken, only the American people may decide.

The general reader may at first be confused by the dates attached to some of the statistics. For example, most figures are for 1968, 1969, and 1970, but some wealth or liquid assets statistics are taken from 1965 or even 1962. This is not a deliberate attempt to hide unfavorable data, but the result of irregular investigation on the part of government and academics. For example, the Federal Reserve Board's study of consumer finances has not been updated since 1962. In all cases I have tried to use the most recent data available. Where dating might make a difference, I have carefully noted the age of the information. As the reader will soon recognize, however, the sad fact of unchanging inequalities has meant that these notations are of little significance: *plus tout change, plus rien ne change.*

Secondly, the general reader may feel that at certain points the book has illicitly fused (or confused) affluence and inequality. Thus, it is imaginable that a country might have an unequal distribution of income and wealth, while everyone in it was still affluent. Imaginable, yes; but in America today, not true. The book fuses the two issues of affluence and equality precisely to demonstrate that such a state of affairs is not our own. Furthermore, I doubt that Americans can be universally affluent without also being equal. I doubt it not only for historical reasons, but for several theoretical reasons, well known to economists, having to do with the distribution of factor shares and the behavior of investment, but which I felt were too technical to be handled well in a nontechnical book.

Economists may have questions or doubts of their own. The field of welfare economics (which covers most of the issues I raise in this book) has long had a notorious reputation as something of a dead end. When one accepts marginalist theory, and with it the concept of Pareto optimality, the ability to talk about the need for radical shifts in the distribution of income and wealth suddenly disappears. One can express an opinion about one's preferred distribution, but trying to prove its preferability to economists inside the apparatus of marginalism is nearly impossible. Efficiency, not equality, is the god of economics, and efficiency is a jealous god.

I have ignored the usual apparatus of welfare economics —the Gini coefficients, the Edgeworth boxes—because in the final analysis I think they do little to help the public understand the problem. Determination of factor shares and the distribution of wealth may have an economic dimension, but they also have political solutions (almost, I might add, because economics has failed to provide its own). The issue is an empirical one: by normal standards, many people are poor and many others are deprived, while a few have enormous wealth. This is a situation I find offensive, and one which I think needs to be made known. It will remain unknown as long as it hides in technical language in technical journals.

Finally, sociologists may wonder why I make almost no mention of the working class as distinct from the middle class. I have not done so, for studies of self-classification show that the overwhelming majority of Americans publicly call themselves middle class, whether technician or laborer, blue-collar or white-collar. I am concerned with this image of America, and not the classification system of social science. "Working class" is a term that might make sense in Europe, where many still consider themselves members of the working class, but here it is artificial. What needs to be made known is the wide disparity of life styles that all pass for "middle class."

The Myth of
the Middle Class

1 | America the Beautiful

If you were living in America during the 1950s, there was a theme you heard endlessly repeated: America is the Affluent Society. Television showed it, professors lectured on it, advertising blared it, the government collected statistics to prove it. America—the Affluent Society.

America had the world's largest Gross National Product. America had the world's highest per capita income. America had more cars, more televisions, more telephones than the rest of the world combined. Americans ate better, dressed better, received better educations and better medical care than any other people in the world. They lived in better homes in nicer communities, enjoyed more leisure, travelled more widely than anyone else. And as if this were not enough, life was going to become better still: automation would gradually take over more and more work, and gains in technology and management would remove the vestiges of burdensome re-

ST. PHILIPS COLLEGE LIBRARY

sponsibilities, leaving us all free to realize our creative potential as human beings.

Furthermore the Affluent Society was unique in man's history because unlike previous societies, the affluence was shared by all. Whereas past societies had divided into the rich and the poor, America was a country in which the vast majority shared the wealth. In ancient and feudal worlds, only a tiny handful had enjoyed such well-being; in modern America the cornucopia flowed for all. Here even the poorest family had a car and a television, and the vast majority had much, much more. Poverty was an "afterthought" in America; for 70% to 90% of the country, the problem was no longer how to acquire more goods, but what to do with the overabundance of goods they already had. In short, modern America was no longer a nation, like others, divided between rich and poor, but a nation of one homogeneously prosperous middle class.

The promise that this uniform middle class affluence held out was stupendous. In place of the conflict which had characterized human societies from their birth, the Affluent Society would be conflict-free. Because the economic deprivation which had caused so many wars and rebellions was gone, decisions would be reached by rational discussion and efficient planning. Debates would no longer be over the quantity of life, but over the quality of life, and on such questions the society could reach peaceful answers. America, as one writer expressed it, would be the first nation in man's history to put an end to ideology. Barring some international holocaust or some horrible accident of nature, America's future would represent the culmination of all men's dreams for a peaceful and prosperous life.

Today, in the early 1970s, it is hard to find anyone who holds such a completely sanguine vision of America. The sixties reintroduced conflict on a massive scale: war, assassination, riot, and rebellion filled the pages of newspapers. The deaths of a president, a presidential candidate, and a major civil rights leader, plus the deaths of nearly 50,000 Americans in battle are landmarks of the last decade. Widespread poverty and even malnutrition has likewise been rediscovered, dealing a heavy blow to the image of homogeneous affluence. Important cities are said to be in a state of crisis, and there is dark talk of impending massive ecological disasters. The tone of today's social commentators is one of gnawing doubt rather than unlimited hope.

But surprisingly this new tone of doubt does not represent a rejection or even a serious modification of the earlier hopeful vision of a homogeneously affluent America; instead it represents an amendment or deferment of that vision. The Vietnam War is viewed as an accidental involvement, unconnected to the structure of America. The crisis of the cities is seen as the result of rising expectations and the relative starvation of the public sector of the economy. The ecology crisis is thought to be a direct outgrowth of America's very affluence—that is, a crisis related to overabundant production and the rapacious consumption of natural resources. Even poverty, which would seem to contradict the notion of affluence most directly, is incorporated into the affluence consciousness by its popular acceptance as a crisis of racial minorities—of black, brown, and red Americans. Only racial discrimination excludes them from the general prosperity.

In other words, the basic image of the Affluent Society in the 1970s is still intact. A recent best seller, Charles Reich's *The Greening of America*, even goes so far as to reject issues of economics as passé, and to lump 80% of Americans into the category "Consciousness I," thereby suggesting the uniformity of both their consciousness and their material condition. Another best seller, Alvin Toffler's *Future Shock*, reasserts earlier postwar images of America by resting social analysis on issues of technology and science, and by arguing that the future requires maintaining and managing an already abundant society. (The fact that Toffler is more ambivalent about the future than many earlier writers does not lead him to challenge their basic attitudes.) In academic journals and textbooks one finds much the same thing: on the one hand, an attempt to reevaluate the goals and character of America, but on the other, an almost matter-of-fact acceptance of its middle-class well-being.

The tenacity of this vision is all the more remarkable because some very authoritative critics have rejected it. Paul Samuelson, Nobel laureate in economics, has warned against thinking that America's wealth is broadly shared by the majority. Displaying his special sense for graphic illustration, he observed of the present income structure: "If we made an income pyramid out of a child's blocks, with each layer portraying $1,000 of income, the peak would be far higher than the Eiffel Tower, but almost all of us would be within a yard of the ground."

Samuelson realized that his description ran counter to popular belief, and sought to buttress his position by further elaboration: "In the absence of statistical knowledge, it is understandable that one should form an impression of the American standard of living from the full-page magazine advertisements portraying a jolly American family in an air-conditioned mansion, with a Buick, a station wagon, a motor launch, and all the other good things that go to make up comfortable living. Actually, of course, this sort of life is still beyond the grasp of 90 percent of the American public." [1]

Yet in America to be middle class is to have "arrived" for the great majority. Few have the possibility of reaching beyond that point, and in a country specifically founded on the desirability of being middle class, few feel it necessary. However this description is appropriated by all sorts of very different people: those who earn $50,000 a year and those who earn $5,000 a year; by college teachers and corporate executives, and by day laborers and file clerks. The distance between these is obvious, but is daily obscured by the meaninglessness of the term itself. Being middle class can mean comfort bordering on opulence; but it can also mean outright poverty, or deprivation that is only one step removed from poverty.

1

Today, the lower boundary of the American middle class is an income slightly below $4,000 a year, the federal government's definition of poverty for an urban family of four. The upper boundary is more difficult to locate because those who, on the basis of income, are rich compared to most Americans, rarely differentiate themselves. *Fortune* magazine illustrated the difficulty in defining the rich by observing that "a man earning, say, $40,000 a year may be hard to distinguish from a man earning $10,000 or $15,000 a year. He is rarely conspicuous in his consumption or ostentatious in his possessions." [2] *Fortune* notwithstanding, a distinction still exists; whether immediately apparent in his spending patterns, life style, goals, or sense of security, the middle class man earning $40,000 is unalterably distinct from his middle class confrere earning $4,000.

Social scientists, having generally conceded the myth by accepting both men as middle class, have however gone on to differentiate between "upper" and "lower" middle classes. This avoids the awkwardness of using a single term to describe two very divergent kinds of lives. But what exactly is a *lower* as opposed to an *upper* middle class, and how do these two very crudely defined groups relate to the rich and the poor who constitute the remainder of our society?

For the sake of argument let us presume the following: that the poor constitute the bottom fifth, and the rich, the upper tenth of the population. Since the government (using its own standards) estimates that poverty afflicts less than 13% of the population, and since the upper tenth includes all those with incomes over $18,000, we can safely assume that we are using a conservative estimate of the size of the middle class. If anything, the remaining seventy percent of the population should show more affluence than if we had chosen a broader model.[3]

Accepting the simple division between the upper and the lower middle class, let us assign the seventy percent by a simple halving. In 1968—the last year for which statistics are available—the upper middle class received 46% of the nation's total money income. In the same year, the lower middle class received 22% or, in other words, less than half the amount received by the upper group.

The situation becomes even more striking if we incorporate the data for rich and poor. According to the Census Bureau, the richest tenth of the country in 1968 received 27% of the money income, while the poorest *fifth* got only 5%. *Stated slightly differently this means that the richest 10% of Americans in 1968 received more money income than the entire bottom half of the population.* Clearly, economic equality is not a prominent characteristic of contemporary American society.

But inequality of income is only one part of the problem in the myth of the middle class in America. For example, liquid assets—checking and savings accounts, shares in saving-and-loan banks, credit unions, and government savings bonds —are strong measures of a family's cushion against disaster and its ability to plan major investment for the future (such as college education for the children). But in 1969, one fifth of the population owned no liquid assets whatsoever, and nearly half of the population had less than $500. Less than a third had more than $2,000. If a father was suddenly put out of work, if a family member suffered injuries requiring long-term care, or if a child won admission to a prestigious college or university, the carefully gathered savings of a lifetime could be quickly wiped out.[4]

Wealth also reflects the imbalance shown in unequal distribution of income. To an economist, the wealth of a family is the sum of its assets—its home, its car, its savings and investments—minus its debts on those assets. Among the rich and the upper middle class, the amount of wealth was understandably large: among those earning ten to fifteen thousand dollars a year in 1962, two-thirds were worth more than $10,000, and the mean was a comfortable $28,000. Among the lower middle class, however, wealth was less generously distributed. The mean was half that of the ten-to-fifteen thousand group, and over half the group were worth less than $6,000. If we recall that wealth includes the value of ownership in the family house and car, $6,000 is paltry indeed.[5]

For those who survived the Depression, figures like these may not seem shocking. But few people judge their present prosperity by the standards of thirty years ago. What these figures mean is that for the poor, life is marginal, and for the lower middle class, danger is never far away. Income is annual, and is spent heavily for the day-to-day maintenance of life; liquid assets and debt purchasing are the chief means for the accumulation of comforts, such as additional appliances, a car, or a college education. And debt purchasing, whatever its popularity, can impose not only exorbitant costs in the form of inflated interest charges, but a heavier psychological burden in the loss of a sense of freedom.

2

In the fifties, a great deal of attention was paid to the transition from the primacy of blue-collar work to white-collar work. Sociologists and popular magazines considered it the harbinger of a great social revolution, the movement to the "postindustrial" society. Theorists saw the growth of the service industries as an early sign of the leisure society that was supposed to be just over the horizon. As automation increased, the number of blue-collar jobs would continue to decline, and the service sector would continue to grow.

The thesis was correct as far as it went, but it overlooked

two important facts: even if both automation and services continue to expand, there is no way to imagine the disappearance of blue-collar workers in this century; more ominously, income for service workers as a whole is lower than income for blue-collar workers, and by a sizeable amount. In many cases, transition from an industrial to a postindustrial economy may mean not an advance for the lower middle class worker, but simply a lateral movement symbolized by a change in the color of his uniform. As a case in point, the hourly wage in the retail trades actually declined as a percentage of the wages in manufacturing between 1940 and the late 1960s.

Today there are approximately thirty-five million blue-collar workers in America. As a group they have made significant gains since the beginning of this century, gains that have won widespread applause from social reformers and political theorists. But how substantial and enduring are these gains? Industrial sociologist Arthur Shostak, in his recent study *Blue-Collar Life*, has suspicions about the working man's economic status:

> On a first reading the record encourages admiration for the progress apparently made by blue-collarites. . . . On a second and more careful reading, however, admiration for these gains gives way to concern for their durability.[6]

Shostak concludes that blue-collar prosperity is precariously supported by heavy installment debt and rapidly declining purchasing power. (The take-home pay of a factory worker was smaller in 1970 than in 1965, because of inflation.) The husband's job is uncertain because of technological displacement and stiffer educational requirements. The wife's role is also unstable, because she frequently has had to enter the labor force in order to provide for the family, and finds the dual life of worker and wife-mother difficult to manage. Even the children, who are supposed to have benefitted from increased educational opportunity, have not been as successful as imagined. "Blue-collar children may spend more years in school," Shostak dourly observes, "but high-quality educational content and not time alone influences postschool achievement."

For the blue-collar worker over forty, there is also the nagging memory of the Depression. Many workers feel equally pressured by unending alterations in their own work. Shostak says that "a vast majority of all manual workers are reveling in their persistent fantasies about escaping the factory, and in their hope that their sons will not follow them into blue-collar work." For those who dwell in the larger cities and in adjoining suburbs, there is the further tension of "encroaching" blacks or other nonwhites. Many times the single debt-free possession of any consequence is the worker's home, and in it he has invested not only his labor but a major portion of his psychic status. To feel constantly pressured from "below," to be constantly reminded of the world from which many came and to which one might so easily return, can be a traumatizing experience for those living on the edge as so many blue-collarites do.

This continuous tension shows itself in many ways. The blue-collarites have a high separation and divorce rate. Their children have high dropout rates and high arrest records. They labor under the weight of "an alarming incidence of little-treated physical and mental illness."

Shostak's study is doubly disturbing not only because it excludes both women and nonwhites—who in general do worse than white male workers economically—but also because, as Shostak himself admits, "these observations . . . refer only to the unique situation of the minority of better-off, modernistic, suburban-dwelling blue-collarites. The vast majority of Caucasian male blue-collarites and their dependents are still less well-off on all counts." And in case anyone has misunderstood Shostak's message, he concludes:

With respect to most blue-collarites, one comes finally to admire not so much accomplishment as endurance and to envy not so much achievement as persistence. Pathos and "affluence" to the contrary, blue-collarites today in America are *not* especially well-off. Many know this and vaguely sense that somehow things ought to "feel" better. How to make things better eludes almost all of them.[7]

3

But if the lower middle class is to be characterized by endurance, the upper middle class is definitely not. The upper middle class may at one time have merely endured; today it has conquered.

For those families earning between $10,000 and $25,000, life displays many of the accoutrements of affluence that many believe to be the property of all. Just as the lower middle class is dominated by the blue-collar and service worker, so the upper middle class is dominated by professionals and managers. One-quarter of the U.S. labor force is made up of professional and technical workers, managers, officials, and proprietors. At first glance this is not at all remarkable: the professionals and managers have dominated the upper segment of the income scale for decades. Nor is it remarkable, because of all the discussion about it, that the professionals and managers have been steadily increasing in number. This increase has in fact been the subject not so much of discussion as of constant praise. It has provided the foundation for feverish speculation about postindustrial life, and as depicted in *The Organization Man* and other such books, has been used as a paradigm of that future life.

But the speculation has been too naive and too optimistic. It overlooks the fact that all men cannot be managers or professionals, and that the upper middle class, instead of merging into a hazy continuum with the lower middle class, has accentuated its differences and raised its admission standards. It would probably be more accurate to say that the professionals and managers display a closer identification with the rich than with the old middle class, and that they see each other as self-conscious members of Galbraith's New Class.

For several years immediately after World War II, optimism was generated by statistics showing a merging of workers' and professionals' incomes. In general, lower groups of workers seemed to be making much faster gains than income groups above them. In some circles, this tendency was even seen as a harbinger of declining income inequality on a vast scale. But what such optimism failed to take into account were the unusual circumstances under which such gains had been made. Wartime conditions, the scarcity of labor, and fat government contracts all accelerated the lower wage levels; once the war was over, however, normal relations began to reassert themselves, and the tendency of lower-paid workers to make more rapid gains than managers and professionals reversed itself by the mid-fifties. Thus, for example, between 1950 and 1960 the median wages for service workers and laborers rose 39%, while for professionals and managers the median rose 68%.[8]

We can see the consequence of these statistics in a different way if we consider the expected earnings of a high school versus a college graduate. In 1968, the median annual income of high school graduates was slightly over $8,000; college graduates, on the other hand, had a median income of nearly $13,000.[9] Projected over a lifetime, this means that the family of a high school graduate will enjoy $230,000 less income than the family of a college graduate. When measured in terms of housing, clothing, education, medical care, or any other index, this is an enormous sum.

The knowledge that his income will continue to rise substantially and evenly allows the upper-middle-class professional or manager to do things which, in lower-middle-class households, would cause financial havoc. For instance, indebtedness has become a crucial way of obtaining the necessities of modern civilization—a house, a car, most major appliances, even health care involves a willingness and ability to sustain long-term indebtedness. For families earning between $10,000 and $15,000 in 1962, fully 55% had debts totalling more than $5,000. By contrast, among those families earning between $3,000 and $5,000 (remember that in 1962 the dividing line between poor and lower middle class was $3,000), two-thirds did not even have liquid assets over $500, and hence could not even afford to contemplate indebtedness on the scale of the upper middle class.[10]

There is a further point to be made about the income of the upper middle class. An income that is, say, X dollars above the national median is very different from an income which is X dollars below it. Living decently requires basic expenditures which consume a large and relatively constant amount of income, varying with the size of a family, the age of its members, its locale, etc. Thus for an urban family of four (considered average by the government), the Bureau of Labor Statistics computes an income of $10,700 as necessary for a "moderate," intermediate standard of living.[11] This sum allows for food, clothing, housing, furnishings, transportation, medical care, household operation, reading, recreation, tobacco, education, gifts and contributions, and miscellaneous expenses. The BLS (a division of the Department of Labor) determined the amounts in each category by examining studies of consumer expenditures that are made every ten years. Examination of the amounts used in the "moderate" budget shows that they are less than extravagant. Clothes are replaced over a period of two to four years and furniture over a longer period. Transportation is by used car unless the city has a well-developed transportation system. The recreation allowance allows a movie every two or three weeks. The education allowance covers only the day-to-day expenses, such as books and paper—it does not include savings for higher education.

This "moderate" budget represents what is felt to be reasonable comfort in America today. It is obviously much higher than the government's definition of poverty, but still short of the two-car-in-every-garage, swimming-pool-in-every-backyard image of affluence that often passes for the norm. One can build upon it with additional income to provide for discretionary tastes, but to subtract from it immediately forces cutbacks in what is surely a modest life. The family would not starve, find itself in tatters, or be forced into a rat-infested tenement, were its income cut back by one or two thousand dollars. But it would find itself deprived of simple comforts, it would begin to detect imbalances in its meals—perhaps a marked absence of meat, or an overabundance of potatoes—it might find itself living in a "deteriorating" neighborhood where crime is a constant problem.

Yet one-half of American families live *below* the Bureau of Labor Statistics' definition of a "moderate" life.

4

We have seen the wide disparity between the lower and upper middle classes; as we shall soon see, there are even greater disparities between rich and poor. Why is it, then, that Americans think of their country as an Affluent Society? How can we speak of America as egalitarian and democratic, when such antitheses contradict equality and endanger democracy?

From numerous interviews, and from cursory observation, it is clear that a majority of Americans publicly identify themselves as middle class (as compared to England, for example, where a majority still identifies itself as working class). Given the fact of this general self-identification, how are we to say that Americans are not middle class without the most patent contradiction?

Part of the answer to these questions lies in the way Americans talk about "the middle class." The American middle class is synonymous with the word majority. To Americans, to be middle class is to stand literally in the middle, to be average, to be the typical man in the street, the Good Joe. The idea of a minority middle class is about as ludicrous to an American as its antithesis was to a European.

Modern social science has reinforced the American notion by incorporating the American concept as part of its analysis. By *assuming* the existence of a broad middle class, and treating it as homogeneous, social scientists have frequently aggregated social economic data in a way that ignores the differences between upper and lower segments of that supposedly unitary class. By stressing the ideal of the middle class's homogeneity over the fact of its diversity, they have assured that the ideal would appear as fact.

But none of this is new; American usage is buried deep in the history of America and in the character of the men and women who founded it. America was born in an age of Rationalist idealism, when the new ideal of equality was sharply contradicted by the reality of European society and, to a lesser extent, by the reality of colonial life as well. It was the hope of many of the Founding Fathers that in America, at least, the ideal would eventually defeat the reality. But instead the idealism of the Founding Fathers launched the country on a wave of anticipation that economic and political institutions were ill equipped to fulfill. Even today it is hard to see how the economic and political systems of America can possibly achieve the ideals which in our rhetoric too often pass for the norm.

It is not hard to see how the myth of the middle class has persisted over time. For lower-middle-class blue-collar and white-collar workers, it removes the sting that a more rigid class structure brings, and gives the workingman the feeling of fraternity in a larger world of equals. For upper-middle-class professionals, managers, and skilled workers, the myth sanctifies above-average wages and privileges on the ground that these are actually available to everyone.

Finally the myth has been enshrined because, over the past two decades, it has helped an elite of the upper middle class to achieve a substantial hegemony over the rest of the community, a hegemony that rarely is challenged successfully because of the New Class's claim to act in the interest of the whole. It is doubtful whether America has ever been the fully participatory democracy claimed by its rhetoric; since World War II, however, this elite of managers and professionals has been able to operate with a freedom that has been only weakly opposed, and then for the wrong reasons.

Their hegemony might not be so bad, were it not for the simple fact that they have misperceived America and perpetuated myths which sustain the inequalities of American life. By naively assuming (or deliberately pretending) that their affluence, advantages, and comforts are universal, instead of unique, and that the middle class includes nearly everyone, they have continued the myth without considering the consequences, neither the injustice which they perpetuate, nor the justice which they promise, but cannot fulfill.

2 | The Affluent Fifties: Approaching the Gates of Heaven

In retrospect, the fifties seem dull and faintly ridiculous. Seen through the turmoil of the sixties, the fifties appear an almost somnolent time. One thinks of suburbs and barbeque pits, of supermarkets and quiz shows, of quiet conformity broken only by the roar of hot-rods or the blare of rock-and-roll. These were the Eisenhower years, the years of Elvis Presley, Ed Sullivan, and Milton Berle. And if this sleepy mediocrity was occasionally interrupted by McCarthyism or the Korean War, we saw these intrusions as no more than that, minor ripples in a placid sea.

It is tempting to generalize in this way, to call the fifties the calm before the storm; but it nevertheless does a serious injustice to the decade. The fifties were an extraordinarily self-confident time, with the very calm that we mock a testimony to that confidence. After emerging from a major depression and a world war, America did not see the fifties as a hiatus between disasters, but as a fundamentally new chapter in world history. America, many believed, had not only consolidated the achievements of its forbearers, but by its achievements in economics, science, and education lay on the verge of an exciting transformation unique in the history of mankind.

This sense of novelty, of having reached a new plateau in human history, is definitely the most remarkable aspect of the decade. Rereading the literature of the period, one finds phrases like "The Atomic Age," "The Technological Age," or "The Postindustrial Age" used with casual abandon. To be sure, some of the terms were not truly novel: the nineteenth century had described itself as the "Age of Science" or the "Industrial Age." But to the writers of the fifties the sheer weight of novelty appeared overwhelming.

David Riesman, for example, announced in *The Lonely Crowd:*

> My concern in this book is with two revolutions. . . . The first of these revolutions has in the last four hundred years cut us off pretty decisively from the family- and clan-oriented traditional ways of life in which mankind has existed throughout most of history; this revolution includes the Renaissance, the Reformation, the Counter-Reformation, the Industrial Revolution, and the political revolutions of the seventeenth, eighteenth, and nineteenth centuries. This revolution is, of course, still in process, but in the most advanced countries of the world, and particularly in America, it is giving way to another sort of revolution—a whole range of social developments associated with a shift from an age of production to an age of consumption.[1]

In other words the fifties marked as decisive a turn in the history of Western civilization as did the entire period from the Renaissance through the nineteenth century.

While other writers were not quite so enthusiastic about the novelty of the postwar era, they were in basic agreement with Riesman. Plagiarizing the dictum that "quantity changes into quality," most social scientists saw America entering a fundamentally new era when the preoccupation with survival and the mere production of goods would be replaced by leisure, when machines would take over most manual labor, education would be available to all, and the general citizenry would enjoy the fruits of automated toil in their abundant spare time. What poverty was left, and whatever inequalities might be created by the shift to automation, could be solved by a government administered benignly by liberal professionals. S. M. Miller and Martin Rein summarized this consensus as it was expressed in the sociology of the fifties:

> The expansion of production and productivity resulted in a much greater economic pie. The graduated income tax, expanded welfare services, and education were more equitably distributing this larger pie. Continued increase in aggregate economic wealth would invariably filter down, more or less equitably, to all income groupings. Marginal economic groups, it was assumed, would in time "gracefully succumb" to continued economic growth and small residual groups not covered by expanded welfare and social security programs would be handily cared for by the public dole.[2]

1

The essential assumption behind all this confidence was economic: we were living in an age of abundance, the new Affluent Society. When John Kenneth Galbraith first coined the term, his notion was that the "conventional wisdom" of an earlier age had imposed upon us a "scarcity consciousness," which had in turn forced us into a preoccupation with the production of goods. The production fetish had in turn led to a serious neglect of the public sector of the economy, and a disruption of "the social balance." This imbalance, Galbraith asserted, was not merely an accident of the conservative politics of the fifties, but endemic to the production mentality, and that the allocation of resources, both physical and mental, would continue to favor the private sector until the "conventional wisdom" was defeated.

The production of goods, Galbraith believed, was now secondary, because "the ancient preoccupations of economic life—with equality, security, and productivity" had by the fifties been satisfied. Americans were no longer in need of more goods; instead they needed refined taste and protection from Madison Avenue hucksterism which tried to tell them otherwise. In a classic indulgence of his polemic style, Galbraith described the common condition of the "average" family in the mid-fifties:

The family takes its mauve and cerise, air-conditioned, power-steered, and power-braked automobile out for a tour [and] passes through cities that are badly paved, made hideous by litter, blighted buildings, billboards, and posts for wires that should long since have been put underground. They pass on into a countryside that has been rendered largely invisible by commercial art. . . . They picnic on exquisitely packaged food from a portable icebox by a polluted stream and go on to spend the night at a park which is a menace to public health and morals. Just before dozing off on an air mattress, beneath a nylon tent, amid the stench of decaying refuse, they may reflect vaguely on the curious unevenness of their blessings.[3]

The sense which such writing left was one of an economy glutted with goods. "Air-conditioned, power-steered, and power-braked" cars, "exquisitely packaged foods," "air mattresses," and "nylon tents" were images that left a sense of surfeit, a sense of overabundance. Clearly, if this was the life of the average American family, America was indeed at a new stage in world history.

Galbraith sensibly tempered his description of American life with the warning that "this is not to say that no economic insecurity remains." But citing the high costs of medical care as his sole example, he concluded that "the preoccupation with economic security is largely in the past." Poverty, where it could be found, was limited to an insignificant minority of "insular" and "case" poor. The former were inhabitants of areas like Appalachia and the rural South, economic pockets where shifting employment patterns were causing "painful, but temporary hardship." The "case" poor were the alcoholics, invalids, and elderly who could not, or would not, get ahead. Poverty in the United States, Galbraith assured his readers, rather than being a major problem, was "more nearly an afterthought."

Galbraith's argument, or at least the idea of an affluent society, fell on sympathetic ears. Economists, many of whom were less than sympathetic toward the implications of his anti-production stance, generally seconded his appraisal of the nation's material well-being. They proudly pointed to aggregate indices of American accomplishment—the continuous growth in Gross National Product, the low level of unemployment, and the highest per capita income in the world—as proof of America's success. Although the economy might be sluggish at times, and "soft spots" might leave many economic groups well below the per capita average, economists were overwhelmingly optimistic about America's economic future. Those who muttered darkly about the possibility of another depression were considered hopelessly pessimistic. The emphasis in the discipline was on growth, and skillful management of the economy as a whole. Economics was no longer "the dismal science," but the key to a bright future for America and the world.

If some responded that aggregate figures gave only a crude measure of well-being, economists had a ready answer. Not only was growth continuous, but the fruits of that growth were being more evenly distributed. Citing studies like Simon Kuznets's massive *Shares of Upper Income Groups in Income and Savings*, they declared that the shares of income and wealth, so concentrated in the hands of the very wealthy before the war, were declining and would continue to decline.*

---

* Kuznets and others had examined tax returns and other data, and found that between 1929 and 1944 the share of the income received by the top 5% of the population had steadily declined.

Correlated with census data which showed that the number of families with incomes below $3,000 had also declined in the postwar period, and information that blue-collar workers had been making rapid advances in income, the economists postulated what came to be known as the trickle-down theory of income redistribution. Briefly stated, trickle-down theory believed that as the economy grew, inequities in income between classes would grow smaller and smaller. On a graph, as the percentage of income controlled by the rich declined, and the percentage controlled by the middle class and poor grew, the income scale would come to act like a spigot out of which income trickled until there was an even flow.

To the consternation of a few doubting economists, the trickle-down theory described better than it explained what seemed to be happening. Apart from some allusions to "strong unions" and "progressive taxation," the exact reasons for trickle-down were not understood, but euphoria over apparently significant changes in income swept such niceties from its path. Arthur Burns, an Eisenhower administration economist, exemplified the mood of many economists when he declared, "The transformation in the distribution of our national income . . . may already be counted as one of the great social revolutions of history." Somewhat less hyperbolically Paul Samuelson expressed the liberal consensus: "The American income pyramid is becoming less unequal."

2

The sense that affluence was now universally available shifted the interest of many academic and journalistic commentators. Americans had always been fascinated by technology; in the fifties technology would follow economics into a new era.

For the early fifties, the predominant image of this transformation was the atom. The atom bomb had ended World War II, and Americans were acutely self-conscious about their new source of power. As the *New York Times* observed, the razing of Hiroshima "made it plain that one of the scientific landmarks of the century had been passed, and that the 'age of atomic energy,' which can be a tremendous force for the advancement of civilization as well as for destruction, was at hand."

The focal interest in atomic energy exemplified a more general interest in science and technology. Development of the transistor and the computer induced a great deal of discussion about the "electronics revolution," and the launching of Sputnik in 1957 so expanded the debate that the decade was commonly declared to be in the midst of a "technological revolution." As with economics and affluence, the debate was rather one-sided. Criticism on all levels was extremely mild, and emphasis was continually placed on the novelty of each development, rather than on its continuity with previous inventions.

Fascination with technology and science, although hardly new in itself, exercised profound influence on the public mind. Scientists and technicians were accorded great status, and the title "nuclear physicist" held mystical powers over popular imagination reminiscent of the shaman in primitive religion. The names Teller, Pauling, Von Braun, and Weiner became the Cabot, Cabrillo, Magellan, and Pizarro of the age, Einstein being its Columbus. The federal government and industry both increased investment in research and development, and a wide variety of future-oriented think-tanks sprouted to solve the problems and anticipate the future of the highly organized technological society.

Technological infatuation created a loosely knit constituency of intellectuals, businessmen, and government officials that saw in the new age nothing but promise. Political scientist Zbigniew Brzezinski held the not uncommon belief that "ours is no longer the conventional revolutionary era; we are entering a novel metamorphic phase in human history." Brzezinski suggested that the new technologized America would produce "alterations in the distribution of power and wealth" that would "affect the essence of individual and social existence," and foresaw "greater devolution of authority" and "massive diffusion of scientific and technical knowledge as a principal focus of American involvement in world affairs." [4]

3

Excitement over the technological revolution corresponded with a third preoccupation of the fifties: education. Stress on the importance of education was certainly not a novelty in the fifties, but the widespread *realization* of educational opportunities was. At the turn of the century, only about 4% of the eligible age group graduated from high school; by the late fifties the figure was over 60%. This mass education of its populace was seen by many as the ranking achievement of American culture, and crucial to the American ideal of equal opportunity.

Mass education, however, inevitably produced negative criticism; imagined lowering of academic standards accompanying the expansion of enrollment caused many to question not only the method but the value of mass education. Widespread complaints, particularly about children's reading ability, were crystallized by publication of the popular critique, *Why Johnny Can't Read*, complaints which were compounded by the launching of Sputnik.

Congress, reacting to public pressure over both the declining quality of education and Russian competition, passed the first National Defense Education Act (NDEA) in 1958. Notably, the expressed aim of the act was not the general improvement of American education. Rather the Act was designed to bolster the physical sciences, in reaction to an imagined technology gap between ourselves and the Russians. Educators sought to develop technological aids and substitutes for teachers: educational television, reading machines, language labs, even computers were tried, and many predicted that by the year 2000 the human teacher would be a thing of the past.

The impact of Sputnik and the NDEA underscored an old conflict—or perhaps plurality—of interests among the several groups involved in education. On the one hand, the educational establishment saw education as a means of popular enlightenment and a bulwark of democracy; Congress and the various state legislatures, while making the proper obeisances to such cardinal virtues, often viewed education as a prime source of labor for an increasingly technology oriented economy—the NDEA itself was passed "to ensure trained manpower of sufficient quantity and quality to meet the national defense needs of the United States"; many of the students themselves viewed their educations as long-term economic investments, similar to the purchase of government bonds.

Amid this tension, the sole basis for accord was the fact that education was reaching more and more Americans than ever before. Between 1950 and 1960, enrollment in public education increased almost 50% from 31 million to 45 million. Higher education especially underwent high-speed change; between 1940 and 1960 enrollment more than doubled.

The success of public education was told not only in the raw numbers of attendance, but in their significance as a percentage of the population. Whereas in 1940 less than 15% of high school graduates enrolled in a college or university, by the mid-fifties more than 30% were enrolling, and by 1960 nearly 40%. The upgrading of general education was felt economically: in 1956 the average college graduate had an income 50% higher than the average high school graduate and more than triple the amount earned by someone who had completed less than eight years of school.

This drastic increase in the output of the American educational machine was generally taken as a further proof of the widespread improvement and equalization of American life.

As with affluence and technology, what little criticism did occasionally arise tended to be criticism of means rather than ends. The appropriate mix of public and private education, how deeply the federal government should involve itself in local matters, how many mechanical teaching aids versus how many teachers—these were the questions most frequently raised about American education. Rarely if ever were there inquiries into the differences between expensive private colleges and under-financed state colleges, or the extent to which children of rich and upper-middle-class families tended to occupy the bulk of the places in better universities. And in many cases, the sanguine assumption that increased education meant an increasingly liberal outlook on society hid the fact that great numbers of students were in fact being educated in conservative, often religiously oriented institutions that merely reinforced the traditional opinions of an older generation.

4

The extension of education was, however, momentous in one way: the sudden upsurge of college graduates in the job market, accompanied by the technologization of parts of the economy, created what Galbraith referred to as the New Class.

The formation of this class had been forecast by earlier critics. In particular, James Burnham in *The Managerial Revolution*, and Adolph Berle and Gardiner Means in *The Modern Corporation and Private Property*, had observed direct control of the giant corporations passing from the hands of individual entrepreneurs into the hands of corporate managers, causing a fundamental change in advanced capitalism. These managers were supposedly a radical departure from their individualistic predecessors: they were putatively group-oriented, socially responsible, and a good deal less barbaric than their robber baron ancestors.

But the New Class was not limited to corporate managers. Managerial structure was dependent on a wide variety of individuals, many of whom were technical specialists rather than managers per se. These included engineers, scientists, lawyers, accountants, advertising and public relations specialists, merchandising personnel—a long and varied list. In addition, expansion of government and education on all levels had vastly increased the bureaucracy, which also required its quota of specialists.

Happily, technology's worship of efficiency did not seem to produce in this class the automatization and regimentation that Orwell, Huxley, and others had feared. Galbraith in fact claimed that the outstanding characteristic of this group was its nonautomated attitudes toward work and leisure:

> It is taken for granted that [work] will be enjoyable. If it is not, this is a source of deep dissatisfaction or frustration. No one regards it as remarkable that the advertising man, tycoon, poet, or professor who suddenly finds his work unrewarding should seek the counsel of a psychiatrist. One insults the business executive or the scientist by suggesting that his principal motivation in life is the pay he receives. Pay is not unimportant. Among other things, it is a prime index of prestige. Prestige—the respect, regard, and esteem of others—is in turn one of the more important sources of satisfaction associated with this kind of work. But, in general, those who do this kind of work expect to contribute their best regardless of compensation.[5]

While the idea that the New Class members "expect to contribute their best regardless of compensation" might sound a trifle exaggerated, it nonetheless underscored the quite important restructuring of social values that the New Class seemed to represent.

William H. Whyte's widely hailed book, *The Organization Man*, gave a much more in-depth evaluation of the New Class than did Galbraith. Whyte was finally more skeptical of the new tendencies in society than was Galbraith, but he offered a similar analysis. In place of the traditional Protestant Ethic which once dominated the consciousness of Americans, there had arisen a new social ethic for the organization man:

> By social ethic I mean that contemporary body of thought which makes morally legitimate the pressure of society against the individual. Its major propositions are three: a belief in the group as the source of creativity; a belief in "belongingness" as the ultimate need of the individual; and a belief in the application of science to achieve the belongingness.[6]

And like Galbraith he departed from earlier social observers who limited their examination of the New Class to the corporate managers alone. The New Class cut a wide swath across occupational categories:

> Blood brother to the business trainee off to join Du Pont is the seminary student who will end up in the church hierarchy, the doctor headed for the corporate clinic, the physics Ph.D. in a government laboratory, the intellectual on the foundation-sponsored team project, the engineering graduate in the huge drafting room at Lockheed, the young apprentice in a Wall Street law factory.[7]

Common to this group of Organization Men, most social critics believed, was a set of fundamental social mores that held revolutionary implications for America. The desire for "pleasurable work" and greater leisure was being realized in the Affluent Society by a more abundant material output, which was made possible by a better-educated work-force and the use of technology. For Galbraith, this change was preeminently desirable: "There is every reason to conclude," he wrote in *The Affluent Society*, "that the further and rapid expansion of this class should be a major and perhaps next to peaceful survival itself, *the* major goal of the society." Other observers were not so optimistic. Whyte, while unwilling to sound too conservative, found in the New Class a discomforting trend toward what he called "private socialism," a collectivization of the society that was in serious danger of losing sight of the individual.

David Riesman elaborated on this latter tendency in *The Lonely Crowd*, referring to the personalities of "the over-privileged two-thirds" as "other-directed" (versus the older—and in Riesman's eyes, preferable—"inner-directed" character). As Riesman described him, the other-directed man differed from the older types of Americans who had settled this country. "What is common to all the other-directed people," Riesman wrote, "is that their contemporaries are the source of direction for the individual—either those known to him or those with whom he is indirectly acquainted, through friends and through the mass media." While at first glance this would appear to be nothing more than normal human gregariousness, Riesman assured us it was not: contrasted with the inner-directed man, the other-directed person learned to respond to a far wider circle than his family. The family was no longer a closely knit unit, but merely part of a wider social environment to which the individual early became attentive.

Since Riesman was aware that this might sound like a return to the preindustrial extended family, he set apart his other-directed man by two special attitudes. First, unlike preindustrial men, the new man was cosmopolitan. "The other-directed person is, in a sense, at home everywhere and nowhere, capable of a rapid if sometimes superficial intimacy with and response to everyone." Second, the adaptation of the other-directed man to his social milieu was more complex than in earlier times. Whereas the traditional society had transmitted behavior and thought patterns in a "cultural monotone," in contemporary society the levels of communication had become exceedingly complex and tension-producing.

What can be internalized . . . . is not a code of behavior but the elaborate equipment needed to attend to such messages and occasionally to participate in their circulation. As against guilt-and-shame controls, though of course these survive, one prime psychological lever of the other-directed person is a diffuse anxiety. This control equipment, instead of being like a gyroscope, is like a radar.[8]

Whyte's interviews with the Organization Man at work, and with his family and community, generally seemed to corroborate the theoretical description that Riesman had drawn. In an in-depth examination of one prototypical suburb, Whyte found that the socialization process was "perhaps the greatest achievement of suburban education." But unlike traditional patterns of socialization, life in Park Forest was built on transience. Men being transferred by their companies around the country were typical of suburban life, rather than the exception, and the expected stay in one community might be as little as two or three years. In the rental units of Park Forest, one-third of the population changed every year, while comparison of the 1954 and 1955 phone directories revealed that in one year's time 18% of Park Foresters had moved to other communities. And even for the 82% who remained, "the transients are still the key. Whether they actually move or not, it is the people successful enough to have the option who set the dominant style of life in suburbia."

The effects of such turnover on the individual confirmed Riesman's description of other-directedness, i.e., "a rapid if sometimes superficial intimacy with and response to everyone." The men and women were joiners—joining the PTA, joining the clubs, joining the neighborhood activities of one kind or another—but none of them participated (as far as Whyte was concerned) at a deep, stable level. Nowhere was one able to find the successful loner, the bright individual, who could continue to resist this cultural *anschluss*.

If this greater communality, with its stress on leisure rather than work, appealed to Galbraith, it disturbed Riesman and Whyte. Whyte exploded about the "socialization" of the middle-level managers:

How futile, how destructive is this solution! Why should the scientist be company-oriented? Is he to be called mal-adjusted because he does not fit the administrator's Procrustean bed? And of what profit would be his integration? It is not to his self-interest, neither is it to that of The Organization. Leave him his other allegiance. It is his work that must be paramount, and efforts to divert him into contentment are the efforts best calculated to bridle the curiosity that makes him productive.[9]

And if Whyte's condemnation smacked too much of shrewd advice given to a corporate president for optimizing productivity, Riesman appealed to the organization men to save themselves:

Is it conceivable that these economically privileged Americans will some day wake up to the fact that they overconform? . . . If the other-directed people should discover how much needless work they do, discover that their own thoughts and their lives are quite as uninteresting as other people's, that, indeed, they no more assuage their loneliness in a crowd of peers than one can assuage one's thirst by drinking sea water, then we might expect them to become more attentive to their own feelings and aspirations.[10]

Whatever their reservations, Riesman and Whyte shared with Galbraith a recognition of the novelty and importance of the New Class. Here was a new social category being created by the success of American production and technology; the class might not be without faults, but it was authentically new, and it held the promise of restructuring American life once it became self-conscious. As Riesman and Whyte had shown, its members were cosmopolitan, a welcome alternative to Main Street babbitry. Because their existence depended on technology and education, they would presumably be enlightened as well. And because affluence seemed so pervasive, and education so widely available, there was the prospect that this class need not be merely an elightened elite, but might someday become the norm for the great middle-class majority of the postindustrial world.

5

These analyses seem remarkable in the faith they display in social change, their acceptance of its scope and almost mechanical inevitability. Reisman, Whyte, Galbraith, and many others accepted wholeheartedly the belief that everyone— or nearly everyone—was well-off, that technology was *the* wave of the future, that more and more education was not only a good thing in itself, but that everyone who wanted it could get it, and that the New Class, highly educated, fluent in technology and administration, could fine-tune both the economy and the culture in a way that promised to usher in utopia.

Given what had gone before, these attitudes were perhaps not so remarkable. Compared with the economic insecurities of the Depression, the fifties were a vast improvement: the economy *was* more affluent than ever before, and more people did share in the fruits of that affluence. And, too, technology was a mesmerizing development—television, atomic power, transistors, rockets, solar energy—all these were truly amazing things, full of great promise. Certainly education offered opportunities where none had existed before. And the New Class did offer new hopes for a more rational, more humane world, a not unwelcome prospect after the horrors of fascism.

And, to be sure, not all comments were dewily optimistic. The purpose of *The Affluent Society* had been not to indulge in a hymn to American production, but to criticize the waste and stupidity of the culture. Reisman and Whyte worried that homogenization of the society, even if many were lifted by it, would produce a bland culture without values or a sense of purpose.

But finally the writers of the fifties must be judged a badly myopic lot. Affluence was not and is not the condition of the majority; poverty, "rediscovered" in the sixties, is even now nowhere on the verge of disappearing, and the lives led by many of the non-poor lower middle class are, as we shall see, far from the image of the affluent middle class that Galbraith and others had in mind. Technology, once thought to be the keys to heaven, has been revealed in another role: it manufactures chemical and biological weapons, plots the course of ballistic missiles, pollutes the land with its waste, and packages crassness. And education, meant to integrate the young into the smoothly functioning world of postindustrial America, now finds itself torn between its need to socialize and its responsibility to criticize.

But most important, and most damning, the writers of the fifties failed to recognize that left to play philosopher-kings, the New Class would create a power elite, appropriating power, wealth, and prestige, making decisions about the future of America supposedly "too complex," too technological to be left to the majority. The comfortable America described in the fifties was really the world of the upper middle class, and many of the disasters of the sixties stem directly from the attitudes many of its members bred.

3 | The Sixties:
The New Class
Comes of Age

Ask not what your country can do for you; ask
what you can do for your country.
                              John F. Kennedy, 1961

If the fifties seemed dull and ridiculous, the sixties gave promise of being something altogether different. When John F. Kennedy took office many of his supporters were convinced that America was entering a Golden Age. The differences between Kennedy and his predecessor were apparently so great, so patently obvious, that his admirers could hardly believe anything less than a new age was dawning for their country.

By the time Kennedy was assassinated this feeling had spread from a small circle of supporters to include a major portion of the American people. The wave of sympathy that swept the country after his murder was so great that Lyndon

Johnson rode to victory with the biggest majority in American history, accompanied by a Congress so packed with Democrats that political commentators seriously debated the end of the two-party system.

Now those years seem terribly far away. The Vietnam war, the deaths of Robert Kennedy and Martin Luther King, the decline of the Peace Corps and the poverty program, and the rejection by many young people (and not a few of their elders) of the New Frontier's "pragmatic liberalism" seem to demonstrate that eras, especially Golden Eras, have a frighteningly short lifetime in America. Nonetheless the three short years of the Kennedy administration are crucial for understanding how our nation has evolved since, and why the myths with which this book is concerned have taken on new forms without altering the fundamental facts of life behind them.

In retrospect, the choice of John Kennedy for president was a highly symbolic act with which to begin the decade. The country, by late 1959, was tiring of the somnolence of the Eisenhower administration. A recession arrived in 1958, and unemployment, although of little concern to professional economists, remained a major political issue to those who remembered the Depression. The Cold War, mellowed somewhat, had not been enhanced by the demagogic "kitchen debate" between Khrushchev and Nixon, nor by Castro's success in Cuba. The issue of civil rights floated just below the surface and threatened to become fully visible at any moment. All in all the mood of the public was one of unease, a mood ready to listen to Kennedy's claim that he would "get the country moving again."

The members of the New Class in particular were ready for a man like Kennedy. In its nascent self-consciousness the New Class had adapted in curious and sometimes contradictory ways to the fifties. These adjustments left them disturbed and uncomfortable. Despite the overwhelming sense of novelty which its writers had seen in that decade, many of them had felt withdrawn from the life around them. Although cheered by the resolution of man's struggle for material survival, they also felt in the Affluent Society a general degrading of culture which they were unable to hide. Thus there were frequent assaults, like Galbraith's, on the crassness of American products, and complaints, like Riesman's and Whyte's, about the degradation of the individual spirit. Faced with the hysterical chauvinism of McCarthy, and the more popular conservatism of the Eisenhower administration, many members of the class retreated into a crabby elitism. Even C. Wright Mills, undoubtedly the most radical critic of the fifties, accepted the fact that workers were no longer revolutionary and that it was up to intellectuals to serve the lonely task as the critical conscience of the society.

Consequently, Kennedy's election appeared to the New Class as a vindication of their hopes and assumptions about America. Their pessimism had stemmed from their inability to affect the course of American history; now with a president who appeared to share their views about the nature of America's problems and the character of its destiny, there would be a new opportunity to lead. The New Class hoped that Americans could be brought to realize how the nature of the country had changed, and why the premises of fifties conservatism were no longer valid. With a liberal Domocrat in the White House, surrounded by advisors from their own ranks, the aspiration for a new American Civilization could be given the political muscle necessary for its realization. Technology could be put to work ending what drudgery remained, educational opportunities could be even further expanded, racism could be blotted out, and the military aid and anticommunism of the Eisenhower era could be complemented (if not replaced) by economic aid for the developing nations, and a detente with Communist enemies. Some even allowed themselves the hope that Americans would accept the *full* impact of science and technology, and consent to wide scale social engineering, not only of the economy, but of the whole society.

This sense of opportunity is captured in two key words of the Kennedy administration: style and service. The style of the country's leaders would show the "overprivileged two-thirds" how affluent quantity could be turned into elegant quality. In place of Truman's piano playing, there would be Casals; instead of Eisenhower's inexpert duffing, there would be tennis, and yachting; and instead of Bess Truman or Mamie Dowd Eishenower (called "Dowdy Mamie" by her detractors), there would be a First Lady who spoke French, came from aristocratic stock, and who promised to restore to the White House its long-lost elegance.

As for service, the New Class would show America the fitness of their vision of the Affluent Society, their ability to administer it, and—hopefully—the congruence of their own interests with those of the nation as a whole. They would show how technology required this New Class, and why its members' ability made them not only necessary, but also desirable. In sum, service would justify Galbraith's plea in *The Affluent Society* that "the further and rapid expansion of this class should be made a major and perhaps next to peaceful survival itself, *the* major goal of the society."

For the New Class in general then it was a heady time. At the Inauguration Robert Frost read his poetry; the next morning the new president's first executive order doubled the quantity of surplus food available to needy Americans. This synthesis of style and service redounded throughout Kennedy's inaugural speech, and to many of the New Class it meant the authentic discovery of a New Frontier.

Discouragement would only come later.

1

Much of Kennedy's behavior in the early months of his administration encouraged those who hoped for a break with the past. Announcement of the Alliance for Progress and the Peace Corps, the arrangement of a summit meeting with Khrushchev, encouraging statements on civil rights and social justice all prompted great expectations. Even the formation of the Green Berets and the invasion of Cuba were not interpreted as essentially reactionary moves, but rather as the pragmatic (or in the case of Cuba, mistaken) judgment of an extremely shrewd but noble president.

Kennedy encouraged the New Class in particular by publicly supporting their viewpoint on the nature of postwar America, on the importance of technology and education, and on their role as a crucial elite. In a famous speech given at Yale in 1962, Kennedy borrowed a favorite theme of liberal intellectuals to express his opinions on American society:

> The great enemy of the truth is very often not the lie— deliberate, contrived and dishonest—but the myth, persistent, persuasive, and unrealistic. Too often we hold fast to the clichés of our forbearers. We subject all facts to a prefabricated set of interpretations. We enjoy the comfort of opinion without the discomfort of thought.

And what were those myths which were the great enemy of truth? They were the myths, Kennedy explained, of the old order, of fifties conservatism, that relied on laissez-faire and good luck for the success of society. No longer could we allow these myths to go on; for, as he told his audience,

> The fact of the matter is that most of the problems, or at least many of them, that we now face are technical problems, are administrative problems. They are very sophisticated judgments which do not lend themselves to the great sort of 'passionate movements' which have stirred this country so often in the past . . .[1]

The assertion that most of America's problems were technical and administrative could not have been better designed to please the New Class. In a few brief sentences, Kennedy affirmed every major assumption that the class had made about American society. By his silence he dismissed the problems of economic inequality and deprivation. By attacking as myths the dominant assumptions of fifties culture he clearly severed any remaining presumption of continuity between that decade and the sixties. By labeling most of America's problems as technical and administrative, he affirmed the strategic importance of the New Class. And finally, by declaring society's opposition to the great "passionate movements" of the past, he foreclosed the possibility of wide-scale public involvement as anachronistic, a modern equivalent of Luddism.

The president also pleased the New Class with his appointments—McGeorge Bundy and Arthur Schlesinger Jr. as Special Assistants to the President, Keynesian economist Walter Heller as head of the Council of Economic Advisors, Adlai Stevenson as chief delegate to the United Nations, and even the self-styled maverick, John Kenneth Galbraith, as Ambassador to India. Sixteen former Rhodes Scholars were appointed to various posts. Appointees who were not identified strictly as liberal intellectuals were nonetheless charter members of the New Class. Robert McNamara, with his cool, analytic demeanor and experience as president of the Ford Motor Company, personified the ideal of every middle-level Organization Man: master of figures, decisive, supremely confident in both the world of men and the world of computers. Dean Rusk, characterized by personal reserve and judicious caution, was a former Rhodes Scholar whose background at the Rockefeller Foundation represented service in one of the newest and most prestigious occupational wings of the New Class. Even Douglas Dillon, the Republican Wall Street banker who many saw as a traditional conservative, suggested Kennedy's ability to achieve consensus support among the managers and professionals of the society.

But ironically, even as Kennedy's words were encouraging support among the New Class as a whole, a small number of the class found itself in increasing conflict with his behavior. By the time Kennedy had taken office, civil rights leaders had built solid political foundations throughout the country with boycotts, sit-ins, and civil disobedience. With the election of a Democratic president, they naturally assumed that federal action on civil rights would soon emerge as a key element in American politics. In the words of one black civil rights leader, "It was the federal government that gave us our freedom; now it's about time they gave us some justice."

But Kennedy moved slowly on civil rights. Contrary to the expectations of liberal members of the New Class, the ascension to power of one of their own was not having the effect they had expected. Rather than resolving the few remaining conflicts at the core of the postindustrial world, Kennedy seemed to be aggravating them. Instead of earning the admiration of Blacks, Kennedy prompted Martin Luther King to remark that his behavior represented only "the limited goal of token integration."

When liberal members of the New Class approached Kennedy, acting in their self-appointed roles as spokesmen for the civil rights movement, the president rebuked them. Joseph Rauh of Americans for Democratic Action went before the president to plead for civil rights legislation; as Schlesinger records the meeting, Kennedy replied to Rauh with "definiteness":

"No. I can't go for legislation at this time. I hope you have liked my appointments. I'm going to make some more, and Bobby will bring voting suits. And we'll do some other things." Rauh said, "You told Bob (Nathan) you would like some liberal pressure on the economic side. I take it you would also like some liberal pressure on the civil rights side." Kennedy replied emphatically, banging his hand on the desk: "No, there's a real difference. You have to understand the problems I have here."

Schlesinger's only explanation of this enigmatic remark is that "undoubtedly he [Kennedy] wanted to keep control over the demand for civil rights and this, unlike the demand for federal spending, might well, if stimulated, get out of hand." [2]

Other actions on Kennedy's part began to increase doubts and dissension. Although his record on civil rights improved, his behavior in the Cuban missile crisis and in Southeast Asia generated more and more criticism, and more and more doubt. Perhaps the wisdom of the philosopher-king was as problematic as Plato himself had realized. Perhaps in fact the New Class, and the myth of the postindustrial, posttechnological, affluent world on which it was based, were as limited as any previous set of leaders and myths. Perhaps this first generation of New Class leaders was worse than many predecessors, because of its unabashed arrogance.

2

No programs better illustrate the bright beginnings and the fading hopes of the New Class than the two wars of the sixties: the war in Vietnam and the war on poverty. Although neither came to the fore until after Kennedy's death, both were planned and anticipated by Kennedy and the men around him. The Kennedy administration saw the war in Vietnam as a test of American resolve on entirely new terms, involving entirely new assumptions, new planning, and new equipment and personnel. Instead of the massive retaliation which Eisenhower had established as the core of American defense, the New Frontier foresaw a variety of wars, from a massive East-West encounter to guerrilla wars, each with its own specific needs. Since America was already prepared for the alternative of massive retaliation, the Kennedy administration planned for the other alternative: under McNamara and Maxwell Taylor, both highly regarded as technocratic "whiz-kids," the Defense Department created the Green Berets, prepared counter-insurgency plans, and made the armed forces mobile enough to be shipped around the world on short notice.

Their accomplishment, coupled with the related activities of NASA and other scientific programs—Comsat for example—brought the Kennedy administration a reputation for technical competence and sound scientific management. The use of computers and cost-benefit analyses, and the expansion of government-financed scientific research not only encouraged much of the New Class, but helped materially advance the well-being of a major portion of its members.

The war on poverty is, however, the best illustration of the behavior of the New Class. The war in Vietnam has caused such a rift within the New Class itself, that to speak of it as "typifying" that class's outlook would involve obvious contradiction. But the war on poverty has maintained a broad base of support within managerial and professional groups. Not liberals alone, but an impressive coalition of upper-middle-class businessmen and conservatives have emerged as supporters of the federal government's antipoverty efforts. Groups such as the Urban Coalition and business leaders such as Henry Ford and Sol Linowitz exemplify the growing interest in the government antipoverty programs by prominent members of the managerial class.

The war on poverty's roots in the principles and personalities of the New Class can be seen in its genesis. If we are to believe the historians of the Kennedy administration, the poverty program was not inspired by uprisings of the poor nor by the agitation of working-class radicals, but rather by a book, Michael Harrington's now-famous *The Other America*. This fact has never been fully appreciated. The silence of the poor, the mask of quiet that hid their misery, the need for a spokesman like Harrington to plead their case—all suggested that the assumption of New Class spokesmen was correct, that the poor, in Galbraith's words, "were more nearly an afterthought." What little poverty remained was only, as Kennedy believed, "a technical problem," and could not be solved by "passionate movements." Like racism, it was one of those minor blemishes soon to be removed from the face of our new technological society.

To his credit, Harrington did not share this optimism. First, he argued that 25%–35% of the American people were poor, thus contradicting the New Class's belief in poverty's numerical insignificance. Harrington furthermore denied that poverty was a "technical" problem open to purely technical solutions. Writing of the plight of the black poor he derided confident assumptions that a few simple correctives would suffice:

If all the discriminatory laws in the United States were immediately repealed, race would still remain as one of the most pressing moral and political problems in the nation. Negroes and other minorities are not simply the victims of a series of iniquitous statutes. The American economy, the American society, the American unconscious are all racist. If all the laws were framed to provide equal opportunity, a majority of the Negroes would not be able to take full advantage of the change. There would still be a vast, silent, and automatic system directed against men and women of color.[3]

Harrington also realized that only one-third of the poor were black, and that for the other two-thirds, the future was equally hopeless. He argued particularly with professional economists who quibbled over their sub-minimal definitions of poverty, and fought with great skill against the abstraction of human suffering into categories of numbers and statistics. In a sensitive display of his own feelings, he tried to draw persons away from the numbers and make the misery of the poor—"the cycle of poverty"—understandable in human terms:

The poor get sick more than anyone else in the society. That is because they live in slums, jammed together under unhygienic conditions; they have inadequate diets, and cannot get decent medical care. When they become sick, they are sick longer than any other group in the society. Because they are sick more often and longer than anyone else, they lose wages and work, and find it difficult to hold a steady job. And because of this, they cannot pay for good housing, for a nutritious diet, for doctors. At any given point in the circle, particularly when there is a major illness, their prospect is to move to an even lower level and to begin the cycle, round and round, toward even more suffering.[4]

Although most of Harrington's warnings about professionalization of the war on poverty have gone unheeded, the basic plea for attention to the poor has not. The manner in which his plea was heeded, however, is worth discussing.

The Office of Economic Opportunity, core of the war on poverty, went into operation in November, 1964, headed by Sargent Shriver. As established by the Economic Opportunity Act, the OEO was to define and deal with the poor, or in the words of the bill itself, to provide "services, assistance, and other activities of sufficient scope and size to give promise of progress toward elimination of poverty or a cause or causes of poverty through developing employment opportunities, improving human performance, motivation, and productivity, or bettering the conditions under which the poor live, learn, and work."

Fine rhetoric aside, when the bill became law, it showed the effects of a collision between New Class assumptions and the American political status quo. As one political scientist put it, "The Economic Opportunity Act is a prime example of executive legislation; it was written in the executive branch and subsequently endorsed by the Congress. It is part of a twentieth-century development in which the president's role as 'chief legislator' has been 'institutionalized' not only in the sense of establishing the congressional agenda, but also for proposing the specific content of bills." The result was that "the classic legislative function—bringing political combatants together to hear their claims, and then resolving these claims—is becoming, in the complex modern polity, less and less the exclusive domain of Congress." [5]

This insight is important because it indicates the extent to which technically trained elites have invaded not only the economy, but the politics of America. The Economic Opportunity Act, instead of "bringing together political combatants to hear their claims," represents an important shift in the sources of public policy. In earlier periods of American history, it was the interest groups directly affected by a proposed law which were brought together in the political arena. Agriculture, business, and labor all had their own spokesmen, organizations, and set of demands. Their leaders were members of their own class. Farm leaders emerged from agricultural ranks, business spokesmen from the business community, labor leaders from the rank and file of industry. But no leaders emerged from the ranks of the poor; the poor developed no organization or set of demands. On the contrary, the entire war on poverty was executed *on behalf of* the poor by elite, technically proficient members of the New Class.

To illustrate the point, consider the events surrounding the bill: it was formulated by a professional economist, a foundation executive, a professional community organizer, and technical experts borrowed from the staffs of executive committees. As the bill developed it was reviewed and amended by other professional administrators and planners. Nowhere in any early stages of the bill's maturation is there any evidence that the poor were consulted about their wants or needs. The entire affair was carried out among a tight circle of professionals. Once the bill was passed and the antipoverty program was launched, the only major new pressure group to speak up in favor of the poor was the Citizen's Crusade Against Poverty, founded and directed by two former members of the OEO's administration. And at no time did it profess to be an authentic spokesman for the poor; rather it was designed to concentrate the influence of "prominent Americans" on the needs of the poor.

Lest anyone doubt the full implications of such a change in

the political process, Daniel Moynihan, one of the original planners of the Economic Opportunity Act and later President Nixon's adviser on the poor, made them clear. The antipoverty program, he said in 1965, is "far the best instance of professionalization of reform to appear. In its genesis, its development, and now in its operation, it is a prototype of the social technique of action that will almost certainly become more common in the future." And how is "professionalized" reform to be distinguished from earlier versions of social reform? "The initiative comes largely from within," Moynihan explains. "The case for action was based on essentially esoteric information about the past and probable future course of events."

To be sure, the Economic Opportunity Act is not the first major piece of legislation in which professional and academic elites have played the determinative role. But now, Moynihan offered, ". . . the main pressure for a massive government assault on poverty developed within the Kennedy-Johnson administration, among officials whose responsibilities were to think about just such matters." Thus America has arrived at ". . . a type of decision-making that is suited to the techniques of modern organizations, and which ends up in the hands of persons who make a profession of it." As a result, decisions are "less and less political decisions, more and more administrative decisions. They are decisions that can be reached by consensus rather than by conflict." [6]

Moynihan's final point—that decisions in the Affluent Society could be reached by consensus rather than conflict—is moot, because the consensus on the poverty program had been reached by a tiny handful of decision-makers who already agreed with each other, rather than by anything resembling a democratic process. The important point is that a large segment of the New Class had come firmly to believe that such decision-making was valid and acceptable; that a democratic procedure involving the tortuous difficulties of mobilizing the American people could no longer be tolerated, and was in fact threatening the smooth operation of a technological world being administered in the people's name.

Yet the enormous mythology required for such an approach has not even now been recognized as mythology. The necessity for an administrative technical elite is viewed as just that—a necessity. Building on the elaborate mythology of a postindustrial world, in which science, technology, and education play all the crucial roles, in which the economy provides abundance for all, it is natural that members of the New Class believe as they do. By assuming the world had changed drastically in the fifties, it seemed logically consistent to them to assume a role in the sixties which only a few decades before would have been denounced as elitist or aristocratic.

A major irony of the New Class's professionalized politics was that the authors of the Economic Opportunity Act considered their chief accomplishment to have been the incorporation at the bill's core of the concept of "maximum feasible participation" for the poor in the determination of their own lives. Seen as a radical attempt at "participatory democracy," and as proof that democracy and elite planning were not incompatible, "maximum feasible participation" never really got off the ground. At first no indigenous natural leaders emerged from new communities, because no political agitation for change had called them forth. And when leaders of the poor finally did emerge they proved too dangerous for the existing power structure to tolerate. In towns like Rochester, Cleveland, Chicago, and New York, the radical character of the new leaders and the militance of their demands challenged not only the local political hierarchies, but also the ability of the OEO to control its programs. The result, as one with a more sober assessment of political realities might have expected, was that "maximum feasible participation" was quietly demoted, and "cost efficiency" put in its place.[7]

Not surprisingly, it has since been argued that the failure of "maximum feasible participation" was not the fault of the New Class, but of its old-fashioned enemies. According to this view, "maximum feasible participation" was introduced in good faith by progressive technicians who were then betrayed by the militance of the poor and the conservatism of big-city politicians.

But such an explanation smacks of ingenuousness or cunning. It absolves the professionals of responsbility for a disaster of which they were the chief architects. It denies that *as professionals* they should have assessed the political climate of the country more carefully before introducing such a major piece of social engineering. Could they possibly have believed that, given the opportunity, the poor would not make the strongest possible demands, or that big-city political machines would have convivially cooperated in their own destruction?

The fact that some, if not all, of the professionals involved in launching the OEO *did* believe much palpable nonsense bespeaks the peculiar outlook on life which membership in the New Class had given them. It allowed them to believe that as the new de facto heads of a technological world they could, without seriously consulting any other group, first identify, then formulate and successfully execute an attack on a social problem as enormous as poverty as easily as if they were building a bridge or solving a problem in higher mathematics. The resultant failure of the OEO and the plight in which this has left the poor will be examined in later chapters; for the moment it is enough to recognize clearly a prime reason for that failure.

3

In broad outline, Lyndon Johnson's Great Society accepted and acted upon most of the major premises of the New Frontier. It believed that America was a fundamentally affluent middle-class nation, in which poverty was a distressing problem for a small minority. It accepted that professional planning was a crucial element in national policy, and that all the other New Class virtues like education, science, and technology were both descriptive of and goals for our modern, technological world.

It is true that the tone of the Great Society was somewhat different from that of the New Frontier. Schooled in the Roosevelt-Rayburn brand of welfare politics, Johnson's rhetoric often betrayed a populist flair foreign to Kennedy. But for the most part the rhetoric remained only rhetoric; after Kennedy's death Johnson sought to retain as many of the Kennedy administrators as possible. And with the exception of the late president's inner circle he eventually succeeded. Rusk, McNamara, Katzenbach, and others all stayed on for several crucial years after Kennedy's death to advise and serve the new president. It remains for future historians to sort out the respective roles these men played as American involvement in Vietnam increased, but it is already known that Rusk and McNamara played crucial parts in persuading the president to deepen involvement. The image of McNamara with his elaborate computer read-outs and intelligence reports, carefully gauging the staying power of a tiny peasant nation and predicting imminent victory, should serve as a tragicomic reminder to those who believe that technology is the solution to our problems.

4 | Looking Backward I: America Before the Fifties

In 1933, I lost my job. . . . It came as a shock.
Cause one day the man tells me I'm set for life, and
the next day he tells me I'm all through. . . .
from Studs Terkel, Hard Times:
An Oral History of the Great
Depression

The Great Depression struck, as one survivor recalled, "like a great scythe, mowing down rich and poor alike." In its wake it left a visible scar across the nation's back: fourteen million unemployed, bread lines, evictions, and suicides. For those with jobs life was not much better: unemployment was always just around the corner, wages were low, and the closely harbored dreams of years—of a home, of education for the children, of a peaceful retirement—were shattered in a single terrible moment.

World War II both heightened and allayed the fears created by the Depression. On the one hand, the war instilled in many an even greater sense of separation and isolation and made the drive for security even more intense. On the other hand, America's victory and escape from devastation was followed by an abundance that seemed a wonderful and unexpected blessing. The comparative affluence of the fifties, fueled by optimism, the forced savings of the war, and the influx of a new educated class fed the headlong race away from the memories of sorrow and hard times.

But for the adults of the fifties and sixties those memories would never entirely disappear, and the fifties are in many ways a consequence of this. There were few adults in the fifties and sixties who did not have some memory of the excruciating years of the Depression. The normal drive for security, for material possessions, for stability, had all been intensified by fifteen years of fear and instability. When Roosevelt said "the only thing we have to fear is fear itself," he captured in the word *fear* the synonym of the thirties, and a part of the explanation for what happened afterwards.

But if the ghost of depression and war haunted the men of the fifties, it also clouded their memories. When Galbraith christened America the Affluent Society, he clearly meant the reader to understand how different this supposed affluence was from America's previous condition. Likewise when he announced that poverty was "more nearly an afterthought," he meant that America had entered a unique phase in her history. "Privation," he observed, "was, a half-century ago, the common lot of at least all those who worked without special skill." But with the triumph of affluence, "the result was to reduce poverty from the problem of a majority to that of a minority. It ceased to be a general case and became a special case." [1] Other writers backed up Galbraith by referring, as Harrington did, to "minority poverty," or alluding, as Riesman did, to "the overprivileged two-thirds" of his countrymen. Without going into detail these writers helped create the impression that American life prior to the fifties had been enormously different in all respects, and most especially economically. Where once there had been scarcity there was now affluence; where once there had been widespread misery there was now an "overprivileged" majority and a minority of poor.

How correct is this image? Certainly there had been great changes since the Depression: bankruptcy, massive unemployment, and desperation were by the fifties no longer the social norms. But the Depression was an unusual experience. Would the fifties appear so uniquely blessed when compared to the normal economic patterns of American history?

The naive complacency of fifties writers left the major question unanswered: was the structure of American life after World War II really revolutionarily, or did it only seem so set against the artificial background of the thirties? Had America suddenly emerged from a past in which a few were rich and many poor into a uniform affluence that abolished such distinctions? Or were the fifties only a slight alteration of older social relations? Could it be that America was a "middle-class" nation long before the Depression, in which the majority was neither affluent nor impoverished, but in which the lion's share of income and wealth went to the upper middle class and the rich, while the poor and the lower middle class were left to struggle along far short of the comfortable life that "middle class" suggests?

The economic data shows that even at its worst moments America did not have the Dickensian poverty so commonplace in Europe in the eighteenth and nineteenth centuries. It did (and still does) have poverty of the most crippling kind, but the economic history of the United States is different from that of England, France, and Germany. The United States was from its birth a country rich in land and poor in population. Even during the second half of the nineteenth century, when industrialism was producing its cruelest inhumanities, much of the populace was protected in ways unavailable to the masses of Europe.

But the absence of dramatic and extensive poverty is not the whole story. The data seems to show that "the middle class" has always been, as it is today, a misleading category, made up, not of one, but of two distinctly different parts: the upper and lower middle class. Even 200 years ago the upper half was filled with professionals and skilled craftsmen, and the lower half inhabited by semiskilled and unskilled workers, small shopkeepers, and minor officials. Of the two, the upper half has always enjoyed the fruits of prosperity disproportionately, while the lower half has existed above poverty, in the strict sense, but not above deprivation. The life style of the lower middle class shades at one end into poverty and at the other end into modest comfort, but defies the comfortable myth of affluence that economic mythology has ascribed to 70% of the nation.

Finally, the evidence shows that the rich, too, have always been with us, a handful of Americans whose wealth was originally dependent on extensive land holdings and prosperous trading, but which is now generated by the nation's industry. Their presence has always troubled historians because the concentration of wealth and income they represent has been a defiance of the myth of equality, while at the same time the goal of American success stories.

This chapter and the next will try to demonstrate that America has had a surprisingly stable social structure throughout its history. These chapters are meant as a challenge to the conventional belief that the fifties were a dramatic break with the past. Far from witnessing any dramatic change, the fifties witnessed the continuity of a social system that generates at one pole a handful of very wealthy, at the other a sizable poor, and in between a set of "middle" classes whose share of the wealth has not varied significantly since the nation's founding.

1

The earliest records of the American colonies tell a great deal about the hope, if not the reality, of America's social relations. When the first ships departed for Jamestown in 1607, a skeptic drily observed of the "New Worlders" that

They would convince one that there are in America none but Elysian fields abounding in products which require no labor; that the mountains are full of gold and silver, and that the wells and springs gush forth milk and honey; that he who goes there as a servant becomes a lord; as a maid, a gracious lady; as a peasant, a nobleman.

But if the writer was not taken in by the promise of the New World, others certainly were. England in the early seventeenth century was experiencing the turmoil of land enclosure, with thousands of peasants being forced off the land as the profitability of sheep-raising became apparent to the nobility. To those peasants and other freemen, the promise of free land and a fresh start was a powerful magnet. Between 1607 and 1770, seven hundred and fifty thousand people crossed from the Old World to the New, often attracted by ditties such as this one distributed by the London Company in 1630:

> *In England land scarce and labour plenty*
> *In Virginia land free and labour scarce* [2]

The English government moreover encouraged its citizens to emigrate. England was still locked in struggle with other European monarchies for control of the New World and wished to populate those areas she claimed. After all, a man who could plough a field would readily carry a gun to defend his property when the time came for England to confront her rivals to North America's vast wealth. Consequently the promise of land in the colonies was most often a promise kept. For those able to pay their own fare (half to two-thirds of those who made the crossing), there was the guarantee of 100 or more acres free or at low cost. In some cases even more generous arrangements were made: Pennsylvania offered 500 acres to anyone transporting his family to America; freeholds in the Carolinas were assigned for every husband, wife, child, and male servant, plus 50 acres for each female servant; in New Jersey a man with a gun and six months of supplies received 150 acres, with a similar amount for each servant and slave, plus 50 acres for each female.[3]

For those who could not pay their own fares, arrangements could still be made. The colonies were starved for labor, and for any able-bodied man or woman willing to accept the position, indentured servitude was the means to a fresh start. It usually meant four to seven years of work for a new master, but at the end of that time the servant received tools and a plot of land. Evidently the conditions were acceptable to many, because it is estimated that about one-third of those who crossed before 1770 did so as indentured servants. However arduous, it proved Captain John Smith's observation in 1616 that land in America "cost nothing but labor."

Widespread distribution of land meant that from the beginning America was buffered from the landless, downtrodden peasantry that formed the base of the European social pyramid. A Pennsylvania immigrant, writing to friends at the beginning of the eighteenth century, exclaimed that American "farmers or husbandmen live better than lords. If a workman only work for four or five days a week he can live grandly." Although this is a trifle exaggerated, it is nonetheless true that wages in the colonies were 30% to 100% higher than in Europe.

Widespread distribution of land did not, however, prevent a few men from accumulating a great deal of it. The original grants made by the English monarchy had gone mostly to titled nobility and wealthy combinations of merchants. A tiny elite held vast tracts of property and wealth. By 1676, for example, there were thirty merchants and landholders in Massachusetts with fortunes of £10,000 to £20,000. Within a half century, through manipulation of the colonial legislature, the wealthy were able to reverse the custom of assigning new villages to the actual settlers, thus permitting land speculators to buy the villages for profitable resale. This led to the creation of a new class of men known commonly as "the lords of the valley," men such as Colonel Israel Williams who held property in no fewer than a dozen towns, or John Reed, a prominent Boston councilman who with a few partners was allowed to purchase 106,000 acres for a pittance. Reed's behavior created a scandal but apparently did not affect his success: when he died three decades later, he left estates not only in Massachusetts, but in Connecticut and New Hampshire as well.

In other colonies the concentration of property was even greater. In New York, the Van Rensselaers controlled over 700,000 acres, the Beekmans 240,000, the Van Cortlandts 140,000. Robert Carter left an estate upon his death in 1722 of 300,000 acres, a thousand slaves, and £10,000 in cash. A group of wealthy Virginia planters (including George Washington) formed the Ohio Company, receiving 200,000 acres in the West plus the promise of 300,000 more if they would settle 100 families there within seven years. In the Carolinas, one group of speculators received a grant of a million and half acres; another, half a million.[4]

Nor did widespread distribution of land prevent the germination and growth of poverty in the New World. In *The Social Structure of Revolutionary America*, Jackson Turner Main estimates that one-fifth of the white population and virtually all of the Negro population lived in poverty. Cities especially showed the presence of sizeable numbers of poor: James Henrietta's work reveals the existence of a propertyless class in Boston that comprised 14% of the adult males in 1687 and 29% by 1771. And events like the numerous slave uprisings and the famous "Bacon's Rebellion" of 1676 testify to the political restiveness created by such conditions.[5]

Yet even with concentrations of power and wealth, and significant poverty, America in prerevolutionary times was never a feudal fiefdom or the breeding ground for a majority proletariat. Extensive rental of land often created the problems associated with the *rentier* relationships of Europe, but agriculture predominated over husbandry and thus prevented the tragedies associated with English enclosure. Imprisonment for debt, which had plagued dispossessed farmers for centuries in the Old World, was minimized, and land was available farther west for those who could not make a go of it the first time. And attitudes toward poverty and indolence, though harsh, were not those of later Social Darwinism, and provision for the aged and infirm reflected the strong communal sense of the pioneers.

2

The American Revolution represented not only a political but an economic turning point in the country's history. Although several modern historians and sociologists have argued that the Civil War was the "real revolution" in American history, the liberation of the colonies from English mastery opened economic as well as political channels for a great outpouring of democratic sentiment.

Where John Locke had written of "life, liberty, and property" Thomas Jefferson substituted "life, liberty, and the pursuit of happiness" as the credo of the Declaration of Independence. The change, so often remarked upon, did not mean the Founding Fathers endorsed absolute economic equality; but they certainly felt that no man should be left impoverished in the new republic. More importantly, the sentiments of men like Jefferson and Paine were not limited to the left wing of our Revolution. Benjamin Franklin argued that no man ought to own more property than needed for his livelihood; the rest, by right, belonged to the state. Even John Adams, a stalwart conservative, fulminated against "the dons, the bashaws, the grandees, the patricians, the sachems, the nabobs, call them what name you please," who connived against the rights of the underprivileged. As one historian observed, "The Revolution was being fought not only against the Tories of England but against the wealthy at home, and disrespect for the rich became flagrant." [6]

The consequence of "flagrant disrespect" was not only the extension of new political rights and freedoms, but economic opportunities as well. Tory landholdings seized by the Revolutionary government were resold with economic equality in mind. New York expropriated the 300-square-mile estate of the Philipse family, as well as other vast properties, so that by the end of the war nearly half of the state was in community hands. Virginia confiscated the 6-million-acre Fairfax estate, and New Jersey took over more than 500 large holdings. Pennsylvania, in one of the great ironies of colonial history, confiscated the holdings of William Penn's family, valued at $5,000,000, and reimbursed the descendents only $650,000. These holdings were then broken up and resold to farmers, with limits of 500 acres or less placed on each parcel in order to prevent speculation. In Virginia, squatters on such lands were permitted to remain, and were charged only five dollars for each 100 acres, payable over a period of two and a half years. Taken as a whole, redistribution signified a major boost to the principle of economic equality.[7]

Even more significant than expropriation of Tory land, however, was the opening of the West. Prior to the French and Indian Wars, England had encouraged her subjects to venture westward, as part of the ongoing struggle to wrest control of the region from the French and Spanish; but with settlement of the struggle the royal attitude took a more parsimonious turn. In 1763, an official decree had limited settlement to the mountain regions immediately to the west of the colonial borders; in 1774, a second decree had not only limited expansion further, but also placed the territory north of the Ohio River under the jurisdiction of the province of Quebec. With the victory of the revolution, however, the territory was reopened. In a stroke of diplomatic genius, the Americans were able to persuade the British to cede the entire territory to the fledgling nation, an area larger than the nation itself. Congress, in the Land Ordinance of 1785, then divided the area into townships of 36 square miles, reserved one-thirty-sixth of each township for the support of public education, put half the remaining territory up for auction at $1 an acre, and left the remainder to be sold in square-mile blocks.

Even then, the rush for land was so great that before Congress's program could go into effect, 7,000 squatters had occupied unsurveyed territory. By 1790 this stream of settlers had grown to a steady flow, and the census found 221,000 Americans dwelling beyond the Appalachians. "Thus the frontier, despite the speculations of the big companies," wrote Sidney Lens, "not only deepened the democratic spirit but offset poverty measurably." An English traveler in 1817 wrote likewise, from personal observation:

The practical liberty of America is found in its great space and small population. Good land, dog-cheap everywhere, and for nothing if you will go for it, gives as much elbow room to every man as he chooses to take. . . . They come, they toil, they prosper. This is the real liberty of America.

3

But the aspirations of Jefferson for an egalitarian, agrarian democracy were not to be fulfilled. It is one of those ironies of history that as Jefferson penned the Declaration of Independence, another man was simultaneously publishing a book that would spell the doom of liberty built on the family farm.

In 1776 Adam Smith completed *The Wealth of Nations*. In its nine hundred pages Smith surveyed as broad a part of the then-extant world as many thought possible, ranging from a discussion of salt in Abyssinia to the sociology of morality. Its view of the world was far from simple, and it was not merely (as later critics accused it of being) an apologia for capitalism. Smith recognized the venality in men and warned that among the eighteenth-century industrialists "the chief enjoyment of riches consists in the parade of riches." But accompanying his keen-eyed distrust of the motives of capitalists was a profound faith in the mechanism of the capitalist market. It contained, he said, "an invisible hand" that would regulate the behavior of grasping men, and if it did create vast riches for a few, it also promised "universal opulence" that would extend itself "to the lowest ranks of the people."

Needless to say, budding entrepreneurs in Europe and America flocked to Smith's doctrine like faithful to the altar. Ignoring his caustic warning that capitalists "generally have an interest to deceive and even to oppress the public," they popularized the doctrine of "the invisible hand" and forged it into a tool with which to battle the Jeffersonian interventions of government in favor of economic equality.

In America, the doctrine coincided neatly with the aristocratic sentiments of the Federalists, who saw equality as a perversion of man's natural and proper state. Communities, Alexander Hamilton had warned the Continental Congress, "divide themselves into the few and the many. The first are the rich and well-born, the other the mass of the people . . . turbulent and changing, they seldom judge or determine right. Give therefore to the first class a distinct, permanent share in the Government."

The growth of capitalist industry, in the minds of these conservatives, was the antidote to democratic degradation. Hamilton, far from being appalled by the dehumanizing consequences of the Industrial Revolution in Britain, was elated.

In his massive *Report on Manufactures* in 1791, he noted that over half the workers in English mills were women and children, and concluded benignly that these people were "rendered more useful, and the latter [the children] more early useful, by manufacturing establishments, than they would otherwise be." [8] According to Hamilton, industry would not only secure the position of the "natural" elite, but would end the "idleness" so common among the masses.

Hamilton's association of industrialism and elitism is a strong theme in American history. Writers and historians from Thoreau and Emerson to the present have seen in the coming of the machine the end of American innocence. They blame industrialization for the destruction of egalitarian democratic society, for the undermining of community, for the transformation of the rugged individual into the corporate cog. They share Hamilton's analysis but reject his conclusions. Where there had once been a humane world of decent comfort shared by nearly everyone, industrialism had erected a stratified society with massive poverty, brutal working conditions, and a tiny but fantastically wealthy elite.

But such a picture of America's industrial transformation, however correct it may be in broad outline, bears a strong tendency toward overstatement in two directions. First, it tends to romanticize preindustrial America into an almost pastoral state, when in fact it was no such thing. We have already seen how a tiny elite of wealthy property owners and merchants existed in colonial America, and we have the evidence of studies like Beard's on the writing of the Constitution to show how these men dominated the political process. And although it may be true that many families were cushioned by subsistence farming, Main's estimate (cited earlier) that one-fifth of the white population and all of the Negro population lived in poverty certainly refutes any easy equation of eighteenth-century America with a world of egalitarian comfort.

Second, such a picture tends dangerously to overexaggerate the negative impact of industrialization in the nineteenth century. Clearly the fifties writers who saw in their own age the novelty of minority poverty were imagining a contrast to the nineteenth century; but were they correct? Apart from the undeniable alterations which industrialization made in the character of life, did it in fact impose such a drastic alteration in the material conditions of that life?

To answer that question fully would require dozens of volumes; but a brief sketch of nineteenth-century social structure can serve to offer the outline of such an answer. First of all, it was in the nineteenth century that the class terms with which we describe contemporary society came into general use. The term "middle class" for example only appeared in England toward the end of the Napoleonic Wars, and shortly thereafter began to appear sporadically in American usage. Tocqueville speaks occasionally of an American "middle class," but his use shows how narrow it was originally conceived to be: generally he means it in the French sense of *bourgeoisie*, a combination of urban business and professional elites plus the landed gentry.

The majority of Americans, in nineteenth-century terms, were not considered to be of the middle class; they were either farmers or members of the working class. But this did not simply mean that they were poor, as was so often the case with their European counterparts. Whereas critics of industrialization in Europe saw these classes being rapidly turned into what Marx called an "immiserated proletariat," the process in America was neither so rapid nor so drastic. As in seventeenth- and eighteenth-century America, scarcity of labor kept up wages for the worker and the availability of western lands protected the farmer.

Although the majority was not "immiserated," a minority did nevertheless become extremely wealthy. This was aptly revealed when the Declaration of Independence was signed not by a broad cross-section of farmers and workers, but by well-to-do lawyers, merchants, and landowners. And as the nineteenth century began, America's tiny elite continuously moved to consolidate and expand its wealth. Harold Faulkner, in his *American Economic History*, shows that while the Revolutionary governments broke up many great estates, many were left intact, and that as great new tracts of land were added in the Ohio Territory and the Louisiana Purchase much of the best land was quickly bought up and incorporated into vast private holdings.

Bending the state laws to their purpose, promoters obtained great tracts of land in the West. They purchased at a discount the bounty warrants of soldiers unable or unwilling to migrate; they sent out servants to secure preemption rights; and they converted state certificates of indebtedness (which represented the values of depreciated currency into claims upon the land). Estates as large as 140,000 acres came into being. So much land, in fact, had thus been obtained beyond the Alleghenies that settlers pushing westward found it difficult to secure titles for reasonable amounts.[9]

In commerce, transportation, finance, and especially in the new manufacturing industries, the same was true: the wealthy and influential maintained their preeminence, admitting successive waves of "new money" as the economy expanded, but in no way contributing to the egalitarian ideal of the American Revolution.

Beneath this tiny elite came the middle class of the day— the professionals, the merchants, the prosperous farmers, the skilled craftsmen. Economically they resembled the upper middle class of today, using the savings from their above average incomes to expand their enterprises or invest in new ones. In one major respect, though, the old middle class was different from today's upper middle class: because the economy of trade and agriculture differs from that of advanced industrialism, no New Class as we have described it existed. There was little need for an elaborate administrative structure either in business or in government; neither was there much need for an educational administration or service sector. Hence the old middle class was smaller in proportion to other groups in the society than it is today.

Beneath the old middle class came the workers and the small farmers. Like the lower middle class of today, the workers and farmers of the nineteenth century were a far from homogeneous group who perceived no common interests. At the top were the skilled laborers, usually a step below prosperous craftsmen, but a step above the semiskilled and unskilled worker. Outside the towns too there were also divisions between farmers owning middle- and small-size farms and below these farmers were the farm laborers.

The working class and small farmers were often an interchangeable lot, with individuals moving from one category to the other with surprising frequency. For example, a man might start out as a farm laborer, amass enough money to buy a small amount of land and become a farmer. Then if times were hard and he found himself dispossessed, he would migrate to a city or town, work as a laborer, or return to working for some other, more fortunate farmer as a farm laborer. Not until well after the Civil War did the factory system impose rigid boundaries on occupations.

For the skilled worker, America was never a bad country. Scarcity of skilled labor is a normal condition in a young country, and scarcity ensured good wages. In the larger cities, craftsmen and skilled workers were further protected from exploitation by craft organizations and workingmen's alliances. The Philadelphia shoemakers, for example, had organized in 1792 and the New York printers established the Typographical Society in 1794. By 1828, urban skilled workers and craftsmen were well enough organized that the Mechanics Union of Trade Associations in Philadelphia proposed to the various unions in that city that they combine in nominating political candidates "to represent the interests of the working classes." [10]

Although not to the degree sometimes thought; as the New Class has grown and the economy has been consolidated in the hands of giant corporations, the number of small businessmen and farmers, who made up the backbone of the old middle class, has steadily declined. Thus it is not accurate merely to say that the upper middle class has been growing, without noticing how that growth was accomplished by the displacement and decline of its predecessor.

If the life of unskilled workers and farm laborers was not the misery of their European counterparts, neither was it pleasurable; real wages were 30% to 50% higher than for comparable work in Europe, but also about 50% lower than the wages of skilled laborers. Faulkner judged that "the unskilled laborer, although commanding greater wages than in Europe, barely made ends meet . . ."

Factory wages, especially during the first half of the century, were also higher than in Europe, but still strikingly low. Even in Massachusetts, where such wages were highest, between 1830 and 1860 men averaged only $5.00 a week, women, $1.75 to $2.00, and children, $1.00 to $2.00. As one went further south, wages were generally lower. Yet even such low wages were subject to fluctuation, rising in the 1830s and 1840s and falling in the 1850s. After the Civil War, for a time, wages rose and fell again, chiefly as a result of mass immigration. By 1900 the average amounts paid in 1860 had almost doubled, but the gains in real wages were by then often offset by unemployment, atrocious working conditions, and ruthless competition for jobs. And most important, the alternative of farming or homesteading, which had forced manufacturers to pay higher wages before the Civil War and allowed unskilled laborers to leave factories when conditions became unbearable, was gone; the frontier, as Frederick Jackson Turner has made clear, was closed.

In the midst of this transformation of America, the poor are curiously difficult to identify. European visitors consistently remarked on the absence of poverty as they understood it, and Americans likewise proudly boasted of its absence; yet poverty did exist. Certainly all slaves were poor; even after their emancipation, the black population lived in grinding poverty. Among the white population, frontier communities and agricultural areas were often poor as well.

But then as now, the worst poverty was urban. As early as the 1820s major cities began receiving large numbers of immigrants, from both Europe and rural America. As a result wages were depressed and daily living conditions worsened. In 1819, soup kitchens had to be opened in New York, Boston, and Philadelphia to feed the poor. The Society for the Prevention of Pauperism estimated that one in fifteen persons in New York was a pauper, and one in ten received some sort of charity. A social reformer in 1829 illustrated declining urban living conditions by describing a room in Philadelphia fifteen feet by eleven feet, in which two couples and four children lived, earning together 25 cents a day by spooling and spinning wool. The New York police estimated in 1852 that 10,000 abandoned homeless children were living in the city. By 1855, one private charity alone was paying out nearly $100,000 a year just to the poor of New York City. If life for the poor was better in America than in Europe, their lot was still poverty.[11]

4

Considered in the abstract, these figures yield an unorthodox conclusion: America of the 1950s possessed striking similarities to nineteenth century America. Great wealth was concentrated in a few hands at the top, while poverty of a significant but not a European kind existed at the bottom. In between was ranged not a homogeneous middle class, but a stratified group of wage earners ranging from prosperous merchants and craftsmen to working class laborers living above strict poverty but well below a level of moderate comfort or security.

Critics might point to regional variations, changes during the century, or the differences between an agricultural and industrial America to refute this conclusion. However our deduction is further supported and enriched by a study of a particular community, Newburyport, Massachusetts.

In *Poverty and Progress: Social Mobility in a Nineteenth-Century City*, Stephan Thernstrom sought to examine upward mobility in a nineteenth-century context in order to check conventional theories of American history against the recorded experience of at least one city. He chose Newburyport not only because it had a long recorded history, full of the data necessary for historical analysis, but also because it had been the subject of an earlier study, Lloyd Warner's *Yankeetown*. Warner's study had concentrated on the twentieth century, and part of Thernstrom's purpose was to examine Warner's claim that Newburyport had undergone a remarkable change since the 1800s.

Poverty and Progress traces the early development of Newburyport through its rise to prominence in the eighteenth century as a merchant and shipping center, its slow decline in the first half of the nineteenth century as its population declined while larger, more prosperous cities achieved economic supremacy, and finally its reawakening under the influence of immigration and industrialization—the period of transition which carried it into the twentieth century.

In his description of eighteenth-century Newburyport, Thernstrom confirms our earlier sketch of pre-Revolutionary America:

Roughly a quarter of the men of preindustrial Newburyport belonged to the merchant and professional class. Among them were the "merchant aristocracy," a group of less than 200 men who effectively controlled the community; the lower fringes of this class took in a variety of petty merchants, traders, and shipmasters. Below them ranked the artisans, who made up almost half of the labor force. Sharply marked off from these two groups were the "laboring poor," the laborers, servants, sailors, and vagrants who made up the bottom quarter of the population.[12]

The situation of the poor and the lower middle class seems to have been more advantageous in the early decades after the Revolution in the nineteenth century:

The town was small—about six thousand in 1800—and its residents were hacked into an area of less than a mile square. The distinct class-segregated neighborhoods of the modern city did not yet exist. There were no working-class ghettos, nor had the merchant and professional class abandoned the central business district as a place of residence. . . . Apprentice, journeyman, and master often slept under the same roof; servants and laborers lived in or near the household of their master and were subject to surveillance and discipline. If a few drifters lived entirely apart, their numbers were small and they had little effect on the affairs of the community.[13]

But Thernstrom warned against exaggerating this life:

The lot of the laborer in preindustrial Newburyport, of course, had been far from idyllic; laboring occupations had been at least as brutish and degrading in 1800 as they were in 1850. What was decisively new in the community was not the depressed position of the working class, but its increased visibility and the weakening of older mechanisms of subordination and social control.[14]

In any case the old colonial social structure was fragile, and under the impact of industrialism, quickly began to collapse. The change which Thernstrom describes could serve as a paradigm for the fate of thousands of small and medium-size towns across the nation:

By 1850 the household economy of the old community had disappeared, and a freely fluctuating market for labor had been established. In the household-based economy even the lowliest laborer was customarily attached to a particular master. The coming of the factory and the mass influx of floating workmen brought a new anonymity and impersonality to the labor contract. . . . Employers had come to think less of individual laborers, more of "labor" as an abstraction, a pool to be dipped into when market conditions made it profitable to do so.[15]

Even so, the process of immiseration, of turning an agrarian peasantry into a vast unskilled industrial proletariat—as had happened in Europe—did not seem to be happening in Newburyport. Thernstrom very carefully catalogued occupations in the town at mid-century and found the following:

Approximately one quarter of the employed males of the city were semiskilled workers, while almost 40 percent were skilled laborers. The diversity of skilled trades was striking—thirty-nine varieties of artisan could be counted on the local census schedules for 1850. It is misleading to classify mid-century Newburyport as a "mill town"; its occupational structure was not heavily weighted toward unskilled and semiskilled callings. The community had a highly diversified craft economy, with almost two-thirds of its labor force in the top two occupational categories and less than a tenth at the very bottom.[16]

For the more prosperous skilled workers, this meant not only a secure income, but the chance for profitable investment. Thernstrom reports that these workers, when they could scrape together the capital, commonly invested in real estate on the edge of town, either moving their families onto the land or renting it to other workers or small farmers. As an example, he traced the financial progress of one Tim Marooney: "Marooney had scraped together $400 by 1867, when he invested it in a shack on the edge of the city. With two cows, a few chickens, and no rent to pay, Marooney found it possible to save a substantial portion of his wages." By further reinvestment and the use of four mortgages, Marooney was worth $1900 by 1880. While Thernstrom did not wish to generalize, he asserted that Marooney was not "untypical" of more adventurous workers.

But it is hard to conclude that the life of the less skilled laborer and small farmer was by any means comfortable. Caught in the middle of a massive social reorientation over which he had no control, the worker or farmer could—depending on his skills—move between occupations and regions, playing on booms and leaving after the inevitable bust. But eventually men of this type became rarer and rarer; families once settled were difficult to move, and the opportunities which made the West so attractive began to disappear towards the end of the century.

By the end of the Civil War, labor in Newburyport and elsewhere began to find out about the new discipline and impersonality of industrialism. "The common laborer," Thernstrom writes, "was, to an extreme degree, at the mercy of the harsh uncertainties of the casual labor market. Without a specific economic function to perform regularly for a predictable reward, he was forced to take his chances daily in the competition for temporary employment." As late as 1875, the mean income for a common laborer in Essex County, Massachusetts, was less than $30 a month.

Moreover, as industrialism continued to remove the necessity for many old forms of labor, and as immigrants began to swell the ranks of job seekers, poverty, which had once been a relatively minor problem for Newburyport, began to grow. The number of welfare applicants tripled, and the local newspaper solemnly swore that certain "foreign influences" were encouraging the immigration of the poor and that handbills were being distributed in England announcing that "Massachusetts is a paradise for paupers."

But there is an important fact to notice about Newburyport: although the *number* of poor increased rapidly, the *percentage* of poor seems surprisingly similar to percentages of poor today. For example, the newspaper reported the common assumption of propertied interests that the Irish neighborhood (the epitome of the poor to the Yankee upper middle class) was full of "teeming lanes and alleys" that provided "the breeding grounds of drinking, crime, fornication, and other immoral activity." The numbers supposed to inhabit "the teeming lanes and alleys" were from time to time referred to as "hundreds of poor." But "hundreds" in a city of twelve to thirteen thousand certainly did not constitute the swarming proletarian mass that recent American mythology might have us believe; indeed it did not even equal the percentage of poor in many American cities today. As a result of the collapse of 1857, the local paper recorded a population loss of "more than one thousand," mostly emigrants in search of a better life: but even this figure still does not suggest that the majority of Newburyport was desperately impoverished.[17]

5

The history of Newburyport reinforces the conclusion that the economic thought of the fifties is misleading. Economists who saw the postwar period as a major break with the past overestimated the amount of poverty in nineteenth-century America. The poor were never a majority in towns like Newburyport. They constituted roughly a quarter to a third of the population; their numbers fluctuated from time to time and were significantly higher in certain parts of the country —in the South and in the immigrant districts of the major cities. But overall, Newburyport was typical of nineteenth century economic conditions.

In other words, America was never a country with an impoverished majority as Galbraith, for example, would have us believe. It has always been, as history books tell us, a middle-class nation. But this means less than many observers, especially those fifties economists, have supposed. Most importantly, it does *not* mean that most Americans have been comfortable and secure; the middle class has always been sharply divided between those who live one step behind opulence and those who have always faced the imminent prospect of becoming poor themselves.

In brief, it seems that America has carefully guarded the rough contours of an unequal society. Indeed it seems that the America of the 1950s, instead of representing a major social revolution, maintained in broad outline a socio-economic structure not markedly different from that of the America of the 1850s.

5 | Looking Backward II: The Prosperity Decade

The country is in the midst of an era of prosperity more extensive and of peace more permanent than it has ever before experienced.

Calvin Coolidge, 1924

We in America today are nearer to the final triumph over poverty than ever before in our land. The poorhouse is vanishing from among us.

Herbert Hoover, 1928

One hundred years ago America was still in transition between an agricultural and an industrial world, with farms and small towns as typical of America as her great cities. Today we cannot say the same thing: agriculture employs only six percent of the labor force, and the majority of Americans live in urban or suburban communities. Instead of horse and locomotive, we use car and plane to travel; instead of coal and oil, we use electricity to light our houses; and instead of brick and wooden homes and offices, we work and live in modern surroundings which steel, plastics, and artificial fabrics provide.

In sum, we have made progress.

But progress, as a number of critics in the sixties have tried to tell us, is no longer the unadorned beauty we once worshipped in the fifties. With technological advances came a raft of undesirable effects as well. Instead of fishing our rivers, we now poison them; instead of cultivating the natural beauty of our countryside, we blight it with billboards and litter; and instead of cultivating our sensibilities, we debase them with television and crass consumption. We have, in one critic's words, become a malignant case of "the bland leading the bland."

All this debunking would be fine, if it were not itself dangerously in need of debunking. For "antiprogress" in the late sixties rapidly took on the mythological character in some circles which progress itself once had, and with the same pitfalls for criticism. The trouble is that much of what passed for novel and analysis relied heavily on some of the hoariest of New Class myths. For example, resistance to growth relies heavily on the casual assumption that after World War II, we became an affluent, middle-class, and (when discussed) roughly egalitarian nation, and that we can now proceed to issues of higher importance—issues of "the quality of life" rather than "the quantity of life." The issue is one of "Social Balance."

The critical belief behind these New Class assumptions which we tried to challenge in the previous chapter was novelty—the idea that because of technology, science, planning, education, and all the other rational forces which professionals and managers direct, America has entered a completely new phase in its, and the world's, history. We saw in the last chapter that the premise on which this belief rested—that America had once been a nation of majority poverty—was false. What if we can show further that technology in the fifties, far from being revolutionarily novel, was merely part of a continuum of technology and technology-worship that spanned several decades, and that as such, instead of having the widely presumed tendency to modify economic and social inequalities, it has maintained them? For after all, agrarian, rural cultures such as that of America a hundred years ago are hard to measure against industrial, urban cultures not only because the material goods which the latter prizes are absent in agrarian, rural cultures, but because the values of the cultures often differ so markedly. If, taking into account the self-evident changes which industrialism has had on American life-styles, we can nonetheless show that over a long span of years, technology has preserved rather than abolished inequalities, we will have come a long way toward a radically different understanding of the myth of the Affluent Society. Moreover, we will begin to realize that the issue today is not one merely of "quality of life" in place of quantity, but how ultimately both will be answered in the context of that understanding of America.

1

Of the three decades before the Depression, the twenties are the most inviting for comparison with the fifties. The first decade of the century was in several respects a continuation of the conflicts of the nineteenth century; the next decade, preoccupied by the Great War, is difficult to compare to a postwar period; the twenties, however, are strikingly similar to the fifties and to a lesser extent to the sixties as well. Politically, the mood of the decade was conservative. The attitudes of its three Republican presidents were not at all dissimilar to those of Eisenhower thirty years later: all believed in a relatively nonactivist presidency, limited government, and free enterprise. During both eras the conservatism of government was reflected in a personal quietism that emphasized private advancement over community agitation, stability over change. Even the terrifying conservatism represented by McCarthyism had its parallels in the Palmer Raids that inaugurated the twenties.

The economic parallels between the twenties and the fifties are even more striking. If fifties economists could believe in the Affluent Society, their counterparts of the twenties were just as enthusiastic about their own decade. Judged by prewar standards, America during the twenties seemed wonderfully prosperous. World War I (like World War II) had given a boost to the poor and the lower middle class: farmers had prospered under the increased demand for food production; factory workers had benefitted with higher wages as American production turned more and more to the supply of European combatants and later, the U.S. Army.

America's belief in its own well-being is suggested by the title of George Soule's book on the period, *The Prosperity Decade*. "Prosperity" was as much a catchword then as "affluence" was in the fifties, and superficially at least the term seemed justified:

Anyone could see [prosperity] for himself just by looking around at the automobiles on the streets and the radios in the homes. As of 1920 only seven million horseless carriages rolled along American streets; nine years later there were twenty-four million. In 1921 citizens purchased ten million dollars' worth of the newfangled instrument, the radio, and in 1929 forty times that much. . . . If the wide-eyed masses could not yet afford to rent the apartments on Park Avenue, with gold-plated bathtubs, advertised for $45,000, their daughters could splurge on lipsticks at $2.50 a tube, and their sons on a package of three razor blades for a half dollar.[1]

But the prosperity of the twenties was much more uneven than such comments suggest, and here too the decade bears a striking resemblance to the fifties.

The farmer, still an important part of the population, had been badly hurt immediately after the war by a sharp fall in prices that left foreclosures and indebtedness in its wake. By 1923 most of the economy had regained its strength, but farming continued to suffer. Senator George Norris of Nebraska bitterly complained that "everyone seems to be prosperous and making money except the farmer."

But the farmers were not alone; labor too found itself shortchanged by the Prosperity Decade, although not with the same uniformity as the farmer. In the twenties, as always, labor was divided between skilled and unskilled, unionized and nonunionized: the skilled and unionized workers regularly did better than their unskilled, unorganized counterparts. As in the nineteenth century, wages for craftsmen were twice the wages of unskilled labor. Even so, average wages for all categories of labor rose only 11% between 1923 and 1929, while profits soared 62% and dividends 65%.

By contrast of course the rich did best of all. Richard Hofstadter recounted the inequities of the period:

> Throughout the "twenties," the slowly rising level of industrial workers' real wages had been outdistanced by the great leaps in profits, savings, and investment. In 1929 more than 40 per cent of American families had incomes of less than $1,500 a year. The 24,000 richest families had a total income more than three times as great as the total income of the 5.8 million poorest families. The savings of the rich piled up out of all proportion to the opportunities for sound investment. For outlets they sought speculative activity in real estate and corporation securities. Speculation itself made the whole economy into a "bubble" that was sure to burst.[2]

The picture of a great many people living in poverty and a tiny handful enjoying great wealth is not an inaccurate characterization of the twenties. Rexford Tugwell judged that during the decade ten million American families were living in poverty—one-third of the population. The Brookings

Institution was even more pessimistic: it concluded that if $2,000 a year provided a family with only basic necessities, then three-fifths of the country was living either in poverty or deprivation. Yet in a single year of that decade John D. Rockefeller, Jr. paid an *income tax* of more than $6.2 million; Henry Ford and his son Edsel together paid taxes of over $5 million.

This picture is something of a caricature, however. It calls to mind the European model of a wealthy elite surrounded by a mass of paupers. From there one is led to the simple conclusion that life today must be a vast improvement over life forty years ago. Neither that conclusion nor its major premise can withstand careful scrutiny.

For example, Tugwell's estimate of poverty in the twenties—one-third of the nation—is almost identical to Harrington's estimate for the fifties. Nor is it far from the percentage we might reasonably call poor today. In 1968, one-third of American families earned less than $6,500, a figure which, though higher than the government's definition of poverty, is more realistic (as we shall see in Chapter Six).

Even the Brookings Institution's conclusions are not as extreme or obsolete as they might sound. In 1970, the Bureau of Labor Statistics defined $10,700 per year as a "comfortable" budget for an average family, yet this exceeded the income of over half of all American families.[3]

Other information supports the conclusion that American classes have undergone little if any change in the twentieth century. Gabriel Kolko, in *Wealth and Power in America*, compiled an income distribution table for the United States between 1910 and 1959. His conclusion, based on extensive investigation of various forms of income and wealth-holdings, was that "a radically unequal distribution of income has been characteristic of the American social structure since at least 1910, and despite minor year-to-year fluctuations in the shares of the income-tenths, no significant trend toward equality has appeared." According to Kolko, throughout that entire half-century, through two world wars and the severest depression in the nation's history, the income of the top 10% of the population remained consistently larger than that of the entire bottom half.[4]

Joseph Pechman, the director of economic studies at Brookings, confirms Kolko's findings in a more recent article. Writing in *The Public Interest* on tax policy and the need for reforms, he commented that "the distribution of income in the nineteen-fifties period may not have been very different from what it was in the early nineteen-twenties." [5] Since income distribution had not changed significantly by the late sixties, Pechman's observation can be extended to the present.

A third economist, Robert Lampman, has drawn similar conclusions concerning the wealth distribution of America. Although his data show a decline in the concentration of wealth, he so qualifies the data as to mitigate most of the decline. For example, he found that the wealth held by the top 1% of adult Americans fell from 31% to 26% between 1922 and 1956, and that the wealth of the top 2% of American families declined from 33% to 28.5% during the same period. But these statistics, he warned, should be scrutinized with care. First, the concentration of wealth had not declined evenly. After World War I the share of the top 1% had been 31% of the total personal wealth, but by 1929 had risen to over 36%; similarly, in 1949 the holdings of this tiny group had fallen to 20.8%, but by 1956 had risen back to 26%. This unevenness was crucially important, because it indicated that in "normal" times the tendency of wealth was not toward greater distribution, but toward greater concentration.[6]

Second, much of what seemed to be a decline in the concentration of wealth was in reality a statistical illusion. As Lampman explained, "The fact that the share of wealth of top individuals fell more than the top families is believed to be due to increasing splitting of wealth within families, principally between husbands and wives." In other words, for tax purposes and other reasons, wealth formerly held in the name of the husband alone was now being registered separately in the name of the wife or the children. "Splitting" had become so common, in fact, that Lampman believed "half the percentage decline found for individuals between 1922 and 1953 would disappear on a family basis." [7]

Lampman's observation about the behavior of "equalizing" wealth is paralleled by Kolko's dissection of income redistribution patterns. In substantiating his claim that "no significant trend toward income equality has appeared," Kolko actually found that in certain respects the income distribution of America was becoming more *unequal*. For example the income controlled by the bottom fifth of the population failed over the period to grow along with the rest of the nation, resulting in a decline of this group's share of the total. Along with a smaller decline by the next lowest tenth, and inappreciable gains by the fourth and fifth tenths, this decline has constituted an actual regression on the part of the bottom half of the American population in its control of income shares. In 1919, according to Kolko, this half received 27% of the national personal income; but by 1959, their share had shrunk to 23%.[8] By 1968, the share of the bottom half had dropped once again, to 22%, according to the University of Michigan Survey Research Center.

At the other end of the income pyramid, however, the rich and the upper middle class were prospering. "The only significant rises in income distribution," said Kolko, "have occurred in the second- and third-richest income-tenths. Their combined shares increased more than one-quarter from 1910 to 1959, and by the end of that period their combined income share was almost equal to that of the richest tenth." By way of confirmation, the Survey Research Center showed in 1968 the top tenth receiving 30% of the income, and the top three tenths receiving 58% of the total, a percentage two-and-a-half times greater than that of the bottom 110 million Americans.[9]

2

Some parallels between the twenties and recent times become clearer if we move briefly from abstract percentages to concrete ground. As with Newburyport and the nineteenth century, the twenties take on a fuller life when we examine what touched the actual daily lives of the people rather than just economic tables.

During the twenties studies such as Thernstrom's on Newburyport first became popular, and none is better known than the classic *Middletown* by Robert and Helen Lynd. Published in 1929, it represented sociology's most ambitious attempt to escape from methodological abstraction, and to borrow from the world of anthropology a coherent frame for the study of human societies. As the book's foreword declared, "To study ourselves as through the eye of an outsider is the basic difficulty in social science, and may be insurmountable, but the authors of this volume have made a serious attempt, by approaching an American community as an anthropologist does a primitive tribe." The Lynds selected Muncie, Indiana, for their case study because it contained features common to a large number of communities in the 1920s, and though not all-inclusive, it displayed a pattern of living that no one could call "untypical" for the time.

For today's reader, many of the differences between that era and the present are obvious: the automobile is now a commonplace nuisance rather than a novel one; religion is less significant in the community's life as a social bond; work hours are shorter and wage levels are higher; television has displaced the radio. Most important, we are a people of the suburbs, and no longer of the small town.

But how much has America really changed? What enormous differences have been wrought by the past forty years in the lives of most Americans? Surely history reveals that each moment is unique; but in the fundamental patterns of living—of mores, customs, and social relations—what has been radically altered in the last forty years?

Perhaps it is the appreciation of technology and science, which writers in the fifties saw ushering in a new age. But three decades earlier, the Lynds wrote with enormous awe of their own changing world:

> We are coming to realize. . . . that we today are probably living in one of the eras of greatest rapidity of change in the history of human institutions. New tools and techniques are being developed with stupendous celerity, while in the wake of these technical developments increasingly frequent and strong culture waves sweep over us from without, drenching us with the material and non-material habits of other centers.[10]

Can we honestly say, for example, that television, or even the computer, has meant as fundamental a revolution in day-to-day human relations as the development of the automobile?

Perhaps we can say that we are now more "urbanized" than then, with all the disruptions such a change implies. But what *does* urbanization imply? For an affluent upper middle class, it obviously means security, mobility, prestige, sophistication, a chance for travel, education, a broadening of horizons. But in *The Levittowners*, one of the most celebrated works of sociology in the past decade, Herbert Gans concludes, "it is striking how little American culture among the Levittowners differs from what Toqueville reported in his travels through small-town middle class America a century ago."

> Of course [Gans continued] he was here before the economy needed an industrial proletariat, but the equality of men and women, the power of the child over his parents, the importance of the voluntary association, the social functions of the church,

and the rejection of high culture seem holdovers from his time, and so is the adherence to the traditional virtues: individual honesty, thrift, religiously inspired morality, Franklinesque individualism, and Victorian prudery. . . . class conflict is as alive as ever. . . . Working class culture continues to flourish, even though its rough edges are wearing smooth and its extended family and public institutions are not brought to the suburbs. Affluence and better education have made a difference, but they have not made the factory worker middle class, any more than college attendance has made lower middle class people cosmopolitan.[11]

But if the mores and customs of many Americans have not changed fundamentally, what has? It is crucial to the myth of middle class equality and the belief in the insignificance of modern poverty that affluence has advanced enormously and been more equally distributed than ever before. On the second point, we already have the testimony of Kolko, Pechman, and Lampman to the contrary. On the first point, we will show evidence that, while not disputing an advance in affluence, challenges some of America's exaggerated assumptions about it.

This evidence could be contested in the sense that the four indices of affluence about to be offered focus only on major spending, rather than the full spectrum of consumer purchases. Obviously, the total number of discretionary items available in the society has increased. But the evidence will suggest that while the total number of intermediate and insignificant items of consumption has grown, the *basic* measures of contemporary affluence were already set in the twenties, and furthermore, were distributed along income lines similar to those today.

In the twenties, a sure proof for Americans that affluence (or rather "prosperity") had arrived was the automobile. In 1890, only 125 Middletown families, virtually all of them upper and upper middle class, had been able to afford horse-drawn carriages. The first automobile appeared in Middletown in 1900; by 1906 there were still less than 200 in the entire county. But at the end of 1923, there were 6,221 cars in Middletown, and over 11,000 in the county, an increase of *five thousand percent* in less than twenty years. Nationally, there were only half a million cars in America in 1910; in 1924, there were fifteen and a half million.[12]

The revolution that the auto brought to American social life has been discussed for decades, but few have summarized it better than the working-class mother of nine who told the Lynds, "We'd rather do without clothes than give up the car."

Admittedly the total number of cars has increased enormously since then, as has the number per capita. The important thing is not simply that there are more cars now than then, but that in the twenties the car was a widely distributed status symbol. Data on 123 working-class families gathered by the Lynds revealed that sixty owned automobiles. Even though the automobile was a great financial burden to working-class families, it was available to a larger percentage of people in the twenties than it had been ten years earlier or would be ten years later.

The second major sign of affluence in Middletown was more traditional: the family home. As the Lynds wrote, "There is a deep-rooted sentiment in Middletown that home ownership is a mark of independence, of respectability, of belonging, a sentiment strengthened by the lag in house building during the war years and the resulting housing shortage which has made purchase necessary in many cases to keep a house from being sold over a family's head." [13]

American society has always made the family home the *sine qua non* of success. Thernstrom's study of Newburyport, although it did not distinguish statistically between family homes and other types of real property, nevertheless stressed the sizable accumulation of real property by working-class families. Presumably the largest portion of this accumulation was the family home. So too in Middletown it was apparent how much importance was placed on home ownership. Of the 123 working-class families interviewed by the Lynds, only a third rented their homes, and only a third of the eighty-one who owned their own homes had mortgages on them.

While this amount of ownership was higher than the national average, it is probably attributable to the character of towns the size of Middletown: unlike larger cities where apartments and rented homes were more frequent, four-fifths of Middletown's housing units were one-family dwellings. What is notable, however, is not only the high percentage of ownership but also the low number of mortgages: today Americans usually think of mortgages as a common fact of life. Approximately 60% of owner-occupied, non-farm homes have been mortgaged at any given time in the last two decades, but in the twenties the average was between 30% and 35%.

Nowadays a third major index of affluence is, ironically, indebtedness. As consumer purchases expand, so does indebtedness, because much of that consumer demand is satisfied by credit or instalment buying. Galbraith acknowledged as much in *The Affluent Society*: "An increase in consumer debt is all but implicit in the process by which wants are now synthesized." But Galbraith was also alarmed by this trend, and worried that consumer debt had increased too rapidly in the fifties: "One wonders, inevitably," he wrote, "about the tensions associated with debt creation on such a massive scale. The legacy of wants, which are themselves inspired, are the bills which descend like the winter snow. . . . Can the bill collector be the central figure in the good society?" [14]

Whether or not that question is answerable, it was already being asked in the twenties. Indebtedness was a permanent fixture of the American landscape long before Galbraith wrote. Contrary to a popular assumption that credit buying in the fifties was a fundamental reversal of puritanical American habits, consumer credit was a standard feature of buying in the Middletown of the twenties. "Today Middletown lives by a credit economy," the Lynds recorded, "that is available in some form to nearly every family in the community. The rise and spread of the dollar-down-and-so-much-per plan extends credit for virtually everything—homes, $200 overstuffed living-room suites, electric washing machines, automobiles, fur coats, diamond rings—to persons of whom frequently little is known as to their intention or ability to pay." As one veteran official of a building-and-loan company summarized the attitude of the Middletowners: "People don't think anything nowadays of borrowing sums they'd never have thought of borrowing in the old days. They will assume an obligation for $2,000 today as calmly as they would have borrowed $300 or $400 in 1890." [15]

Finally, the purchase of electric appliances allows a fourth measure of the increased affluence of Middletown in the twenties. According to the Lynds, by 1924 all but one percent of Middletown's homes were wired for electricity, and between 1920 and 1924 there was an average increase of 25% in the household use of electricity. Where much of this electricity was going can be seen from the following: the Lynds found that the major electrical appliance shops, in one six-month period, sold 1,000 irons, 700 vacuum cleaners, 460 toasters, 370 washing machines, and 114 heaters. Clearly, Middletown's inhabitants were not living much differently than their counterparts in the fifties. And to complete this picture of twenties "prosperity," the cost of living in Middletown increased 117% from 1891 to 1924, but a sample of the earnings of workers and professionals shows gains of 140% to 190% in the same period. So, uncontestably, life in Middletown by the twenties was "affluent" by previous standards.

But, as in the fifties, too much attention to prosperity alone can produce a badly skewed judgment of the times. First, the Lynds' study excluded both the rural farmer and the big-city poor. Second, within the confines of the city there still existed both poverty and low-paid deprivation. From fragmentary tax data, the Lynds speculated that the majority of Middle-towners earned less than $2,000. In a more specific survey, they found that a majority of 100 working-class families earned less than what the U.S. Bureau of Labor considered a "minimum income" for a "standard family of five." In fact the median income for these families fell almost $500 below the bureau's "minimum" level.[16]

Even when the common signs of affluence were present in these lower-middle-class families, their presence was often a source of great worry. The automobile offers a case in point: a working-class family was assumed to spend about a quarter of each month's pay for the cost and upkeep of the family car. In extreme cases, the home might even be mortgaged in order to make the payments.

For the worker, the stresses produced by inequities in income and well-being were often accentuated by the unstable character of affluence itself.

According to its [i.e., industry's] needs, large numbers of people anxious to get their living periodically are stopped by the recurrent phenomenon of "bad times" when the machines stop running, workers are "laid off" by the hundreds, salesmen sell less, bankers call in loans, "credit freezes," and many Middletown families may take their children from school, move into cheaper homes, cut down on food, and do without many of the countless things they desire.[17]

While it is an exaggeration to claim that such conditions were "common," they still suggest the character of life for many members of the lower middle class. Although possession of a car, of a home, of a variety of appliances served as a rude measure of membership in the middle class, the difficulties surrounding the possession of such symbols illustrates how tenuous a grasp most Americans held on their newly found prosperity.

3

It is not being suggested here that there has been no change in two hundred years of American economic history. Our goal is only to counter the fatuous assumption that since World War II America has made a quantum leap from the past.

Reciting the litany of progress has the effect of incantation, and mesmerizes the listener. There are complicated elements mixed into the notion of progress that standard measurements overlook: values that have no dollar equivalent are lost, but their loss goes unnoticed in the statistical indices of our forward movement. It is apparent that while the standard of living has risen, much of the rise, even when we discount inflation, has depended on far-reaching changes in our attitudes toward work and leisure which may or may not represent progress, depending on one's point of view. For example, it is clear that the role of the wife in supplementing family income plays a more crucial role than ever before. According to census figures, at least 42% of families with median incomes require *two* wage-earners to achieve that level, as compared to 10% of median income families in the twenties. This means that the wife must give up tasks which she normally performed in the home in order to be a part of the labor market. But in giving up many of these tasks she has been forced to substitute labor-saving devices at higher cost that she did not need in the twenties. This means that in one sense there has been only a lateral movement in a major area of income increase. Whether the substitution itself is desirable or not depends not on one's economic attitudes, but on one's attitudes toward the role of women in the society and the role of the family.

Second, the use of aggregate or average figures has had the effect of concealing the plight of the poor, and ignoring the difficulties faced by the poor and the deprived lower middle class. The facile assumption that medians or averages somehow represent the general condition of all citizens has only recently received severe criticism, but shows no signs of disappearing.

Finally, while conceding that the general level of well-being has risen, we have attempted to indicate how radically different that change has been from what it is popularly assumed to be. American historians have been of two minds on this question: either they have accepted the myth and described America as a homogeneous middle-class nation; or (borrowing from European, and especially Marxist, historiography) they have described America as a nation of proletarians who, as industrialization proceeded to further impoverish them, clung futilely to the delusion that they were members of the middle class.

Historians of the former school have conceded that hard times did occur, especially in the late nineteenth century and again in the thirties, but they have insisted that the fundamental prosperity and equality of America was only for those brief periods in any doubt. The performance of the economy since the Depression has supposedly vindicated this view.

Historians of the latter school insist that from the outset, America has been beset by class conflict of varying intensity. Terms such as "masses" and "proletariat" become meaningful because the basic reality of American life has been poverty, against which the common man has struggled valiantly, and with scant success. Not surprisingly, this view enjoyed more popularity during the Depression than it did in the fifties or sixties.

But between these two views there is another course to which these two brief chapters can only serve as an introduction. This view relies on the income and wealth data we have been able to collect, and the social structure we have been able to infer from it. On the one hand, this view would suggest that America has not in the past twenty or thirty years been emerging from a dark past of "majority poverty," but rather has exhibited a fairly stable social structure—modified over time with transitions from agriculture to industry, but preserving in its broader contexts the same relative shares of income and wealth over at least a half-century. On the other hand, this third view hardly gives credence to the bland assumption that social stability has rested on a broad base of economic and social equality. Rather it would seem that the vast homogeneous middle class which appeared so striking to so many European commentators has actually divided rather loosely into upper and lower halves, across which there has not been enough movement to obliterate the meaningfulness of the distinction. Both poverty and great wealth have remained prominent features of American life, perhaps not on the classic European scale, but prominent and permanent nonetheless, with the poor continuing to constitute a quarter to a third of the population, and the rich continuing to receive more income each year than the poorer half of the American people.

If this view is defensible, it strongly suggests the myopia of numerous economists, sociologists, and historians of recent years, and seriously undercuts their credibility as social critics. Moreover, it leaves us with the realization that the great accomplishments of recent decades are more accurately just modifications of long-standing social and economic conditions. And if this is so, it raises the possibility that our present social and economic structure is notably ill-equipped to lead us toward a more equalitarian and democratic future.

6 | Contemporary America: The Poverty of New Beginnings

The poor ye have always with you.
St. John, 12:8

The existence of hungry and abused men, women, and children in the midst of what is supposed to be the most prosperous and humane country on earth makes a mockery of American claims to "liberty and justice for all." Public rhetoric has occasionally admitted the presence of these human beings in our midst, but always with the promise that they would soon disappear, swept up eventually by the well-being that enfolds the rest of middle-class America.

In fact, the poor have not disappeared, but are now, and always have been, a basic feature of American society. Moreover, there are no signs that this situation is changing.

To most people that statement will sound exaggerated. Since 1960 the number of officially defined poor people has steadily declined, and seems to be declining further still. The government has increased its expenditures to fight poverty and in the past decade has founded an agency specifically concerned with poverty's abolition. The country at large seems to be more aware than ever before of the existence of poverty, and more willing to do something about it.

But the statement must nevertheless be made, because Americans have developed over the years a temporizing attitude toward the coexistence of extreme poverty and extreme wealth. It is, as a friend once called it, the "new beginnings" approach to social change. According to the "new beginnings" approach, poverty (or any other social problem) is admitted to exist, but is immediately removed from the realm of social criticism by two corollaries. The first corollary states that the existing problem is bad, but is better than it was, say, fifty years ago. The second corollary is that however meager the solution offered, it represents a "new beginning," a fundamental change in American consciousness and behavior, a change that will presumably solve the problem under discussion. Eventually.

Unfortunately for the poor, America seems to be constantly making new beginnings, only to slide rapidly into indifference and inaction. As the Southern Rural Research Project reported on malnutrition in late 1969:

The poor and the hungry had their brief moment in the sun: America may lionize its victims, but the vogue of compassion passes quickly on; the hungry have now become somewhat passé. Americans seem to take it for granted that once such alarming conditions are publicly known, the appropriate authorities will automatically step in and clear the matter up.[1]

A good illustration of how the new beginnings approach works can be seen in an article that appeared in *Time* magazine in 1970. *Time* announced optimistically to its readers that during the sixties, "The war against poverty was not won, but there were some notable victories. As of 1969 the number of Americans classified as poor dropped to 24.3 million, down from 39.5 million in 1959." [2] The article offered no explanation of how the poor had disappeared so quickly, where they had gone, or what their chances were of becoming poor again; it merely stated the fact that the poor were "disappearing."

Time's failure to recognize the persistence of poverty was the result of some simple but misleading assumptions. Its statistics were drawn from the U.S. Census, and the census figures were based on the government's own official definition of poverty. But that definition, as we shall see, is crucial to understanding why the poor are disappearing only on paper.

When Lyndon Johnson declared "an unconditional war on poverty" he was speaking of an enemy that was statistically unfamiliar. Like the enemy in Vietnam, poverty blended well into the landscape of the country; *The Other America* and subsequent studies had proved the existence of the poor, but how many remained a mystery. Harrington had estimated at least a quarter of the population; others suggested as high as a third or as low as a tenth. A few neolithic congressmen even insisted that there was no poverty at all, but they remained a minority.

Accurate estimation of the extent of poverty was an obvious precondition to any war against it: but that task posed problems which remain at the center of the antipoverty program today and which go a long way toward explaining why poverty is not "disappearing." First, federal planners had to decide on a definition of poverty. Were economic conditions alone to be the criteria? If so, which economic conditions? Low income alone? Low wealth? Some composite of the two, plus other factors? Second, and more to the point, what definition of poverty would satisfy Congress? Any definition of poverty thus had to pass not only economic but political scrutiny, and passage of the antipoverty program depended in no small way on its ability to win support among men who would not instinctively support such a measure. Liberal congressmen could be counted on, but they were not enough. If poverty were defined too "generously" crucial congressmen would balk, both because of what it implied about America and because of the costs for its correction.

The definition of poverty that consequently emerged was characteristic of most political compromises: it satisfied neither supporters nor opponents but was not unsatisfactory enough to block passage into law. The heart of the compromise was acceptance of a $3,000 "poverty line," which meant that the government would thereafter consider poor any urban family of four whose annual income fell below $3,000.

The rationale for the $3,000 figure was that since food prices are more easily measured than other prices, and since food takes up a large part of any family budget, the proper way to compute a "poverty budget" was to follow Department of Agriculture guidelines on minimum food budgets. Because a 1955 government study showed that the poor spent a third of their incomes on food, the Department of Agriculture figures could then be tripled and a "poverty" budget arrived at; each succeeding year, changes in food prices could be adjusted, and changes in the cost of living provided for. Although the economist for the Department of Health, Education, and Welfare who devised the formula specifically warned against its strict use, it was made official by the OEO. Since then, the so-called Orshansky formula has served as the official definition of poverty, and the basis for the census figures used by *Time*.

1

If the $3,000 limit seems arbitrary, on close consideration it is something else as well: austere. Even austere seems a generous adjective when the budget is considered in detail. The food costs upon which the budget depends inspire disbelief. The government's comment that "assuming the homemaker is a good manager and has the time and skill to shop wisely, she may prepare nutritious palatable meals. . . . for herself, a husband, and two young children" on a budget of *seventy-five cents per person per day* caused one pundit to comment that "Betty Crocker herself would starve." A statistician for HEW described how the housewife was expected to spend her meager allowance:

> For a meal all four of them ate together, she could spend on the average only ninety-five cents, and to stay within her budget she must allow no more a day than a pound of meat, poultry, or fish altogether, barely enough for one small serving for each family member at one of the three meals. Eggs could fill out her family fare only to a limited degree because the plan allows less than two dozen a week for all uses in cooking and at the table, not even one to a person per day. And any food extras, such as milk at school for the children or the coffee her husband might buy to supplement the lunch he carries to work, have to come out of the same food money or compete with the limited funds available for rent, clothing, medical care, and all other expenses. Studies indicate that, on the average, family members eating a meal away from home spend twice as much as the homemaker would spend for preparing one for them at home. The twenty-five cents allowed for a meal at home in the economy plan would not buy much even in the way of supplementation.[3]

This is the food budget which, adjusted annually for price rises and multiplied by three, becomes the poverty budget each year. Its inadequacy is so serious that the Department of Agriculture itself found 63% of those who tried to live on it suffered from malnutrition.[4]

Because the food budget is so low, the entire poverty budget is low as well. Oscar Ornati, in *Poverty Amid Affluence*, summarized a typical sixties "poverty budget" for a family of four:

> It provides for simple clothing to protect against the weather and maintain cleanliness. A woman's coat, for instance, must last five

years. Leftover food must be retrieved. A cup of flour spilled means no thickening that week; a blown bulb, no light for that month; and a chair broken in anger cannot be replaced for a year. The meat budget allows for stewing lamb, beef liver, or heart, picnic shoulder, fillet of haddock, or perhaps a boned veal roast. No frozen foods are provided for. It allows nothing for an occasional glass of beer, tobacco, or telephone calls. The budget assumes a small rented five-room flat. The family living room might have two chairs. A mattress and spring on legs may serve as a couch, a dropleaf for eating; two straight chairs may also be there. Linoleum may cover the floor, and there can be a lamp or two. An electric refrigerator and iron are allowed. The family may listen to the radio an hour a day, but television is not included in the budget. There will be money to buy aspirin but none for "miracle" drugs. The husband may get a haircut once a month, and the wife a home permanent once a year. She can use a self-service launderette. There will be no money to buy the children candy or ice cream, or to go to the movies, or to offer the visitor a cup of coffee.[5]

The government's budget for the poor is unrealistic on numerous other scores. It insists the poor should spend a third of their income on food, though the average family spends only 22% of its income on food. It fails to take account of the overpricing and shoddy quality of food in poverty areas. It ignores the high costs of items such as housing and furniture (usually 10% to 25% higher in poverty neighborhoods, according to one Census Bureau economist) which drive up expenses in the other two-thirds of its budget. In farm areas, the budget still relies heavily on the presumption that rural families produce much of their own food, although home-grown items have fallen from 70% to 36% of farm diets in the past twenty years. It makes no allowance for the higher education of poor children. It assumes no major medical expenses in the family, although most of the poor are inadequately covered by medical insurance. Finally, it does not even allow for a savings account, presuming rightly that the poor will have nothing to save.

2

The natural result of the government's gross underestimation of poverty is that poverty *by the government's standards* is disappearing: from 1959 to 1969 the percentage of Americans officially classified as poor declined from 22% to 12% of the population.* But the obvious question is whether this statistical sleight of hand deserves to be called a "notable victory."

For example, we have already seen how the government's definition of poverty includes only the poorest of the American poor. Now consider how even *those* poor have been lifted from poverty. In 1959, the "poverty level" was $3,000; ten years later it had been raised by $721, or roughly 25%, to account for rises in the cost of living. But how well does the 25% increase cover the actual rises in the cost of living?

Over the same ten years, the consumer price index rose almost 35%; if rises in federal, state, and local taxes are added, economists estimate that American families required a 41% increase in income just to maintain the same standard of living. In dollars, that meant that a family earning $3,000 in 1959 needed $4,365 in 1969 just to remain as poor as they started out. Similar figures apply to higher incomes.[6]

But the OEO has its own set of economists. By adjusting the $3,000 index upward by $721 instead of by a more realistic $1,300 or $1,400, they guaranteed that inflation would play a bigger role in eliminating poverty than all the poverty programs combined; at the present rate, using its own definitions, the OEO will be out of business by 1980—the poor "gone," carried into heaven in the arms of inflation. But if instead one uses consumer price index estimates plus awareness of other economic pressures, the poor will be still here, as nu-

---

* In 1970, however, poverty *as defined by the government* actually increased by 5%, an interesting testimonial to President Nixon's economic programs.

merous as ever. In 1959, the percentage of families below $3,000 was one-fifth of the nation; in 1969, the percentage below $4,365 was still one-fifth of the nation.

Other figures tend to corroborate the belief that poverty is not disappearing. For example, census studies of income distribution showed that the bottom 20% of the population had received only 5% of the income in 1959. Ten years later the poorest 20% were receiving the same amount of income. Had some major advance been made during the intervening ten years to abolish poverty it ought to have shown up as a change in the percentage of the total income going to the poor. Instead the bottom fifth (and the entire bottom half) of the population showed no appreciable gain in their share of the total income.

Even for those who do "escape" poverty, the escape can be short-lived. The President's Commission on Income Maintenance Programs observed:

Between 1965 and 1966, the number of households classified as poor declined by almost 3 percent. This net change, however, obscures considerable movement of households into and out of poverty. Some 36 percent of those households classified as poor in 1965 had, for one reason or another, left poverty by 1966. Of those classified as poor in 1966, 34 percent were not poor in the previous year. This flow indicates that the risk of poverty is considerably more pervasive than has been imagined.[7]

Moreover, for those who fall below the poverty line, the fall is precipitous. The Census Bureau reports that 70% of those living below the federal poverty level live at least $500 below it, and one-half live $1,000 below it.

Ironically enough, the complete inadequacy of the government's poverty budget has been made obvious even by the government. The Department of Labor's Bureau of Labor Statistics prepares annually what used to be called a "minimum but adequate" budget, but is now merely called a "low" budget, perhaps because of the political stir it caused.* The BLS budget for a family of four is only slightly less penurious than the OEO budget—it assumes rental of housing because ownership is considered too costly, but allows only $120 per month for "shelter, housefurnishings, and household operations." Its food budget allows for more meat, poultry, fish, fruit, and vegetables than does the OEO budget, but still relies most heavily on large quantities of potatoes, dry beans, dry peas, flour, and cereal, and assumes that "users of this plan will select lower cost food items." Its transportation budget allows for one six-year-old car, few repairs, no comprehensive insurance and no out-of-town travel on "planes, trains, or other public vehicles." The total allowance for "recreation, reading, tobacco, alcohol and miscellaneous expenses" is $350. No savings are assumed.[8]

Yet the BLS estimate for a "minimum but adequate" budget for a family of four in 1970 was $6960—nearly double what the OEO defines as a poverty income. Is it too lenient to call the life such a budget allows poverty? If it is not, one-third of all American families—seventy million human beings—are poor.

3

In reevaluating the government's assessment of the extent of poverty, we have to remember a simple fact: poverty in the sixties was an important political issue. The turmoil around the compromises of the first antipoverty bill, the uproar over the bill's encouragement of "maximum feasible participation" of the poor, and the bitter resentment over cutting the War on Poverty budget in order to fight the Vietnam War only partly evidence the entrance of national politics into the lives of the American poor. Diagnosis of poverty goes

* This low budget should not be confused with the "intermediate" budget prepared by the BLS, mentioned in Ch I. The Bureau regularly prepares three budgets,—low, intermediate, and high—the first two of which are used in this book.

hand-in-hand with its remedy: if one sees limited, marginal poverty, one needs only limited, marginal solutions. A few job programs here, a day care center there, nothing more than the few billion spent each year to remedy poverty, even though each year ten times that much has been spent to assure victory in a country whose population is smaller than the number of poor in America.

To say the government has only venal or cynical motives in dealing with the poor is unjust and incorrect, but sincerity on the other hand does not feed the hungry nor teach the illiterate. The inability of the government to identify and deal with the poor is the consequence of the American political system. The present definition of poverty is the result of political compromise; both liberals and conservatives are committed to the definition, and, having committed themselves to it, they are anxious to show that they, as politicians, are capable of vanquishing poverty. No one likes poverty, and the politician who is able to dispose of it (for the least amount of money) will be well regarded at the polls. Government bureaucrats, dependent on the politicians for their annual appropriations, find themselves providing the *desired* information, and not necessarily the *correct* information. Thus a Senate subcommittee headed by George McGovern was forced to complain bitterly about the behavior of government statisticians in classifying the poor. "In 1968, government statistics estimated there were between twenty-two and twenty-seven million Americans living in poverty." Yet less than a year later, "the higher of these two figures was dropped without explanation" and the twenty-two million figure used thereafter as the official estimate.[9] Obviously the Defense Department is not alone in having problems with accounting.

4

Saying that the decline in poverty over the past ten years has been largely a statistical chimera is not to say that all the decline was spurious. Some poor have been helped to find jobs, have been retrained for new skills, have been given a sense of worth. But their numbers are exceedingly small, even as a proportion of the officially-defined poor.

Nearly half of the poor in America today are either elderly, disabled, or part of a family headed by a woman. According to the government:

> Included among the 45 million designated as poor or near-poor in 1966 were 18 to 20 percent of the nation's children and from 30 to 40 percent of the aged. Counted poor were nearly two in four of the minority persons living on farms as against one in seven of the nonfarm population. The total with low incomes included 12 to 19 percent of the white population and 41 to 54 percent of the nonwhite. In 1966, households with a female head accounted for nearly one-half of all poverty units. In 1966, one in three of all poor children were minus a father in the house and the poverty rate among children in female-headed families was now four and a half times as high as families headed by a man.[10]

The consequence is that for many poor the kind of salvation that relies on growth of employment is useless.

Even for those who do find jobs, the future is often not as bright as one might imagine. A man working at the federal minimum wage, forty hours a week, fifty-two weeks a year earns only $3,300. Even so, over ten million jobs in the United States pay less than the minimum wage. These two facts help explain why 70% of non-aged poor families already work but are unable to escape poverty, and why for those who move out of official poverty the move is frequently one of no great consequence: according to unpublished tabulations from the government's Current Population Survey, of those persons who moved out of poverty between 1965 and 1966, one-eighth remained within $200 of the poverty line and one-quarter remained within $500 of the poverty line.[11]

And for those fortunate few whose success was greater in dollar terms, the success may well be temporary. The sixties was a decade of impressive economic expansion; today America is a trillion-dollar economy. But much of the economic expansion, especially from 1965 on, was fueled by the war in Vietnam. From the early sixties, unemployment dropped from over five percent to less than four percent by late 1967; but now unemployment has risen again to above five percent and is expected to go higher. As companies lay off workers, they lay off low-seniority, low-skill men first; since the poor almost universally fall into that category, they will find themselves in the same position they were in before, condemned to unemployment, or poorly paid menial labor. To offer only one illustration of a wider phenomenon, the unemployment rate in Watts, the black ghetto of Los Angeles, was 61% higher in 1970 than in 1965, the year of the Watts riots.

Yet according to the government, a great deal is being done to help all the poor, both outside and inside the economy. The HEW, for example, attempted to give substance to this point of view by listing total welfare expenditures under public programs—federal, state, and local—at over $150 billion in 1970, a sum which represented more than two-fifths of all governmental expenditures that year.

One hundred and fifty billion dollars is an intimidating amount of money. It would suggest that the poor are not forgotten. But consider how the money is spent. It is divided about equally between federal and state and local governments. One third of it goes for education—education not just for the poor or deprived, but education of all the young. Thus the children who live in a wealthy family benefit as much as do the children of the poor—or even more considering the well-known disparities between the schools of the affluent and the schools of the poor. Another third is consumed by social insurance, especially Social Security. But what is life like on Social Security? In 1967 the average retired worker got $91 a month, or $1100 a year: a retired couple averaged $142 a month, or $1700 a year. Even allowing for the lower cost of living for a retired couple, these figures dramatize how inadequate Social Security is. The government's own Bureau of Labor Statistics considered $2,671 a "low budget" for a retired couple the same year, which was nearly a thousand dollars more than the average payment. Pensioners exist on fixed incomes, but the economy is anything but fixed. Prices rise—for food, for housing, for medical costs; pensions do not. Last year Congress voted a 15% increase in the average payments, but few believe this will come anywhere near to meeting the extra costs which inflation has imposed on the elderly.

Because Social Security is self-financing and because education does not single out those who need it most (and in fact, often impedes their advance through poor schooling), this leaves less than $40 billion of the $150 billion. From this another $9 billion should be subtracted for the very special, and numerically insignificant, case of veterans programs, leaving roughly $31 billion for all public aid, health aid, aid to housing, and what the HEW refers to as "other social welfare."

While $31 billion is significantly less than $150 billion, it is still an enormous sum—almost as much as we were spending annually in Southeast Asia in the late 1960s. But scrutinize the expenditures which HEW lists under this heading, and consider how much is directed toward those who need it most. Under the $9 billion "health and medical programs," to choose one example, the department includes Defense Department expenditures for military personnel and their dependents, and medical research. The former is patently *not* directed toward the poor, and the latter is only vaguely directed their way. The health crisis of the poor is not one of medical research, but medical care. Despite an already highly sophisticated medical system in this country, the poor continue to suffer from all kinds of preventable illness because they lack the proper care. America's infant mortality rate is among the worst in the industrialized world, concentrated among the poor. Hollingshead and Redlich, in *Social Class and Mental Illness*, found that three times as many poor people had psychiatric illnesses as did persons in upper income groups. Yet three times as much money had been spent on the fewer cases of mentally ill at the top of the income ladder as on those at the bottom rung. And according to government investigations, infant mortality rates failed to decline in the sixties despite increased provision of health facilities.[12]

Continued deductions of this kind from the figure of $31 billion further diminish the amount actually used for the poor, so much so that Michael Harrington remarked idly, almost as if it were a matter of common knowledge, that "only half the poor are getting half of what they need" from public welfare. His remark becomes understandable when the actual benefits received by the poor are examined: Aid to Dependent Children (ADC), the largest single public assistance program, furnished an average of $187 per family per month in 1970. This is only $20 more than a retired couple receives, and comes to less than $2,250 a year. New York, the most generous of the fifty states, actually provides an average of $292 a month, but this is still less than the government's definition of poverty *five years ago*. In the Deep South, where half of all poor families are located, payments regularly average less than $70 a month, and in Mississippi, $46 a month.

5

Perhaps the most poignant and the most instructive example of how the antipoverty program works, and how it fails, can be seen in the lives of the poorest of the poor—the fifteen to twenty million who go to bed hungry or malnourished each night.

The malnourished were the last "discovery" of the decade that "rediscovered" poverty. Mention of them had appeared as early as 1961 in several papers as a result of nutrition surveys by private doctors and health organizations, but it was not until 1967, when Senators Joseph Clark and Robert Kennedy visited Mississippi, that the underfed began to receive serious attention. The senators' visit to the shacks of black dirt farmers and their shock at seeing the swollen, deformed bodies of hungry children convinced them that something had to be done.

At first, they believed that what was required was an expansion and renovation of existing federal food programs for the poor. After all, the Department of Agriculture could already list in operation the Commodity Distribution Program, which delivered surplus food to county welfare agencies: the Food Stamp Program, which allowed the poor to purchase food in local grocery stores: the National School Lunch Program which furnished food and money to states in order to provide hot, nutritious lunches for school children: and the Special Milk Program, which subsidized the cost of milk for school children. Taken together, these programs seemed to contain all that was necessary to guarantee an adequate diet for every American.

But the question immediately arose: why, if these were adequate programs, were there still so many hungry Americans? Providing food for the poor was not new in the United States—private charities had always made the Christmas or Thanksgiving basket a symbol of their doles to the poor. And if these were no more than symbolic gestures, the federal government had been distributing food to the poor since 1934, when President Roosevelt authorized the Federal Employment Relief Agency. By 1939, 13 million Americans were eating surplus food.

The answer to that question lay in the total inadequacy of each of the programs. For example, the Commodity Distribution Program by 1959 reached 1300 counties, but provided a family of four with only the following: twenty pounds of flour, ten pounds of corn meal, nine pounds of nonfortified dried milk, two pounds of rice, and occasionally four pounds of butter and ten pounds of cheese per month. States and counties could exercise their option not to take certain items, and so this was often a maximum, rather than an average cross section of the food provided. There was no meat, limited protein and calories, and no vitamin C.

Senator John Sherman Cooper of Kentucky, seeking relief aid for unemployed coal miners in his state, inquired of Secretary of Agriculture Ezra Taft Benson why there were such limited provisions. Benson explained that for surplus commodities the first priority was overseas sale for cash; the second priority was the international Food for Peace program, with payment in soft foreign currency for U.S. use abroad. Then finally came the poor, and the Commodity Distribution Program. As Benson's undersecretary explained, "We are most sympathetic to the plight of needy persons. We must, however, not lose sight of the fact that the primary responsibility of the Department is to carry out the farm programs that benefit farmers." [13]

The undersecretary's point was not without merit. Farmers were often impoverished, and the complex system of agricultural subsidies had originally been designed as much to help these poor as to ensure the stable production of food for the nation. But the agricultural subsidy program, like most projects designed to benefit the less fortunate, ended up benefitting those who needed help least. By 1967, less than a million farmers grew most of the nation's food supply and reaped the bulk of the federal price support program. And of these wealthy commercial farmers, 25% received 75% of the subsidy payments. What little money filtered down to the remaining farmers might help ease their burden, but obviously not as much as it enhanced the profits of the richest few. Put more graphically, the largest 264 commercial farmers received $52 million in federal subsidies: this was as much as the 540,000 smallest farmers received. This worked out to an average of $197,000 apiece for the wealthy, and an average of $96 for the poorest half-million.

The bitter irony was that, despite all this dispensation of

federal largesse, the plight of those who needed food most did not improve. The poor farmer was still poor, and many of the poor were still hungry. Sent by the Department of Agriculture to investigate charges of malnutrition in the South, a team of nutritionists reported back that the diet among the southern poor in 1967 "was uniformly worse than had been that of the average southern family with less than $2,000 annual income in 1955"—twelve years earlier. The National Food Consumption Survey likewise reported in 1955 that almost 25% of American families living in poverty had "diets seriously lacking in essential nutrients"; a decade later the number had risen to 36%. In other words, the impact of federal food programs had been nil, and the position of the poor had been actually deteriorating.

The Agriculture Department, under liberal Orville Freeman, tried to modify this situation by redesigning distribution of food to the poor. Using a pilot program begun by President Kennedy, Freeman attempted to shift emphasis from commodity distribution to a food stamp program. In theory, the food stamp program was simple and direct, and should have provided significant benefits for the poor. The eligible poor pay the government each month what they would normally spend for food, then receive in return an equivalent value in stamps plus a bonus to buy extra food. Grocery stores accept the stamps as money and redeem them from the government for cash.

Practice was something else. Within a few months of their inception they were being referred to among the poor as "Scrooge stamps." The amount of money paid is dictated by the size of the family and its monthly income. Presuming a monthly income of $70, not uncommon in the South, a family of four paid $34 to receive $64 worth of groceries. This left $36 a month to pay for rent, utilities, clothing, medicine, and all other expenses. Thus a typical welfare mother in the South spent half of her monthly budget for food when the national average was closer to 22%. Furthermore, even the Department of Agriculture admitted that $64 a month for four persons was inadequate. It suggested $100 a month as minimum, and at least $120 as a modest but adequate food budget. This left the government supplying only half what was required for a balanced diet, and calling it "a break-through."

This inadequacy was compounded by a second: as counties throughout the nation changed over from surplus commodities to food stamps, many dropped out. Forty percent of participating counties withdrew, leaving one million poor who had previously received aid without any government program whatsoever. Even in those areas where the food stamp program was accepted, the participation among the poor was only 16%, reflecting not only the pride of the poor, but the failure to disseminate information, and the costly nature and low benefits of the program. To these problems was added a third: stamps had to be paid for on a monthly or bimonthly basis. As one observer of the scene wrote:

> Anyone with a realistic conception of extreme poverty knows that most families with $70, $100, or even $200 monthly incomes spend money as they get it. As the pressure builds to cover necessities such as rent, doctor bills, or a pair of shoes so a child can go to school, the budget for food often is whatever money is left. If the family with limited but regular income had trouble saving for the lump sum payments, the family with irregular income finds it impossible.[14]

Finally, in late 1967, the Agriculture Department admitted the extent to which the food stamp program had failed. Testifying before the Senate's Poverty Subcommittee, officials revealed that the average food stamp recipient got only $200 worth of food annually (for $123 of his own money), while a fully adequate, low-cost diet would cost at least $345. The department estimated that it would spend $330 million to aid

5.8 million persons with food stamps and commodities in fiscal 1968, but acknowledged that a reformed program to feed nine million malnourished (the low estimate) would cost at least $1.7 billion, or *five times* what was currently foreseen. By 1969, the program was cut back to only $225 million, because of budget pressures from the Vietnam War, congressional opposition, and White House indifference.

The inadequacies of the food stamp program could be repeated ad infinitum for the other federal food programs. After studying the school lunch program in 1969, a panel of eminent nutritionists chastized it for the high fat and low protein content of many school meals. The panel found three-quarters of the meals lacking adequate calories, two-thirds lacking sufficient iron and magnesium, and one-third missing essential vitamins. Yet even this deficient diet was unavailable to many poor children. In 1967 at least four million children from families with less than $2,000 income were denied the free or reduced price lunches to which they were entitled by law. Nine million American students attend schools with no lunch program whatsoever, and only 19 million out of the 50 million school children participated at all. In many cases, these children were from middle-class homes, while those without free lunches attended inner-city or rural schools that could not afford the cost of kitchen facilities or their operation. Boston, America's "cradle of learning," had one of the worst programs, with Detroit and Philadelphia close behind. Clearly the programs fell far short of even their own mandates.

The toll which this has taken on the children of the poor is inestimable. Even hardened conservatives, opposed to welfare for poor adults, have recognized that the only way the young will escape the deprivation of their backgrounds is by supplementary aid. But at every turn, that aid has failed to live up to the clear-cut needs of the poor. Its consequence, as one medical researcher called it, has been "a morbid chain" of physical and mental illness. As described by Dr. Charles Lowe of the National Institutes of Health, "Poverty means improperly fed pregnant women . . . which means ill-fed foetuses in their wombs . . . foetuses which fail to synthesize proteins and brain cells at normal rates . . . which means a high rate of mortality among infants . . . and further lack of brain and body growth during the crucial first four years of life." In bloodless statistics, this means that poor children in the South receive only 50% of needed calories, and worms reduce even this inadequate nutrition. It means that the premature birth rate of the poor is three times that of the affluent. Because up to half of premature children mature with inadequate mental development, this helps explain why children of the poor show impaired learning ability up to five times as often as other children. Put most bluntly by Dr. Joseph English, former administrator of health services in the HEW:

Five percent of the children in the United States are born mentally retarded, yet by the time that age group reaches 12 years of age, 11 percent are retarded, which indicates that we *produce* almost as much mental retardation as is born. And when you consider the fact that 75 percent of the mental retardation in this country comes from poor urban and rural areas in poverty and when you consider the role malnutrition can play, then I think you can see how serious this problem is.[15]

6

The inability of the poor, and most especially the hungry poor, to translate their needs into effective social results is neither new nor should it be surprising. It is the natural consequence of temporizing that makes the coexistence of extreme poverty and extreme wealth a natural fact of American life. We always claim that more Americans have become middle class and that poverty has declined. Then to dispose of our last hard core of poverty we say we must work together for a "new beginning." Our successive waves of "new beginnings" have no doubt begun with uniformly good intentions, but have ended with uniformly bad results. Thus the poor in America have been promised redemption from their poverty on innumerable occasions, only to find themselves forgotten a decade later.

In 1904, in the midst of an early new beginning, a precursor of Michael Harrington wrote a book titled simply *Poverty*. *Poverty*'s author was a young social reformer named Robert Hunter whose sympathy for "the neglected poor" was undeniable. Anticipating *The Other America, Poverty* was both a statistical and a personal description of poverty at the turn of the century; the striking feature of the book is not so much its description of poverty, however, but its estimation of the number of poor. Hunter was a zealous social reformer, dedicated to a new beginning and surely unlikely to underestimate the extent of poverty in America. Yet he ended up estimating that twelve percent of the population was poor, a figure identical to the government's today. Hunter's figures were immediately attacked as exaggerated.

In an attempt to correct Hunter's "exaggeration" and provide a firm methodological base to understand poverty, Professor Jacob Hollander of the Johns Hopkins economics department authored a small treatise, *The Abolition of Poverty*. A distinguished scholar, later to become president of the American Economics Association, Hollander used a number of evaluation techniques that directly prefigured the War on Poverty a half-century later. Devising an income line approach that provided for "minimum physical adequacy, with little or no margin for savings or the amenities of life," Hollander estimated that an average family of five would require an annual income of $825. (Using the consumer price index as a guide, this is roughly equivalent to the $3,000 figure for a modern family of four.) Thus equipped, Hollander reviewed Hunter's findings and, to the surprise of himself and many others, his own figures corresponded almost exactly with

Hunter's. Twenty percent, Hollander found, of the population in industrial states, and ten percent in the nonindustrial states, were poor.[16] If we revise Hollander as we have revised the government's similar recent estimates, one quarter to one third of the American public were, and are, poor.

America is presently on the verge of another of these new beginning." Michael Harrington warned that the President's the most important potential reform in welfare in thirty years. In place of complicated welfare provisions, he would substitute a "guaranteed annual income" for the poor. The program's advantages are manifest: it would abolish much of the red tape associated with welfare; it would pay even the working poor; and it would finally remove the inequities between various state systems, some of which provide a great deal more aid to the poor than others. Although stalled in the Congress at time of this writing, the "guaranteed annual income approach" has been widely hailed as a "new beginning" in our treatment of the poor.

Perceptive critics, however, have seen beyond this "new beginning." Michael Harrington warned that the president's program might result in "guaranteed annual poverty"; another critic called it a "family deprivation plan." What both objected to was not the systemic reforms, but the level of payments. President Nixon proposed a maximum assistance for a family of four of $4,200 a year. While $4,200 might have been a meaningful definition of poverty in 1959, by the mid-seventies, when the program goes into effect, it will be as deficient as the present definition is today. Furthermore, because it supplements the income of the working poor, it may well tempt employers to freeze wages for the poor at the present low levels, a situation which President Nixon seeks to permit by allowing a "special" minimum wage of $1.20 an hour in place of the statutory $1.60.

To counter the Nixon proposals, welfare groups have offered their own alternative plans. One plan is to use the existing $3,720 poverty level as the minimum, and the Bureau of Labor Statistic's $6,960 figure as the maximum. Another plan, offered by the National Welfare Rights Organization, uses the BLS figure as the minimum, and allows families to retain a third of their earnings above that up to $10,000. But neither of these programs is expected to meet with the approval of Congress for the simple reason of money: the former would cost $28 billion, the latter at least $50 billion.

Eventually, something along the lines of the Nixon plan, perhaps slightly modified by a liberal Congress, will become law. It will not meet the standards set forth by welfare groups, and given the politics of Washington, it will probably not even satisfy establishment liberals. But it will be accepted and touted as a "new beginning" for the American poor. No one will ask why previous new beginnings failed, why "maximum feasible participation" was abandoned, or why the OEO program limps along on a deficient budget. No one will ask why Social Security, which likewise began with low payments that were supposed to be radically increased "later," still leaves the elderly poor barely ahead of inflation. The American conscience will, as it has so often before, quietly pass over the poor, confident that they have been taken care of. And the poor will still be with us.

7 | The
Rich

*Let me tell you about the very rich. They are
different from you and me. They possess and enjoy
early, and it does something to them, makes them
soft where we are hard, and cynical where we are
trustful, in a way that, unless you were born rich,
it is difficult to understand. They think, deep in
their hearts, that they are better than we are because
we had to discover the compensations and refuges
of life for ourselves. Even when they enter deep
into our world or sink below us, they still think
that they are better than we are. They are different.*

F. Scott Fitzgerald

Unlike the poor, the rich have somehow
never been considered outside the boundaries of the mythical
middle class. When F. Scott Fitzgerald tried to convince Er-
nest Hemingway that "the rich are very much different from

you and me," Hemingway responded in the best American tradition, "Yes, they have money." American social mythology has rarely accepted any distinction between the wealthy and middle class save that the rich have more money. Whereas European wealth was always associated with the hereditary distinction of aristocracy, with exclusive schools and exclusive privilege, American wealth has more often been seen as an outgrowth of middle-class virtues themselves: riches were the reward for hard work, frugality, and clean living.

This homely notion is a long-established corollary of the myth of the middle class. As early as the 1830s, Tocqueville claimed to see in the behavior of the American rich a significant departure from European habits. Americans of great means, he declared, unlike their European counterparts, "think more of satisfying their slightest needs than seeking extraordinary delights. They indulge a quantity of little wants, but do not let themselves give rein to any great disorderly passion. They are more prone to become enervated than debauched."

Whether Tocqueville would have said the same of the robber barons later in the century must remain a mystery. More important is the fact that, except for such occasional remarks, he preserved a discreet silence on the subject of the American rich, a silence which is still observed by many social critics today. For a nation born in violent denunciations of unfair privilege and vehement praise of equality, the question of vast wealth concentrated in few hands would seem a natural subject for concern and debate. Yet today the American rich go literally unchallenged—though poverty is widespread and the rich's share of our national wealth has not changed appreciably since the days of the Depression.

To be sure, the American rich have been challenged before: during the Revolution, we noted earlier, there were several attempts to redistribute highly concentrated land holdings; during the first half of the nineteenth century the struggle between Andrew Jackson and the Bank of the United States symbolized the challenges that were made against wealth; in the latter half of the same century, the fantastic riches of the new industrialists fed the hatred of militant laborers throughout the country; and in the thirties, the popular feelings of unemployed millions literally caused many of the rich to tremble with fear.

But none of these challenges was successful, if by success we mean a significant redistribution of the nation's income and wealth. We saw how the attempts of the radical revolutionists to redistribute Tory lands was undone soon afterward by the development of great new speculative landholdings in the West. Jackson, though he defeated the Bank of the United States, was entirely unable to stop the growth of industrialism which undermined his base of support in a rural agrarian democracy. The creation of unions, passage of minimum wage laws and supposedly progressive income taxes, the most tangible measures of the success of labor agitation, did no more than slow the drift toward greater and greater concentration; such measures were entirely unable to reverse the already high concentration of wealth and income. So too for the New Deal: although statutory rates of income tax on the rich were raised, the effective percentage of income actually paid by the rich fell because of loopholes bored into the tax laws.

Today the almost complete absence of any noticeable hostility toward the most affluent is surprising. Especially in view of the wide-scale poverty known to exist in America, one would expect at least a few major voices raised in protest against the rich. Along with demands for a "minimum" income, one might expect to hear demands for a "maximum" income as well. Instead, an almost perfect silence reigns. Why?

Shortly after World War II, when the silence became noticeable, New Class theorists took it as validation of their theories. Not only was affluence widespread, but the high concentration of wealth and income was believed to be undergoing major, and permanent, change. Studies like Kuznets's and Goldsmith's encouraged belief in the trickle down theory of income redistribution; Arthur Burns, as noted earlier, called the imagined redistribution "the greatest peacetime revolution in history." As the years wore on, however, it became more and more apparent that "trickle down" was not working; in fact by the mid-fifties it was apparent that the richest segments of the society were actually *increasing* their share of the national income and wealth each year.

Consequently, more and more social theorists sought means to explain the marked decline in hostility toward the rich; until the fifties it had been such a normal part of life that its absence now seemed meaningful. Galbraith, to take just one example, tried in *The Affluent Society* to develop an explanation for the widespread silence. First, he suggested, Marxist economists had predicted that as capitalism matured, the concentration of wealth and income in the hands of fewer and fewer capitalists would increase so drastically that the workers would be further immiserated and forced to revolt against their masters. Since this communist prediction had not come true in the United States—that is, inequality in wealth and income had not drastically *worsened*—we had one reason for the silence.

The second factor, Galbraith believed, was that the rich were now less conspicuous than before; in contemporary jargon, they had adopted a low profile. Galbraith did not argue that the rich were less rich than before, only that conspicuous consumption was less a part of their behavior. "The depression and especially the New Deal gave the American rich a serious fright," he said. "The consequence was to usher in a period of marked discretion in personal expenditure." In addition to fear, taste had played a role: "Increasingly in the last quarter century the display of expensive goods, as a device for suggesting wealth, had been condemned as vulgar." Taken together, these two factors had effected a change in the visible, if not the actual, face of the rich.

The third factor, undoubtedly the most important in Galbraith's mind, was affluence. "As more people feel more secure, they become less interested in redistributing the wealth of the rich," he observed. Even "the liberal has partly accepted the view of the well-to-do that it is a trifle uncouth to urge a policy of soaking the rich." To his credit, Galbraith (unlike many New Class critics) was both too perceptive and too forthright to argue that the existing state of economic inequality was either good or acceptable, affluence or no affluence. For example, at one point in his discussion of the rich, he quoted R. H. Tawney with obvious approval:

Those who dread a dead-level of income and wealth do not dread, it seems, a dead-level of law and order, and of security of life and property. They do not complain that persons endowed by nature with unusual qualities of strength, audacity, or cunning are prevented from reaping the full fruits of these powers.

At other points, Galbraith casts a cold eye on conservative arguments that wealth creates incentives, or acts as a buffer against cultural uniformity and monotony. Most significantly, Galbraith gave equally little respect to the orthodox liberal assumption that growth, rather than redistribution, would by itself completely eliminate poverty. "Increasing aggregate output," he warned, "leaves a self-perpetuating margin of poverty at the very base of the income pyramid. This goes largely unnoticed, because it is the fate of a voiceless minority." [1]

But Galbraith, despite his own warnings, chose not to consider inequality as a major issue. Perhaps too preoccupied with making his point about the Affluent Society, perhaps too discouraged by the conservatism of the fifties, Galbraith chose to let inequality remain a secondary, insubstantial issue. Such inequality, one presumed, was trivial in the developed postindustrial world.

Unfortunately for us, neither Galbraith nor any other New Class critic has come forward to explain how inequality could be abolished (or even diminished) or how the wealth of the very rich could be rechanneled to the aid of the poor and the deprived. Quite the opposite has been true: nowhere has silence about the wealth of the very rich been more apparent than among the New Class.

1

The extent of present-day inequality, and the reason that the concentration of income and wealth is far from being irrelevant or secondary can be seen from just a few figures: according to the U.S. Census, the top one-fifth of the population in 1968 received 43% of the total money income in the United States; the top tenth received 27%, and the top 5% received 17%. By contrast the bottom half of the population earned only 22%. In slightly more graphic terms, the top one percent of the American population got more money in one year than all the men, women and children the government defined as poor; in fact the top one percent of the American population received in one year more money than the poorest 50 million Americans.[2]

To be sure, not all Americans in the top fifth of the population were rich by conventional standards. The top fifth contains a large percentage of New Class members, in addition to the extremely wealthy; in 1968, even the top 10% included anyone earning more than roughly $16,000 a year, hardly a definition of extreme wealth (even though almost 60% of America earned less than *half* that amount). Only as one passes into the top five percent can one begin to speak properly of the rich. *Fortune* magazine perhaps wisely chose the much smaller two percent who earn more than $25,000 for its criterion of the rich.

As the number of people in a particular category declines, however, per-person income and wealth rises—fantastically. Paul Samuelson's analogy between American income structure and the Eiffel Tower—"almost all of us live within a yard of the ground"—is apt, because it suggests how well-to-do the very well-to-do really are. To offer one simple example, in 1962 the mean wealth of those earning $15,000–$25,000 was a substantial $63,000; in the much smaller $25,000–$50,000 category, a very healthy $291,000; and in the $100,000 and above bracket, a munificent *average* of $386,000. These figures compared with a national average—including these very wealthy—of only 1,700,000.[3]

Robert Lampman's *The Share of the Top Wealth-Holders in National Wealth, 1922-1956* indicated moreover that even among the rich, wealth is continually stratified toward the top, with fewer and fewer holding increasingly larger amounts. He noted that in 1956 the top one percent of the adult population accounted for 26% of the nation's private wealth-holding. But, he also noted, the top *one-half* of one percent accounted for 25% of private wealth-holdings. In other words, the top half of the richest one percent of the population accounts for all but a small portion of the holdings of that entire one percent.

Lampman's work is helpful, because it sets such figures in perspectives that are easy to understand. He found for example in 1953 the average estate size of the wealthiest 1.6% of the adult population was over $186,000; the average estate size of the remaining 98.4% of the population was a mere $7,900—about enough to cover clothes, furniture, a used car, a TV, and a heavily mortgaged home. More frightening was the fact that even among the 98.4% wealth was very unevenly distributed: the average estate size of the lower half of that group was only $1,800.

How incredibly wealthy the very tiny minority of rich Americans was, and what influence they held over the American economy, Lampman went on to point out. *"This group of 1.6 percent owned 32 percent of all privately owned wealth, consisting of 82.2 percent of the stock, 100 percent of the state and local (tax-exempt) bonds, 38.2 percent of federal bonds, 88.5 percent of other bonds, 29.1 percent of the cash, 36.2 percent of mortgages and notes, 13.3 percent of life insurance reserves, 5.9 percent of miscellaneous property, 16.1 percent of real estate and 22.1 percent of debts and mortgages."* [4] (Italics added)

Lampman traced the progress of this concentration from the early twenties up to the mid-fifties, and in general remarked on its decline. But he discovered that the decline which had characterized the holdings of this tiny minority had ceased in 1949. Since that time the decline had not only ceased but reversed itself, and by the mid-fifties the wealth of the nation was again showing a tendency toward high concentration in the hands of the few.

Lampman's suspicion that wealth was again tending to concentrate in a few hands was confirmed in 1965 by two statisticians employed by the Internal Revenue Service. Extending Lampman's findings up to 1958, they found that the "top wealth-holders owned 27.4 percent of gross and 28.3 percent of net prime wealth in 1953, but increased their share to 30.2 percent and 32.0 percent respectively by 1958." They concluded categorically: "These data support Lampman's conclusions that the share of top wealth-holders has been increasing since 1949." [5]

Their findings were then extended by Ferdinand Lundberg, who used the basis of rising stock prices and general economic prosperity. "Actually," Lundberg declared, "in view of market valuations, the share of top wealth-holders at this writing is easily the greatest in history. It is my hypothesis that the share of the top ½ of 1 percent now exceeds the 32.4 percent of this group for 1929." [6] Lundberg's estimates for the most part remained exactly that; his methodology was not as exacting as Lampman's.

The important thing, however, is not the debate over the exact percentage point, but the massiveness of the holdings themselves. Ten years ago, when the government last published these statistics, the total wealth of the richest 2% of Americans was greater than the *U.S. Gross National Product.*[7] The same is true today.

2

The rich, then, incredibly more than any other group, enjoy the benefits of the Affluent Society. The popular notion of that society—of families able to enjoy their well-being, secure against debt and worry, able to offer their children education and a hopeful future—seems if not a monopoly of the rich, at least unlikely to be enjoyed by many others. *Fortune*'s investigation of the rich emphasized this fact: "Something thoroughly satisfying happens to people when they cross an income threshold of around $25,000 a year. Until then basic family wants tend to outrun income, but afterward income moves ahead of needs. The family pays off debts and stays out of debt. And major costs are met from current income. Most families find that even sending children to college is not financially binding." [8]

Because survey data on the very rich is lacking, *Fortune* limited its survey to "the simple rich," the families earning between $25,000 and $75,000 per year, slightly more than one percent of the population. Yet as a group the simple rich earned $56 billion in 1968, more than what 30% of the entire population earned. With such phenomenal buying power, they are three times as likely to own a color television or hi-fi as those Americans earning below $15,000, five times as likely to serve Scotch, seven times as likely to drink imported wine regularly, and eight times as likely to own a dishwasher.

Even so, such spending habits should not perforce be considered opulent: *Fortune* warns:

The upper-income American uses his extraordinary income for ordinary purposes. His desire is comfort, his goal security, his diversions passive and innocent. He buys the same things that anyone else buys but he buys more of them and usually chooses models with the most buttons and gadgets. He is neither adventurous in his spending nor a taste maker. The country club satisfies his modest social ambitions.[9]

But *Fortune*'s caveat should not be taken strictly at face value. By more conventional standards this infinitesimal group consumes at a rate unknown to most Americans. Automobiles are still a good register of major consumption. As expected, a large minority own Cadillacs and other luxury cars, and those who do not usually own a Pontiac, Buick, or other expensive car, compensating for their modesty with numerous accessories. Housing is also a status signal. While the home itself might or might not be estate sized, it is generally located in the best neighborhoods, with the best schools, the best shopping centers, the best landscape, within easy reach of the best country clubs for exercising those "modest social ambitions."

Home furnishings were, *Fortune* discovered, a common expense. Frequent remodeling was apparently a favorite habit of wealthy housewives, and homes were often equipped with several TVs, central vacuum cleaning, and gold plated faucets. One man reported that he had recently purchased a snow blower for use in the winter months. "I used it twice and now it hasn't snowed since. I always buy the luxury model. I like the little extras. Even just a fancier knob on an item could make the difference . . ." A contractor defined luxury as a TV set and car for every member of the family. Second homes—mountain or seashore retreats, often costing more than the average American home—are also becoming popular items in the budgets of the wealthy.

A major departure from earlier patterns of well-to-do living since World War II has been the marked decline in "help"—butler, maids, and chauffeurs. *Fortune* found only one in five homes with regular help. (The specific sample for this conclusion included only fifty-three homes, so the proportion may be understated.) Many expressed a common complaint to the *Fortune* interviewer that "good help just isn't available any more," but Gabriel Kolko remarked of this attitude, "It is clear that the 2.5 million butlers, maids, chauffeurs, and cooks employed in private households are paid by someone." [10]

A favorite pastime of the rich is travel. Even in *Fortune*'s generous terms, it was "the one real extravagance" of the upper-income Americans. Many people who lived "modestly" at home apparently thought nothing of spending freely abroad. As one Boston businessman put it, "When I travel, I travel deluxe." Both business and pleasure will take the very affluent to exotic places like the Caribbean, Africa, and Asia, and most take at least two, and more often, three or four vacations a year. "A winter vacation in Miami or the Caribbean has become normal," *Fortune* announced, "a cultural expedition to Europe with the children is common, and quick trips to Mexico and Canada and around the U.S. itself are routine."

An equally popular pastime is drinking. The preference for imported wines and the use of hard liquor, both for diversion and escape, was made apparent by a recent survey of executives and their drinking habits. Those who had four or more drinks a day had a median income of $27,500 a year, while one-drink-a-day men averaged a mere $18,500. An ad in an issue of the *New Yorker* stressed the benefits of buying 12-year-old Scotch by the case—at a "reasonable $150 per case."

Naturally enough, as this tiny minority of Americans becomes secure in its annual income, savings increase. According to the Federal Reserve Board, half the families with incomes of $25,000 or more saved at least $5,000 in

1963—more than the average income of two-fifths of the population that year. The mean wealth of people with 1962 incomes between $15,000 and $25,000 was $63,000, and that of the $25,000 to $50,000 group, $291,000.

As this wealth increases the composition of the family's estate changes with it. Savings accounts, real estate, and U.S. savings bonds dominate most small estates, but as incomes grow, a larger portion is invested in common stock. Asked what they would do with an additional $2,500 in income, most said they would invest in more stock. ("Only one person considered giving it away; charities do not seem to be uppermost in the minds of the affluent," said *Fortune.*)

3

Yet even with large incomes, savings, and rates of consumption, the men and women who earn $25,000–$75,000 often have more in common with those who earn less than with the super rich who earn more. After all, the super rich by all terms are an elite. Fewer than a fraction of 1% of American households report incomes of greater than $100,000; yet in many ways they dominate American life. It would be hard to find the top executive of any major company in the country who earns less than this; most earn more. The president of the United States earns twice this amount and eight of his cabinet members are millionaires in their own right. Although the official salary of congressmen is half this amount, many earn much more. A Washington columnist has found that 46 of 100 U.S. senators are millionaires. Virtually without exception, a $100,000-a-year income has become a synonym for the pinnacle of success in America today.

Not surprisingly, as one enters the highest reaches of affluence occupational diversity tends to narrow. The opportunities for making really big money in American society are limited to business. The arts provide a few well-heeled exceptions, and philanthropy contains a very few well-paid executive positions in the largest foundations; but almost without exception a man who wishes to die wealthy must first become a businessman.

For those who choose business, and who succeed, the rewards are magnificent. In a survey of the heads of America's 500 largest corporations, well over 80% reported incomes of between $100,000 and $400,000 annually, with another 10% admitting incomes even higher.[11] Although few ever achieve the astronomical heights of a Rockefeller or DuPont, such salaries do at least guarantee a comfortable retirement.

As for Tocqueville's belief that the tastes of the rich differ inconsequentially from those of the middle class, the question becomes one of degree. At some point the continual addition of quantity produces a subtle change in quality; the steady accrual of wealth and power has a powerful psychological impact on a man's loyalties and tastes, and from a casual perusal of the habits of the very wealthy, it is doubtful that they are middle-class habits.

For example, virtually all own their own homes, and 60% claimed vacation "getaway" homes as well. Half of the executives in the survey said they collected original works of art as a hobby. Far and away their most popular form of relaxation was golf, followed by fishing, boating, hunting, tennis, and swimming. Few prefer TV for relaxation, and even fewer prefer movies or plays. A significant number listed such un-middle-class tastes as rare-book collections, flying, horse-racing and owning, and sports-car driving.

As for friendships and acquaintances, the super rich show a distinctively self-conscious segregation from the rest of society. Three-fifths said they preferred to fraternize with other executives. Only 12% preferred the company of doctors, lawyers, or other professionals, and only 6% had academics as social companions. While such patterns are understandable in terms of the work required and the natural desire of men to associate with peers, it also suggests how cut off this potent group is from anything that might be called the mainstream of American life.

But background has carefully prepared business leaders for just this kind of seclusion. Little more than 20% of the major executives interviewed started out as stock boys, junior clerks, or hourly shift workers, and to balance those nearly the same proportion started at the top of their companies— as president, chairman, or founder, a pattern reflecting the family environments in which they were reared. Only 16% were the sons of blue-collar workers or farmers, despite the fact that most were born at a time when these two categories accounted for the majority of jobs. The rest grew up in comfortable upper-middle-class and upper-class homes, where the father himself was usually a businessman. Forty-five percent of the fathers, in fact, were at the very top of the business world either as founder, chairman, or president of a company, or as a self-employed businessman.

In preparation for their roles as business leaders, even further exclusivity was practiced. Ninety-four percent of them attended college, and a full 44% held graduate degrees, an outstanding record considering that only about 10% of their generation ever attended college. And of the college graduates, many attended the very best: 35% attended Ivy League schools, another 45% some other private college.

In matters of religion, the leaders of the business world show this same exclusivity: 80% were Protestant, and less than 10% each were Catholics or Jews. And among Protestant denominations, the "upper-class churches"—Episcopal and Presbyterian—tended to dominate, although these two denominations together contained only seven million members nationwide. (In banking and insurance, 93% were reported to be Protestants.)

The sum total of all this segregation, both in upbringing and in contemporary association, is a negation of Tocqueville's hope that the American rich would retain their middle-class habits. The rich, the very rich, *are* very different from you and me. Equipped with money, power, and prestige, they move freely throughout the world, living life as 99% of the world could never imagine. They are successful, and self-consciously so. Their clubs are exclusive, and so are their vacation spots. If the Versailles and Schoenbruns are no longer being built, it does not mean that smaller, but still lavish estates are not. James Ling, head of the Ling-Temco-Vought conglomerate, built himself a million-dollar home to celebrate his success, and for his efforts was considered something of a *parvenu*. Texas money, it seems, still carries the mark of the newcomer in high society.

For the very rich, money is no longer the basis of life but the means of amusement. One advertisement in an exclusive magazine recently recommended a $33,000, 13-carat champagne-colored diamond ring as an "end-of-a-vacation present." A circular put out by a travel company catering to the very wealthy began: "For 200 million Americans Thursday will dawn dull and drab—another ho-hum, humdrum day. But for 84 people—and you can be one of them—Thursday will mark the beginning of the greatest travel adventure of their lives." The brochure was for an $8,000 round-the-world tour. The *New Yorker* regularly carries advertisements offering such diversions as a crystal trout with 18-carat gold fly, complete with ruby eyes, "for only $700." Another magazine might offer such necessities as a golf putter with a solid gold head, or perhaps the classic of "conspicuous consumption," a gold-plated swizzle stick, battery-powered.

Insights into the lives of men and women who can afford such luxury are rare, but when they do appear they strikingly illustrate how different the rich are in all respects from the two hundred million "others" living in America. One woman, who chose to remain anonymous, described the "difficulties" of upper-class life:

Two years ago we went to Europe and zipped about for five weeks. Last year we were in Europe for eight weeks. We went to Istanbul and came back on a ship through the Greek islands. And I bought a fur coat in Germany. And a topaz pin in London. We mostly buy jewelry and paintings. And my husband has started collecting rare books. I adore to get new things. I'm mad about it. I've always felt this way. Probably because I'm basically a rotten capitalist. I like life to be as comfortable and beautiful as it can be. Because it makes me sweeter and everyone else around. Usually we just buy things because they strike us as something we'd like to have. If it's beautiful and within our means we'd buy it. . . . I consider traveling first-class on ocean liners and staying at the best hotels in Europe a luxury of which I never tire. . . . When we are in New York, which we often are, we hire a chauffeured limousine. . . . The things I look forward to are trying to stay conscious and feeling alive and trying to guide my children to being conscious and feeling alive. So few people are conscious. It's hard.[12]

But if this woman's crises and life-style seem fantastic, it is probable that the crises and life-styles of the very richest in America are as equally unknown to this woman herself. For at the very top of the income pyramid sits a tiny handful of individuals and families whose uniqueness it is impossible to understate. Names like Rockefeller and DuPont and Ford immediately come to mind, but for the most part, the men and women of the very top remain anonymous to most Americans.

In 1968, slightly more than 1,000 families reported an annual income of $1 million or more, and another 3,000 reported earning between $500,000 and $1 million. The fact is that these people probably earned a good deal more. Even so, these 4,000 families together claimed a total income of nearly $4 *billion* dollars.

Income of that magnitude is difficult to conceive, even in an age of multi-billion-dollar government and a trillion-dollar economy. In 1968, $4 billion was more than government expenditures for feeding the poor, and two times more than the government spends on anti-poverty programs. In that year $4 billion exceeded all the money given away by foundations. In that year $4 billion was more than what the federal government spent on education, and four times more than the federal government spent on all natural resources. In 1968, $4 billion would have provided a poverty-level income for over one million families. Instead it was shared by 4,000.

Ferdinand Lundberg, discussing the problem of comprehending such sums of money, put it this way: "If a prudent, hardworking, God-fearing, home-loving 100 percent American saved $100,000 a year after taxes and expenses it would take him a full century to accumulate [$10 million.] A self-incorporated film star who earned $1 million a year and paid a ten percent agent's fee, a rounded 50 percent corporation tax on the net and then withdrew $100,000 for his own use (on which he also paid about 50 percent tax) would need to be a box-office rage for thirty-four unbroken years before he could save $10 million." [13] Yet it is clear that several thousand Americans are worth much more.

Perhaps the most spectacular cases of such supreme wealth are the multi-millionaires. In early 1968 *Fortune* published its list of "America's Centimillionaires," those precious few Americans worth $100 million or more. *Fortune* was able to locate 166 such individuals, and admitted to missing quite a few more. Among this infinitesimal set, several, it turned out, had made their fortunes only in the postwar years.[14]

This fact must be comforting to the ideologist of American enterprise, because it indicates to what an extent "new wealth" is still being created, and, by implication, how much is still available to those who earnestly seek it. Such a fact seems to affirm the strength of American capitalism, and the benificence it is able to bestow.

But in the case of the centimillionaire, "new money" is the

exception, not the rule. If one looks at the list closely, it becomes obvious that in fact most of the very wealthiest are the sons and daughters, and often the grandsons and granddaughters of the very rich. Of the 66 individuals *Fortune* concluded were worth more than $150 million, over half came from clearly recognizable "old money" families, that is, families socially prominent for over two generations. (Indeed, a quarter were either a Rockefeller, a DuPont, a Mellon, or a Ford.) And of the remainder, a majority came from families which had left them a great deal of wealth. Rather than confirming the fluidity of the American social structure, and the opportunities available to any industrious individual, such facts suggest that America has created a stable moneyed aristocracy, admitting few newcomers but capable of surviving the upturns and downturns of all political and economic climates.

Close scrutiny deals a sharp blow as well to the idea that the "new money" demonstrates the viability of free enterprise. Many of the few new super-fortunes have been made at the expense of the government, or in industries protected by government. No less than a dozen of the new centimillionaires made their millions in the oil industry (protected for so long by the oil depletion allowances and import quota system), or in defense hardware of one kind or another. It is hard to imagine what their success would have been in truly competitive markets, unsubsidized and unprotected by the benevolent hand of government.

4

One of the most spirited arguments of the postwar years concerned the extent to which the rich still dominated American economic and political life. For a time it was popular to believe that the New Class was in control; sharp distinctions were drawn between ownership and control, and the fact that a tiny handful owned and profited from so much of America's wealth was dismissed as irrelevant. Since the New

Class managers were making the decisions, it was they, rather than the rich, who should be watched.

But the vast wealth-holdings and income of so few Americans can no longer be seen as irrelevant. On the one hand, it has been shown that many of the managers themselves are rich, and have opinions on the redistribution of wealth that are similar to those held by their wealthy stockholders. More important, the extent of poverty and deprivation should make the argument over who holds power secondary to the concern for economic justice. Can we possibly call our society just, let alone affluent, when the richest handful enjoys more money and more wealth annually than most Americans may enjoy in their lifetime? Do we want a social system which encourages the mindless pursuit of the material, when the great majority have no chance for its fulfillment?

The existence of the very rich today is testimony to the imbalance of our economy and the society which it sustains. Yet it is an imbalance which the New Class has carefully neglected. Unlike the poor, whom the New Class has been quite willing to view as a technical problem to be disposed of on the road to the postindustrial utopia, the rich have somehow escaped careful scrutiny. The fact that the rich man's salary might be a hundred times larger than the poor man's dole seems to discomfort few; or if it does discomfort, the discomfort has been overlooked because, as with Galbraith's liberal, advocating a policy of equality might be thought "a trifle uncouth."

8 | The Lower
Middle Class

*A young guy will start working at Dodge, and
after a week he'll be so shocked at how dull the job
is and how unpleasant the working conditions
are that he'll figure it has to be better somewhere
else. So he goes to G.M. for three days, and then to
Ford—and then he sees it's all the same. The
young guy asks: "Is this all there is to America?"*

Eugene Brook

In April of 1970, Assistant Secretary of Labor Jerome Rosow placed on President Nixon's desk a
memorandum entitled "The Problem of the Blue-Collar
Worker." It began, "The social and economic status of blue-
collar workers has become a subject of increasing concern in
the last few years." [1] Within a month blue-collar construction workers had organized "support Nixon" demonstrations
throughout the country, and speculation began to sweep the

ranks of political pundits that the New Deal coalition of workers, intellectuals, and the Old South was finally about to collapse. This fact alone made blue-collar workers not only the object of "increasing concern" but of rapt attention.

But Rosow's memorandum, whatever its political implications, was not concerned with the political future but with an economic present. New Class opinion had generally viewed the postwar years as a time of arrival for the American working class. Unionization, according to their mythology, had brought most workers under its protection and now guaranteed them not only a modest but often a prosperous income. Automation and technology might present some future threat, but unions would help displaced workers make the easiest possible transition to the society of leisure and technology. Workers enjoyed unemployment insurance, sick leave, Social Security, and paid vacations, none of which had existed fifty years before. Finally, the traditional disadvantages of blue-collar labor—low status, dull work, and poor working conditions—would disappear as machines replaced men, and the men who had tended the machines would somehow move into new, more rewarding white-collar employment or high-skill crafts, achieving what modern psychologists have termed "self-actualization."

Rosow, however, dealt a death blow to the New Class myth. Instead of finding security and contentment, he argued, many workers were finding themselves as hard pressed as ever. Forty percent of American families—a total of seventy million people—lived on incomes of $5,000 to $10,000 a year during the late sixties. While this might seem a regal sum to survivors of the Depression, for today's worker caught in a web of never-ending debts and responsibilities it was more often barely enough to stay solvent. Rosow described the entrapment bluntly:

The head of the household is usually a vigorous, fully employed blue-collar worker with heavy family responsibilities although many of this group are also in white-collar or service jobs. It is precisely when his children reach their teens and family budget costs are at their peak that two things happen to the bulk of such male bread-winners:

- They reach a plateau in their capacity to earn by promotion or advancement;
- their expenses continue to rise, as the last family members are born, as they become homeowners, as car and home equipment pressures mount, as the children may become ready for college, or support is needed for aging parents.[2]

Put simply, income was not keeping pace with need, the more so as needs became most critical.

Tracing the life of a typical steelworker, Rosow found that income exceeded need while the worker was young (presuming no savings and an extremely modest standard of living), but that by the time he had reached an earning peak in his mid-forties, family needs had completely outstripped his ability to satisfy them. Thus, although his income increased progressively, it increased at such a rate that he found himself falling farther and farther behind in the race to provide opportunities for his family. Moreover, as Rosow admitted, steel is one of the best of the blue-collar professions.

But this was not the worker's only problem; it was just the most evident one. There have traditionally been three routes of escape from such a life: promotion to a supervisory post, becoming a small businessman, or moving into a white-collar job with better income expectations. (Although, as we shall see, not all white-collar jobs offer such increased expectations.) This was the formula stressed by all nineteenth-century apologists of capitalism, and is still the most touted means of escape today for lower-middle-class workers.

Contrary to the myth, however, chances for advancement are dramatically scarce. A study of eleven major industries showed that one-third of all nonsupervisory jobs were "dead-end" (i.e., offering no further advancement), and that another significant proportion offered only single-stage advancement. Rosow noted that lack of opportunity was compounded by the lack of adequate adult education for workers, either on the job or in the community colleges originally created to aid the worker. And to these factors he added discrimination against older workers, lack of detailed free information about other kinds of jobs, and the high cost of private employment agencies for those who try to escape.

"The result," declared Rosow, "is that, when general wage rate increases are added to increased individual earnings due to promotion, real income has somewhat less than doubled in the past two decades, which is still not enough to cover the cost of the same standard of living throughout the period. Males aged 45 to 54 in 1968 who had one to three years of high school—the educational level typical of blue-collar workers in that age group—had increased their incomes by only 84 percent between 1949 and 1968." [3]

Thus, if a worker wished to maintain the standard of living he enjoyed before marriage, Rosow concluded he must do so by one of the following means:

1. Having saved when he was young (which he didn't do); or
2. moonlighting on a second part-time job; or
3. having his wife work even in spite of the obstacles to doing so; or
4. continued pressure for wage increases. [4]

The folly or hardship of these choices is not difficult to discern: Rosow ruled out the first; the second, moonlighting, means working on top of a regular 40-hour week that often includes overtime, which imposes a physical burden as well as a familial hardship; and the fourth, continued pressure for wage increases, has led to reciprocal price rises that only feed the inflationary spiral.

The only viable alternative left to the blue-collar family is sending the wife to work. Thus in two out of five blue-collar families the wife already works and census statisticians predict that this percentage will rise over the next several decades. But unlike professional families, where the wife's labor is seen as a welcome contribution or a natural outgrowth of her desire for varieties of experience, in the blue-collar family employment of the wife may impose sizeable burdens. Among unskilled and older families especially, the new roles imposed by economic necessity have undermined role differentiation between husband and wife, left children without proper care, and forced upon families life-styles that have led to conflict and divorce.

1

The plight of the blue-collar worker is not as surprising as the recent growth of interest in it. Until the late sixties little concern had been generated over the condition of the working man. Neglect fed on the mythology of their middle-class affluence and the news media's interest in more explosive problems. Working-class attitudes were rarely presented, and then only in a critical light. Blue-collar resentment against blacks, for example, was constantly interpreted by liberal journalists as a sign of prejudice. Accounts of fair-housing demonstrations similarly stressed the right of the Negro to equal housing, without regard for the blue-collar worker's unwillingness to see his neighborhood and home threatened by social experimentation. Construction workers' protests were given short shrift by many of the big city newspapers and weekly news magazines as examples of histrionic xenophobia.

What few reporters took time to point out was that, whatever the immediate issue—race or the Vietnam War or longhaired students—much of the workers' dissatisfaction stemmed from an underlying dissatisfaction with the quality of their own lives. To some critics continued dissatisfaction seemed impossible: Herman Miller, a well-known specialist on income, for example, tried to deny the "blue-collar disenchantment" by pointing to both the vast quantity of material goods available to workers and the opportunities they still had for advancement. He concluded, "The success of blue-collar workers can be most clearly seen in their own expressed attitudes. Opinion surveys how that union members now see themselves as part of the solid majority and not as a group that is alienated or that is struggling to establish its identity."

Miller's statement is misleading. To consider a "solid majority" as alienated may seem a contradiction of the term "alienation," but in fact it is at the root of the crisis of the lower middle class. Modern psychology has tended to restrict the term alienation to individual crises, but in its nineteenth-century conception it was a designation for a class crisis. Thus Miller's claim that "union members now see themselves as part of the solid majority" overlooks the possibility that the entire "solid majority" feels alienated in the original sense of the word—a sense of powerlessness over their lives and a sense of revolt over their apparent destinies. In a cover story entitled "The Troubled American: A Special Report on the White Majority," *Newsweek* found after months of interviews and investigation that "the white majority [is] profoundly troubled. . . . There is a heavy undertone of resentment—a dark suspicion that the rules are being changed in the middle of the game, that the dice are loaded in somebody else's favor. But at bottom, the mood adds up to a nagging sense that life is going sour—that, whatever is wrong, the whole society has somehow lost its way."[5] Rosow found this same quality of dissatisfaction and discouragement, and underlined "the fear of being forgotten" as a common condition of the lower-income American.

The fear of becoming "the Forgotten American," as President Nixon has called the lower middle class, has several dimensions. On the most immediate level, that of job satisfaction, the worker is acutely aware of the declining status of manual labor. "While the nation has in recent years sold the importance of science and technology to our younger people," declared the Rosow report, "it has neglected to communicate the importance of some ten million skilled blue-collar workers who are responsible for transforming the ideas of scientists and the plans of engineers into tangible goods and services." Consequently, "according to union leaders, the blue-collar worker increasingly feels that his work has no 'status' in the eyes of society, the media, or even his own children."

Second, this loss of status is an accurate reflection of economic reality. Automation has carved deep into the ranks of blue-collar jobs: for example, between 1951 and 1963 employment in the steel industry declined by 20% while steel output remained the same. The resulting insecurity makes blue-collar employment unattractive to new workers. Young men seek out other kinds of employment, while older men continue to work, waiting for retirement and hoping their union will protect them in the interim.

Third, the much vaunted material progress made by workers is in many ways illusory. Most often overlooked is the critical fact that blue-collar workers have actually lost the economic momentum they reached in the early postwar years. From the rapid gains of wartime, workers have again fallen behind managers and professionals in their drive to increase income. Price increases have cut sharply into blue-collar buying power: in the past five years, because of inflation, workers have actually lost ground in terms of real purchasing power (measured in 1957–59 dollars), from a high of $88.06 per week in 1965 down to 85.35 five years later. Added to this are the especially rapid rises in the cost of necessities that hit the lower middle class the hardest: between 1958 and 1968, according to the *Wall Street Journal*, daily hospital care went up 101%; auto insurance 44%; physicians' fees 38%; property insurance 36%.

Arthur Shostak summarized the quality of workers' lives by means of the BLS's "intermediate" family budget plan.

Between 1960 and 1967, the weekly after-tax take-home pay of an average factory worker with three dependents increased by 11 percent. In the same time period, however, the amount of money such a family needed to "live moderately" rose by 24 percent. . . . The budget itself was held to *very* moderate standards ($1.50 a day for food, $6 a month for recreation, $15 a month for clothing; no allowance for college expenses, savings, or installment buying). Nevertheless, the budget in 1967 required a net income $3,500 more than the 1967 earnings of the average blue-collarite.[6]

The situation Shostak surveyed was bad enough to refute Miller's easy confidence that workers share in affluence and no longer feel alienated in their lives: "Budget inflation, inadequacy, and disparity demonstrate the serious erosion that has occurred in the worker's economic position. For all the talk of joining the 'great central mass,' most workers have actually failed to share in the semiaffluence of the postwar years; many in 1967 could not even manage a stringent 'moderate' living budget."[7]

But the dilemma of economic status and security represents only one level of the workers' alienation. Over the past decade, workers have watched what they consider a steady degradation of the values and customs they consider essential to "the real America." The civil rights struggle of the early sixties placed a great strain on social mores that had evolved over many decades, mores workers considered almost inviolable. Often these values were not explicitly racist, but did contain (as Blacks correctly charged) an implicit racism equally damaging to the civil rights cause. But these values seemed logical and necessary to workers. They accepted the traditional American belief that "each man makes it on his own," and had little understanding or sympathy for the special treatment they thought blacks were receiving from the government. After all, many of the workers were from ethnic minorities themselves, and whatever the facts, they firmly believed they had made their own way; as a consequence, they were dismayed by much of the civil rights movement.

Compounding frustration over civil rights were the protests by the young against the war in Vietnam. Workers, irrespective of their personal gripes over jobs or income, have always been strongly "pro-American" and "anti-Communist." The "Americanism" of many of them is easily parodied but not easily ignored: George Meany has forced cancellation of an American contribution to the UN's International Labor Organization because a Russian had been appointed as one of the organization's five assistant directors. None of this means that workers in general are either racists or xenophobic super-patriots. A pluralism of viewpoints exists in the labor movement as strongly as it does elsewhere, and many of the attitudes expressed by workers are still strongly progressive. Before his death Walter Reuther organized the Alliance for Labor Action, a coalition of the UAW and Teamsters designed to seek "social justice" for all Americans. One of its first projects was the unionization of the black and white workers in the Atlanta area. Likewise, after the Cambodian invasion an important group of West Coast labor leaders declared their firm opposition to President Nixon's action. Thus working-class sentiment is far from uniformly reactionary.

On the other hand, the lower middle class is the strongest supporter of traditional American virtues by persuasion and necessity, and their crisis is caused by what they perceive to be the steady erosion of these virtues. "The values we all held so dear are being shot to hell," one man told *Newsweek*. "Everything is being attacked—what you believed in, what you learned in school, in church, from your parents. So the middle class is sort of losing heart. They had their eye on where they were going and suddenly it's all shifting sands." *Newsweek* listed several of the values it saw as "changing": "the work ethic, premarital chastity, the notion of postponing gratification, and filial gratitude for parental sacrifice." Or as Paul Jacobs said, "When the hippies go to Woodstock, they are building a new community of their own. The worker's community is disintegrating. He doesn't know where to find a new one. So he keeps harking back to the old days and the old values. But it is not possible to go back. And there is no new community to replace the old."

The feelings of loss, of confusion, of being caught going down an up escalator are all exacerbated by government and the media. The lower middle class often feels, justifiably, that the attention given various protesting minorities vastly outweighs their numbers, and that the lives and worries of the "un-black, un-young, unprotesting middle American" goes neglected in the news.

2

The old adage that America practices "socialism for the rich and free enterprise for the poor" is also strongly felt by the deprived lower middle class. Faced with agricultural subsidies, oil depletion allowances, expense accounts, and various other boons to the rich, and welfare, job opportunity programs, small business loans, and now perhaps a guaranteed income for the poor, the lower middle class reacts with either numb resignation or bitter resentment. They feel they are forgotten by government, a suspicion supported by the government's investigators themselves.

Rosow, for instance, pointed out several deficiencies in the government's aid (or lack of it) to the lower middle class. Although an official of the Nixon administration, he bluntly argued that the Tax Reform Act of 1969 "does not provide adequate relief" for the lower middle class because the basic tax structure "gives only small recognition to family size considerations." A married couple with an $8,000 income and two children will receive some tax relief when the bill takes effect in 1973, but the saving is almost insignificant.

Furthermore, present tax deductions for dependents are "token in character," says Rosow, and actually "provide more at higher income levels than at lower or moderate levels." [8] Moreover, the size of the tax deduction bears no relation to the age of the children, even though budget costs are higher for older children. Finally, the government makes no provision for tax relief as family education costs rise, a burden that becomes especially acute when families try to send their children to college.

Added to the failures of the federal tax system is the clear regression in state and local taxes, which hits the worker harder than anyone. Last year the average state and local tax bill for a lower-middle-class family was $700. Because state and local taxes rely so heavily on property and sales taxes, necessary expenditures such as food, housing, and gasoline are taxed, while discretionary income (which makes up continuously larger portions of affluent income) escapes. The result is that the poor and the lower middle class pay, while the upper middle class and rich go free. In percentage terms, the President's Council of Economic Advisors made this pattern clear: in 1965, those earning less than $2,000 paid 25% of their income in state and local taxes; those earning between $2,000 and $6,000 paid 10.5%; and those earning between $6,000 and $10,000 paid 9%. By contrast, those earning more than $15,000 paid only 7%. No elaborate arithmetic is needed to see what this progression means.[9]

To add to his difficulties, many of the welfare programs financed by the worker's taxes are legally unavailable to him. Child-care expenses, necessary for a working mother, are not deductible for families earning more than $6,900 a year, and with the passage of President Nixon's welfare reforms this situation will become worse. Welfare mothers will be able to leave their children at day-care centers free of charge or at subsidized rates; working-class mothers will have to bear the full expense themselves, often as much as $40 per week.

Other programs such as job retraining and welfare subsidization are similarly closed to the lower-middle-class worker, even though the margin between a worker and a welfare recipient may be only a few hundred dollars.

The theme of neglect, of being forgotten, reappears constantly in the worker's life. In buying a home for his family he is faced with the same tight market faced by the poor. The House Banking Committee's finding that less than a quarter of new housing now sells for under $20,000 means that many workingmen must either settle for older housing, or content themselves with trailer or apartment living. If he chooses to go ahead with a home purchase (as most Americans still do) he will find himself strapped with a mortgage that over a 20 or 30 year period will cost him more than double the initial cost of the house. Interest alone will consume 3½ years of a blue-collar worker's wages.

If he or a member of his family falls ill or suffers a serious accident, neglect will often be the common treatment. Workers, because of the higher incidence of work-related injuries and because of their general attitudes toward health care, are more likely than the affluent to suffer illness or injury, but are less likely to receive decent medical care. A 1962 study of medical care received by New York City teamsters found that "45 percent of all cases hospitalized under union insurance plans received substandard care; 60 percent of the children hospitalized received less than optimal care . . . and 67 percent of nonsurgical cases received less-than-optimal care." Another study done at the same time showed that the average white-collar worker spent $169 per person on health care, service workers only $134, and blue-collar workers $123 (unskilled workers, $104).[10] As Richard Lichtman bitterly observed, "We are involved in nothing less than distributing the chances for physical and mental well-being on the morally invidious basis of economic class." The president of the American Medical Association admitted as much, in slightly elliptical terms, when he told a reporter, "Sixty percent of Americans receive good medical care." [11] Discounting an optimistic exaggeration on his part, this leaves about half the nation *without* good medical care.

What may be said of medicine may also be said of the law. America is a nation which prides itself on law; law-and-order is a big issue in the lower middle class, but it is the lower middle class (and the poor) who suffer most from the law's neglect. The president of the American Bar Association, quoted in *Time* magazine, acknowledged this fact and further remarked that the poor, because of legal aid and new legal services created by the War on Poverty, may actually be receiving better service from the law than the lower middle class. It is still true that lawyers are attracted by clients best able to pay, and too frequently workers and their families fall outside this category. A single call to a lawyer may cost $25 nowadays, and minor litigation seldom costs less than several hundred dollars. For the rich and the affluent, this may be expensive but not burdensome; for the poor, the state may often pay the bill. But the worker may be discouraged by the fees from seeking any help at all. In such cases, the lower middle class has little protection from the hucksters, loan companies, and dishonest merchants that are regular features of life on a marginal income.

And what is said of medicine and the law can be repeated *a fortiori* for most of the workingman's social relations. Life below the median income is life below the comfort zone. The outward signs of affluence—the home, the car, the paid vacation, and the occasional frills of modern appliances—that celebrants of American society have publicized are deceptive indices of security. Purchased to give security, as often as not they have only increased anxiety. An income of $5,000 or $7,000 or even $9,000 cannot buy security for any family in America today; *at best* it can provide a sense of superiority over those millions who earn less. Such incomes provide little margin for saving; they are consumed almost entirely in the present, leaving the years to come in a limbo of union benefits, beneficent employers, and uninterrupted economic growth.

3

It has been popular for the past few decades to imagine that blue-collar workers have been making significant progress. The traditional reasons for such thinking have been rising wages and increased educational opportunities; a more novel one has been the gradual shift of the economy from an industrial to a service economy. We have seen that, rather than rising to some new plateau of security, workers have been caught in a bind of rising prices and more rapidly increasing financial obligations that made security harder and harder to achieve. But education, we commonly hear, is changing this situation, at least for some. Universal education through high school and ready access to college means social advancement for the bright and ambitious, and escape from the drudgery of the lower middle class.

This upward movement of a vast segment of society, however, is not all that it seems at first glance. First, the economy itself, as it comes to rely more and more on the skills of technology, continually upgrades educational requirements; thus like income, educational levels have continuously risen but so have educational requirements for good jobs. A B.A. or B.S. degree is no longer either a prestige symbol or a guarantee of financial security.

Second, it is not at all apparent that the quality education necessary for professional and managerial jobs is being won by the lower-middle-class young. This is certainly true of the Ivy League schools and other private institutions of similar rank, where the median family income of students regularly falls well inside the top ten percent of the population. But it is also true of public schools, which were designed to overcome the elitism of private colleges and universities. Education officials in California found that enrollment at the state's universities and colleges followed class lines. A similar survey of the University of Wisconsin in 1964–65 showed that the median income of students' families was 50% above the median for the state as a whole. What seems to be happening is that higher education, rather than abolishing class lines, is acting to stabilize them.[12]

The third factor in the alleged amelioration of working-class life is technology. Automation has taken over more and more jobs; during the same period blue-collar labor has declined as a percentage of the total work force. To theorists of the New Class, this has meant that America is in a new phase, about to enter a new society in which the drudgery of labor will vanish in the movement toward leisure and the development of human potential.

But this hopeful notion neglects two facts. First, the non-manufacturing sector, into which the bulk of new workers are pouring, actually pays lower average wages than does manufacturing. Second, the white-collar and service jobs seem to produce few of the benefits New Class writers predicted for them, such as less drudgery and more meaning in work.

In 1967 the average spendable (after tax) weekly income of production or nonsupervisory workers—blue- and white-collar alike—was less than $91. In manufacturing the average was $10 higher (and in construction, $43 dollars higher), whereas in white-collar finance, insurance, and real estate the average was $85; in retail and wholesale trade the average income was only $75 a week—just above the poverty level. The low average in trade is caused partly by a fairly large number of part-time workers, but not entirely. For example, the average *hourly* income in retail trade in 1967 was only $2.01, before deductions. Whatever the number of hours worked, $2.01 still ranks as a miserably low wage, especially if it must support an entire family. And in the service sector, the fastest growing segment of the labor market, wages are often worse. For example, building service workers and laundry and dry-cleaning workers earned only $64 a week; motel and hotel employees did even worse with only $56 a week. Yet these three fields alone employ over one million workers.[13]

The National Industrial Conference Board, a private economic research organization, discovered similar patterns among white-collar office-workers. They found that in large metropolitan areas (where wages would normally be highest) a wide variety of office jobs paid only one or two thousand dollars more than a poverty income. Thus the median income for secretaries ranged between $4,000 and $6,000; that of typists and stenographers between $4,000 and $5,000; and that of specialized clerks between $5,000 and $7,000.[14]

Some economists have argued that such low wages are often supplemental incomes, and so do not have the dire consequences they seem to imply. That is, such wages are often earned by wives or children supplementing family incomes. It is true that roughly two-fifths of working class families have a second wage-earner; but that fact yields several conclusions. First, it means that children are left unattended by their parents, with obvious psychological dangers, as noted before. Second, it suggests that there are a great many miserably low-paying jobs in this country, if so many incomes need to be supplemented in this way.

Put more directly, these figures suggest that much of our so-called affluence has been achieved, not by any redistribution of income or wealth, but by a widespread adaptation to economic necessity. Rather than benefitting from an improved wage structure, workers have responded to the desires or imperatives of affluence by sending wives or other family members into the labor market. And apparently even then, if we take seriously the quantity of sub-median family incomes in America, these families have not been successful in reaching anything that might be called affluence.

Finally, the testimony of white-collar workers suggests that technology has meant little change in the basic conditions of labor. The conditions associated with factory assembly lines —the routine, the infinite division of labor that makes each task pointless and boring, the strict regimentation—have in many cases simply been transferred to the office building. *Newsweek*, in its investigation of middle America, surveyed not only production-line laborers, but white-collar workers as well, and found their complaints disturbingly similar. One man who worked in the headquarters of a large insurance company observed, "It's a womb-to-tomb life. . . . They lead you into the bathroom. You piddle. And then you go back and do your job. It becomes frustrating. You go home wondering, 'What the hell did I do today?' " A colleague apparently more content in his resignation said, in a grotesque parody of Willie Loman, "What the hell, I made this bed. I made the choice, so I have to live with it. I'm just an average slob. They wind us up in the morning and we go all day. But is that so bad? On the whole I'm happy." [15]

The fact is that the shift from a blue- to a white-collar has not altered the way many workers live their lives. An insurance salesman whose father was a foundryman, or a grocery checker whose father was a coal miner, retain values that popular sociology attributes to blue-collar workers exclusively. They retain traditional values because America has left them with traditional lives: forty-hour weeks and fifty-week years of uninviting, uninspiring, soul-destroying work. Perhaps they are better off sitting silently at their desks, peering around them at identical desks stretching in all directions, rather than standing in a noisy factory amid rows and rows of machines; but the final verdict is not yet in. The promises which the transition to a white-collar economy were supposed to fulfill have not been met: automation has not meant the end of drudgery, most jobs have not become more meaningful, and the leisure which we were all supposed to get ready for remains the reward of the privileged minority.

4

Back in the early sixties, when the poverty program was just getting under way, Leon Keyserling proposed that instead of limiting federal aid to the poor (officially, those with incomes below $3,000), a second category—which he called "deprived"—should also be eligible for government assistance. The deprived were to be distinguished by the fact that they fell within our conventional notion of the middle-class majority: they were to be those families whose incomes ranged from the poverty line up to $5,000 a year.[16]

Keyserling, as a former member of the President's Council of Economic Advisors, probably realized that this plan had no chance of success. Even though the "deprivation" budget he put forward fell far short of anyone's idea of affluence, it was politically and economically explosive. First, in a Congress not clearly disposed to the idea of a War on Poverty of *any* kind, a War on Deprivation might well have sunk both programs. Second, Keyserling's program would naturally cost much more money. And third, and perhaps most important, had Keyserling's definition been accepted, 77 million people—one-third of the American population—would have been officially revealed to be either poor or deprived. To a nation convinced of its own happy affluence, this would have been an intolerable insult.

And yet Keyserling's suggestion made perfect sense. Adjusted upward for inflation, his figures now approximate the Bureau of Labor Statistics' "lower" budget of $6,567. Earlier, we classified all those families falling below the BLS budget as "poor"; the distinction is worth retaining. Keyserling's term deprivation is better employed to describe the condition of those millions of Americans who today live above such a poverty budget but below the Bureau's more reasonable "intermediate" budget, which allows for few of the "luxuries" of an Affluent Society.

For such Americans, affluence is something to read about in advertisements; it is not something to experience. They may own a car and a television, and may look forward to some day owning their own home. But they are not affluent. They do not spend carelessly, because there is no room for carelessness; they may enjoy a few of the superfluous goods which advertising would have us believe are the basic equipment of the American family; they may even hope that some day—in that automated, technologized Arcadia promised by the New Class—they too will be affluent, like the happy families on TV. But while they are a majority of the Affluent Society, they are not yet affluent themselves; most of them never will be.

9 | The Upper Middle Class

In late 1970, with a myopia that should by now seem characteristic of New Class assumptions, the *New York Times* proudly announced: "Opulence Becoming a Way of Life for the Middle Class." Under that headline the *Times* documented the life of the McRea family: a Seattle teacher, his wife and children, and their newly found well-being. According to the article, the McReas made about $14,000 a year—which let them "typify a vast number of American families for whom in the 1960s, the affluent society appears, current inflation and recession notwithstanding, to have become the opulent society." [1]

The Opulent Society. Having surveyed the extent of poverty and deprivation in this country, the idea that opulence is typical of American life borders on the absurd. The *Times* was aware of the absurdity, but only to a limited extent. Instead of explaining the breadth of income maldistribution, and the serious situation of those below the median income level, it merely acknowledged "the deep poverty that endures among 10 percent of American families"-and took heart because "even that number has dropped sharply from the 1960 poverty total." No mention was made of the rich, none of the poor (except for the government's officially tiny minority), none of the lower-middle-class blue-collar and white-collar workers who spend their lives in continual economic anxiety, able to own some of the attributes of a modest life, but at heavy expense.

How can a newspaper with the resources of the *Times* present such a one-dimensional description of American society? Earlier we argued that true affluence was a characteristic only of the upper middle class, a group whose most prominent segment was the professional-managerial elite Galbraith called the New Class. The New Class, surveying its own well-being, and imagining the prosperity of others to be as great, concluded that America had entered a new era in world history, a postindustrial, technological age in which the ancient pursuit of material comfort had been finally and permanently won.

This same myth, subject to slight modification, seems to be reasserting itself today. Despite the disclosure of widespread poverty in the early sixties and the increased concern for lower-middle-class workers in the late sixties, it seems apparent from the *New York Times* article and other sources that a great many upper-middle-class Americans still believe in the truth of an Affluent Society. Somehow the assertion of inequality at the heart of American life is considered passé, displaced by principled pontifications about the greatness of America's economy and political system, and the need for only minor reforms—"new beginnings." The new beginnings, however, are usually the same new beginnings we've seen for 70 years: proposals for a graduated income tax that "really works," for closing loopholes in corporation tax laws, for health programs, for education programs, for a "real" antipoverty program. Had there been any truth to the myths of American affluence and equality in the first place, none of these reforms would have been necessary—not 70 years ago, and certainly not today.

1

As if embarrassed to be restating such a hoary myth, the *Times* rather quietly acknowledged the uneven distribution of material goods in the United States. But instead of giving us any useful details, it tried to comfort us with the comment that "More families have two cars than have none and as many families have television sets as have toilets."

In fact the census shows that while "as many families have television sets as have toilets," most families are significantly less well off than families like the McReas. For example, it shows that while three-quarters of all U.S. families have at least one car, the distribution of cars is heavily skewed toward the top income brackets, ranging from 96% of the richest bracket to only 44% of the poorest bracket. Moreover, the report directly contradicts the popular image of the average American family with its two cars, color TV, and expensive home. Only 30% of all U.S. families reported owning a second car, and this figure concealed the concentration of second cars in the hands of the upper and upper-middle classes. For example, nearly two-thirds of the families earning between $15,000 and $25,000 owned two cars or more; among those earning between $5,000 and $7,500, only a quarter could report the same.

Similar observations can be made about other major consumer items. In the upper-income bracket (i.e., $15,000–25,000) 55% of the families owned color TVs, 71% owned clothes dryers, and 52% owned a dishwasher. By comparison, among those families in the lower income bracket ($5,000–7,500), only about 30% owned color TVs, only 30% owned clothes dryers, and less than 10% owned a dishwasher. (The dishwasher figure is especially ironic because it is one of the items which the *Times* highlighted as belonging to the McReas and "the vast number of Americans like them.") [2]

A substantially more ominous tone could be sounded about housing. The *Times*'s casual reference to the McReas' $34,-000 home neatly overlooks the already-mentioned House Banking Committee's belief that 50% of American families cannot afford mortgages on even $20,000 homes, let alone homes costing $34,000. Moreover, the 1960 census found over a quarter of all housing in the United States either deteriorating, dilapidated, or lacking in such elemental facilities as hot running water or indoor plumbing. (In states like Alabama and Mississippi, the percentage was almost half; only 44% of Mississippi's housing was considered sound by Federal standards.)

In December, 1969, *Fortune* declared that a "housing crisis" was overtaking America. "The shortage of acceptable shelter that has long been afflicting the poor and the black is spreading to the white middle class and even to quite affluent families. It may be that conditions are at their worst right now. But a real turn-about will not come quickly, for the housing industry is at present simply not well organized or well enough financed to make rapid solutions possible."

Measured in terms of government estimates, the nation needs 26 million new housing units in the next ten years. At the present rate of construction, not even half that figure will be reached, and the rate itself has been falling. But this is nothing new: President Truman in the late forties set a five-year target figure for the construction of new public housing which had not been reached two decades later; what *was* new was the breadth of the crisis. Unless drastic reversals can be achieved almost immediately, the consequence will be an increased burden of older, less adequate housing, and a tightening of the market which will drive up the price of even these older structures. Although egregious conditions such as the absence of indoor plumbing or hot running water will presumably decline, the overall quality of housing remains in doubt. "Ticky-tack" housing, built at minimum cost with minimum care, was a prominent feature of the early postwar period and now seems firmly established as a characteristic of American housing.

As might be expected, the burden of inadequate housing will fall most heavily on those least able to pay. Home ownership has always enjoyed a sacrosanct position in American ideals, but examination of ownership's realities reveals how unevenly the ideal has been realized. The Federal Reserve Board published in late 1966 a monograph entitled "Survey of Financial Characteristics of Consumers." The study showed that for the population as a whole, home ownership accounted for a larger share of total wealth than any other single asset. Among those whose income was above $15,000, for example, nearly 90% owned their own homes (and an appreciable number owned a second, and in rarer instances, a third, home). But among the poor ($3,000 or below), home ownership fell drastically to 40%. For those between $3,000 and $5,000 the figure was still half that of the upper-income group, a modest 45%. And even for the lower middle class (those between $5,000 and $7,500 annually) the rate of ownership stood fully a third below that of the most affluent, at 60%.

This maldistribution of home ownership, moreover, does not reflect the wide variation in quality of the housing in which Americans reside. In contrast to the McReas' $34,000 home, the census reported in 1970 that the median value of single-family, owner-occupied homes was $17,000 and that only about 9% of American families owned homes as expensive as the McRea's. The fact that the median price of a new home rose to nearly $26,000 by 1969, when the House Banking Committee was worried about mortgages over $20,000, suggests that the situation is getting worse rather than better.[3]

2

Another indicator of opulence, according to the *Times*, is college education. Mr. McRea is a schoolteacher, and hence a college graduate (with presumably an additional year of post-graduate work for a teaching credential).

Here we encounter in its new form the fifties' infatuation with education. For example, the number of college students in the United States doubled between 1960 and 1970, and nearly 40% of high-school graduates enrolled in some college or university. Taken at its face value, this feat is worthy of unadulterated self-congratulation. But should the feat be taken only at its face value?

Much of the admissions bulge of the last decade was created by the coming-to-age of the postwar baby boom—a bulge which had been foreseen for some time—and is not likely to repeat itself in the near future. This would suggest that the absolute rate of growth will taper slightly, although total enrollment will not. Yet even if growth does continue, college graduates will not constitute even a near majority of the population by 1985. The census predicts that there will be approximately 20 million college graduates in the United States by then, less than a tenth of the total population.

This is an important figure to bear in mind—less than a *tenth* of the population as late as 1985 will have graduated from college. Even if computed as a percentage of persons over 25, the percentage does not rise that significantly—to roughly 16% or 17%. In addition, another 12% will have attended college without graduating; combined with graduates this means that by 1985 less than three in ten Americans will have *ever attended* an institution of higher learning.[4]

While the McReas are "typical of a vast number of Americans" in a strict sense, they are, and will remain, atypical of the vast majority of Americans—an enormously greater number. This is extremely important; for college education, as the country by now so well knows, is the key to success in a technology-oriented economy. In 1968, the college graduate could expect to earn over $586,000 in his lifetime, whereas the high-school graduate could expect to earn $350,000. In annual terms, this means that the college graduate could expect his income to be roughly 60% higher than the high-school graduate's, which easily spells the difference not only between "opulence" and "affluence," but more importantly between "affluence" and "deprivation."

Given that fact, one can reexamine income distribution with an eye to educational attainments. Measured by total money income, in 1968 over 60% of the families headed by a college graduate earned more than $12,000; by contrast, less than 30% of the families headed by a high-school graduate had similar earnings. Moving the cutoff line to a more affluent $15,000 per year, the number of high-school families earning more fell sharply to only 15%, while the number of college families fell only to 40%. That year only one out of ten college graduates reported earning less than $7,000, as opposed to one out of four high-school graduates.

This can be stated slightly differently in order to highlight the contrast between the incomes of high-school and college graduates. In 1968 four out of five college graduates earned more than the median income, while three out of five high-school graduates earned less. Alternately, this meant that the mean income of college graduates was a full $5,000 above that of high-school graduates in the same year.[5]

3

The usual caveat added to such comparisons is that anyone intelligent and studious enough to attend college has the opportunity to do so. America, unlike aristocratic societies, offers wide opportunity to all individuals and rewards men for their ability rather than their parentage. Stated most crudely, this is the Horatio Alger cliché; in somewhat more sophisticated terms it is called upward mobility.

There is already a sizeable literature in sociology which

suggests that there is in fact very little upward mobility in America. It should be interesting to find out what effect higher education has had on this reported lack of mobility, since the claim of higher education is that in addition to providing the manpower for operating a technological society, it also tends to equalize the conditions of life.

It is apparent that a college degree is a prerequisite for most high salaried professional and managerial work. It is also apparent that college graduates are drawn to such occupations, especially the professions. The most recent studies show that over 80% of college graduates enter either professional or managerial categories, predominantly the former.

This is neither surprising nor disturbing all by itself: one would expect that in any society those best qualified would rise to the top. What *is* disturbing is the prospect that opportunity to gain these qualifications is being severely restricted. That is, it appears that acceptance into colleges and universities is going disproportionately to the children of college graduates, a fact which greatly increases our similarity to aristocratic societies, and fundamentally challenges even a limited notion of "equal opportunity."

There are substantial bases for this claim: the first is a study in the *American Economic Review* on the income backgrounds of students at California colleges and universities. The study is illuminating for two reasons: first, because California's system of higher education is generally ranked as the best in the country, and second, because the study covered only the *public* university and college system, excluding the private institutions which have historically drawn most heavily from upper-class and upper-middle-class families. The study shows that average family income correlates with the rank of the university or college attended, and suggests the difficulties which low income families face in sending their children even to publicly financed institutions. This meant in money terms that while the average income of California families in 1964–65 was $8,000, the average income of families with children in the University of California was $12,000 and that of families with children in the state college system, $10,000.[6]

The authors concluded:

> Paradoxically, the most common justification for the redistribution in the case of higher education is that it helps achieve greater equality of opportunity. The lower the tuition, the easier it is for students to attend. But low or even zero tuition has still not been sufficient to permit sizable numbers of young people, particularly from lower-income families to attend public institutions.

The discrimination against lower-income families is even more striking in private colleges which now enroll fewer students than public schools but which still contain the majority of top-ranked institutions in this country. In *The Open Door College*, a survey of freshman students from San Jose, California, Burton Clark found that while 45% of enrollees at San Jose State College and 17% of those at Berkeley were from blue-collar families, only 6% of Stanford's freshmen were from such families. This correlated closely with Gabriel Kolko's information about Harvard, which showed that 80% of the incoming college students were from professional and managerial families, whereas only 8% were from blue-collar families.[7]

4

Proper understanding of this upper-middle-class elite is made doubly difficult through its being obscured by the myth of the great homogeneous middle class. To be sure, the class's more visible characteristics have been observed and commented on, but most comment has been confined to the supposedly odd or sensational case. Thus, Thorstein Veblen's explorations of the technocrats remain at the fringes of academic consideration, and C. Wright Mills's description of a

Power Elite seeking organized hegemony over decision-making was dismissed as gross exaggeration and fundamental misunderstanding.

Rather, the presence of a small elite at the core of economic and political decision-making has come to be seen as inevitable and even desirable. Thus we have Galbraith's already cited claim that the increase of the New Class should be a primary goal for America. His more recent reformulation in *The New Industrial State* of the New Class as the "technostructure" aroused hardly a word of criticism. In addition, we have the testimony of innumerable political scientists that elitism is necessary, rather than antithetic to the democracy of advanced postindustrial America.

Perhaps the best example of how confused, and conversely how clear, the understanding of this new group of college-educated, affluent Americans can be appears in a well-known work of political science in the sixties, Robert Dahl's *Who Governs?* Dahl's thesis is that equality has increased in America as the elites of the eighteenth and nineteenth centuries have given way to a newer, more broadly based "pluralism" of interest groups more representative of the community as a whole. From an age of Patricians, the city which Dahl examines (New Haven, Connecticut) evolved through a generation of Entrepreneurs to a generation of Ex-plebes until its present domination by what Dahl, in an unintentional paraphrase of Galbraith, calls the New Men.

Significantly, Dahl does not claim that this evolution proceeded directly down a path from great inequality to low or marginal inequality, as other critics would have us believe. Instead, "this silent socioeconomic revolution has not substituted equality for inequality so much as it has involved a shift from cumulative inequalities in political resources . . . to non-cumulative or dispersed inequalities."

Whether one accepts Dahl's history of New Haven or agrees that it is typical of America in general is not the immediate issue. What is important is the conclusion Dahl reaches about the present distribution of equality and inequality and his judgment about class division.

In Dahl's opinion, the balance of power, influence, and involvement clearly favors the middle class. But who is the middle class? Here lies the major confusion: in a footnote the middle class is specifically defined as "executives, managers, professionals, administrative personnel, small businessmen, clerks, salesmen, technicians." This excludes the majority of the population, but an even more exclusive definition is still to come. For when Dahl writes of the middle class in the text, he has a distinctly smaller group in mind, a group defined by what "might loosely be called the possession of 'middle-class' attributes and resources: *a college education, above-average income, a white-collar occupation, and the like.*" [8] (Italics added.)

As we have seen, these attributes—aside from white-collar occupation—are not widely shared even among what Dahl technically defined as his middle class. College education is concentrated among "executives, managers, professionals, and administrative personnel" and is only infrequently a characteristic of "small businessmen, clerks, salesmen, and technicians." The same is true of "above-average income": the former group uniformly enjoyed incomes significantly above the average, while the latter group often found itself concentrated much more closely around the average, and quite often below the average in times of economic reversal.

Nonetheless, Dahl's confusion (or better, his dual definition of the middle class) is enlightening because of the attitudes it reveals. It demonstrates the subconscious image that characterized social commentary from the end of World War II on, and explains in part how tremendous optimism and complacency could be generated by the idea of a post-technological world. Dahl takes a set of empirically verifiable facts about American life and grafts onto it an image of life that ignores equally verifiable but less encouraging facts. The result is a congeries of fact and fancy that fairly typifies the upper-middle-class world but which is grotesque when applied to the nation as a whole.

The consequence of this definitional confusion is not difficult to detect. Academics, journalists, editors, and politicians could measure their own situations as members of Dahl's "middle class"—with "a college education, above-average income, a white-collar occupation, and the like"—and see themselves as no different from, or not very far ahead of, the rest of "middle class" America. And as the men and women who effectively created America's image of itself, they could celebrate our entry into a new age of affluence, where the destiny of the nation could be trusted to conscientious managers and professionals who would oversee our lives for the good of all.

There can be no doubt about the power of such mythology to influence public opinion. If there is any doubt it should be banished by the example of the *New York Times* article discussed earlier. The belief that the McRea family heralds the Opulent Society—that two cars, a boat, and a $34,000 home typify the lives of "vast numbers of American families"—merely repeats all of the fundamental socio-economic misconceptions of the postwar period.

5

The economist Robert Lekachman once observed, "What everybody knows is frequently not so." This comment might serve as our motto for the New Class, for it suggests the conclusions we have drawn about New Class myths. The idea that America could be captured in simple phrases like "The Affluent Society," "The Technological Society," "The Post-industrial World," or that it could be described as "middle-class," "egalitarian," or "affluent" should by now seem not only faintly ridiculous, but cruelly deceptive.

It would be preposterous to imagine that such images were

deliberately created by a tiny cabal in order to cheat the majority of decent lives, but so too would it be wrong to imagine that the myths which govern our world do not unequally benefit the minority who most firmly accept and promulgate them. It has not been the purpose of this book to suggest that a tiny elite consciously imposes its will upon the majority in all areas of politics, economics, and social life; rather the purpose has been more clearly to define the inequalities which are the facts of American life today.

We live in a world advanced far beyond the feudalism of medieval Europe and the systematic discrimination of ancient monarchies, and we have achieved much of which we can be proud. The majority does not live in fear of starvation, and the minimal requirements of food, housing, and clothing are broadly distributed. Measured against many nations we are far better off no matter what the criterion.

Having said this much, however, there is much that remains to be done. America today is still, despite all our hopes, all our efforts, and all our dreams, a vastly unequal society. The most affluent third of Americans receives each year two times the income of the other two thirds. One half of America lives on less money than the richest 10%, and poverty of the grim, soul-breaking kind endures for nearly one out of three of our countrymen. And yet a handful of Americans enjoys wealth on a scale that even European nobility would have found hard to imagine.

For the McReas and New Class families like them— white-collar, college-educated, and well above average in income—America has become a pleasant place to live. If questioned they would probably display the same confusion as Dahl, speaking of themselves as characteristically middle-class; they would then tell the interviewer that their lives are probably little different from those of most Americans: comfortable, secure, affluent, and on the verge of becoming, in the *Times*'s words, "opulent."

But most Americans encounter such a life-style only in the

media. It simply cannot be said that the majority is "comfortable, secure, and affluent." Most Americans seek such goals; but until more of them draw more critical conclusions about the nature of American life today, most of them will seek and never find.

10 | The New Class and the Seventies

*Given twenty years of stability in relative measures
of income distribution and twenty years of
widening absolute differences, there is no reason
to suppose that the nature of the American
economy is about to change. The burden of proof is
certainly on those that think the income distribution wil
take care of itself. Unless positive evidence can be
found of structural factors that will alter the
nature of the American economy, there is no reason
to think that our income distribution problems will
solve themselves.*

Lester Thurow
M.I.T. economist

It is easy in retrospect to see the mythology behind Horatio Alger and how markedly it differed from the
facts of nineteenth-century industrial life. Likewise it is easy
now to expose the mythology behind our zealous desire to

"Christianize" and "civilize" nations like Panama, Cuba, and the Philippines at the turn of the century. We even find ourselves able to admit the intentions behind the decimation of the American Indian and the enslavement of the American black.

But myths do not die easily, or willingly. The Civil War released the black American from legal enslavement but not from the myth of his intrinsic inferiority. So too with the myth of a vast, homogeneous, equalitarian middle class. It is hard to see even fissures developing in its durable surface.

In a way, the durability of the myth should not be surprising. The French anthropologist Claude Levi-Strauss has remarked that "every civilization tends to overestimate the objective orientation of its thought." This is so, Levi-Strauss argues, because myth is a distinct mode of man's scientific reasoning, i.e., a way of organizing and informing the vast quantities of fact and data which besiege him in his day-to-day life. Levi-Strauss is saying that myths are the necessary glue of a society, one of the chief ways it holds itself together. What his observation does not explain is why the American myth of the middle class should be so nondescriptive of its own society and therefore so different from other myths. The American myth of the middle class is the assumption that prosperity and relative security are characteristic of the majority. Europeans commonly speak of a middle class, but mean by it a much smaller, and distinctly segregated group within the society. In England, for example, when questioned by interviewers the majority still identify themselves as working-class; the middle class is a term reserved for a fifth or a quarter of the population. The same is true in Germany, France, Italy, and the rest of the world; only in America is it common to hear the majority described as middle-class.

To its staunch defenders, the use of the term middle class is a testimony to the triumph of the American economy. But measured against the statistics carefully gathered in this book and elsewhere, the usage bears the marks of cruel deception. A country cannot easily continue to call itself middle-class when twenty million malnourished live in its midst, or a third of its populace lives in poverty, or the majority do not have what the government's own agencies describe as a "moderately comfortable" standard of living. Somewhere myth has sharply diverged from reality.

In Chapter One, it was suggested that faced with a divergent reality, the myth of the middle class gains its strength by serving a two-fold purpose: on the one hand, for the lower-middle-class blue- and white-collar worker it removes the sting that a more rigid, carefully divided class structure brings, and allows a leverage in economic negotiations for higher wage demands; on the other hand, it sanctifies the high pay, status, and security of the upper middle class because ostensibly these advantages are common or available to the middle class as a whole.

Such an explanation, however, does not reach the crux of the matter. After admitting that there is no vast, affluent middle class in America and that income and wealth stratification exist to the disadvantage of the majority, we must then ask if such stratification is really necessary, and if it is not, what may be done to abolish it? In other words, does the structure of industrial society impose on us a permanent economic inequality, and if not, what are the mechanisms available for its change?

1

To the first question, the answer is tentative but depressing. Historically, the industrial societies of the West have shown no striking trends toward equalization of income or wealth. For most of the first half of this century, distribution remained static (or actually worsened, as in America during the 1920s). When shortly after World War II, respected economists like Simon Kuznets announced that this long-standing trend was being reversed and that income and wealth were finally starting to trickle down from the rich to the rest of society, the announcement was greeted with great rejoicing, and played a crucial part in developing the image of the affluent society. But the rejoicing was short-lived because subsequent studies like those of Kolko and Lampman showed that wealth and income had returned to their high levels of inequality, and that what little had trickled down had trickled no farther than the upper middle class.

Furthermore, what was true of the United States was true also of the industrial countries of Western Europe. R. H. Titmuss's study of the British economy shows even higher concentrations of wealth than in the United States. Titmuss concludes that Britain's own so-called postwar income revolution was a largely inadvertent or accidental consequence of wartime economic conditions, and that the trend toward equalization had been clearly reversed.[1] Even in those few countries such as Sweden and Norway where income and wealth redistribution have been an avowed aim of public policy, the net effect has been small. A recent study of trends in Norway, for example, shows little measurable improvement since the war.[2] If inequalities have not been removed or, indeed, even significantly modified by labor agitation, heavy taxation, two world wars, and a major depression, it would seem that inequality on a major scale is here to stay.

This view received a further boost several years ago with the publication of a book by the Yugoslav Communist, Milovan Djilas. Until that time it had still been debatable whether or not inequality could be abolished through the initiation of public ownership and socialism. Theoretically at least, inequality seemed removable through a conscious choice of allocation schemes aimed at that end. But Djilas argued by implication that such a situation was impossible because socialist industrialism had created its own bureaucracy of managers and professionals who allocated not only income, but also power and prestige to themselves rather than divide it among society as a whole.

Djilas called this bureaucracy of managers and professionals the New Class. Unlike Galbraith, however, Djilas did not see the New Class as a benign group of public-spirited people whose emergence marked a hopeful era in man's history; he saw them instead as powerful enemies of the public good.

The American New Class widely accepted Djilas's judgment of the socialist New Class without turning the criticism back upon itself, which says a great deal about the Americans' perceptions. Schooled in the myth of America as a middle-class society and careful to avoid any sharp self-differentiation, the American New Class obviously felt themselves fundamentally different from their managerial and professional equals in the Eastern bloc. What they failed to consider was Djilas's own observation that the Communist New Class felt itself (publicly at least) just as much a public-spirited part of the majority.

The importance of Djilas's work was that it underscored the common structures of both capitalist and socialist industrialism and the common role of the New Class in both. Western political scientists may rush forward to argue that democracies and authoritarian societies are quite different, but for our purposes here this is beside the point. What Djilas shows, and what is confirmed by the studies of income and wealth distribution throughout the industrialized world, is that political structures have not altered the fundamental economic inequalities which exist throughout. Where industrialism exists, the New Class exists, and where the New Class exists, profound inequities remain.

Consider Djilas's views in light of recent proposals for major reform of American society. Galbraith, in *The New Industrial State* for example, takes up the issue in his final chapter on "The Future of the Industrial System." There, after persuasively arguing the point that all industrial systems are organically similar, he reasserts his old defense of the New Class left over from *The Affluent Society*. Focusing on the intellectual and scientific community, he argues that it is their responsibility to defend the diminishing liberty of individuals within the industrial society, and to advance the civility of arts and letters against the tide of mass production and monopoly control by the state and big business. If this community is successful, it will mean a new and humane postindustrial world for all, a world in which

aesthetic goals will have pride of place; those who serve them will not be subject to the goals of the industrial system; the industrial system itself will be subordinate to the claims of these dimensions of life. Intellectual preparation will be for its own sake and not for the better service to the industrial system. Men will not be entrapped by the belief that apart from the goals of the industrial system—apart from the production of goods and income by progressively advanced technical methods—there is nothing important in life.[3]

But the beauty of Galbraith's utopia, like that of so many others, is marred by the author's murkiness on how to reach it. For he admits that the present direction of industrial society is in exactly the opposite direction. We are headed now not toward the humane world which is Galbraith's ideal, but toward one where

our wants will be managed in accordance with the needs of the industrial system; the policies of the state will be subject to similar influence; education will be adapted to industrial need; the disciplines required by the industrial system will be the conventional morality of the community. All other goals will be made to seem precious, unimportant, or antisocial. . . . We will be bound to the ends of the industrial system.[4]

Galbraith's hopes for the New Class are made all the sadder by his awareness of its limitations inside the industrial system. To speak of the New Class as if somehow that group were free from countervailing and crosschecking forces does disservice to reality. The New Class is only slightly freer than other groups in the society, because it is the class on whom final decisions fall and which has the information and ability to understand the workings of the society it administers. But conversely it is less free than any other group in the society because its identity and very existence depends more heavily than any others' on the continued existence of the industrial system.

It does not matter whether there are a plurality of groups within the New Class competing for power and authority, as in America, or whether the groups are more tightly consolidated under the hegemony of a single party, as in the Soviet Union. The outcome is the same, because in both cases the New Class is bound to an outlook and social structure which is unable to deal with the need for increased economic and social equality. Concessions are made, but as the past history of stable income and wealth distribution shows, the final effect is nil.

Undoubtedly this is a bitter pill for many to swallow, because it means that the goals which men like Galbraith write about seem out of reach. Such a judgment eliminates hope, and at present the greatest need in America seems to be for hope, for a way out of the morass of confusion and dissension into which we seem to have sunk. And furthermore, it overdraws the case: socialist societies *have* overcome the kinds of inequalities of wealth found in the United States by the simple expropriation of property out of private hands; they have also reduced the degree of inequality found in the capitalist societies of the West, though by no means completely. But finally such a pessimistic view seems a premature assertion, rather than a conclusion, because it skims over the ways in which income and wealth distribution might conceivably be altered.

2

America offers two methods of change: the first is growth, the second is redistribution.

Of the two, growth has been more popular, and in its limited way, more successful. Over the past half century growth has accounted for the bulk of what social improvement has taken place. Growth has increased our output of goods and raised our wages; growth has made possible the myth of the affluent middle class.

But, as we are increasingly discovering, growth has been achieved at enormous cost. New-found awareness of our environment and of the necessity for ecological balance makes us realize that we pay for what we consume. Pollution, despoliation of our countryside, noise, and the decay of our major cities are the price we have paid for reckless growth.[5] Moreover, as this book has shown, we have not been rewarded with the affluent society we thought we were buying. The maldistribution of affluence, the persistence of poverty and malnutrition have accompanied pollution and the degradation of our natural resources. It was once pleasing to think that we had been given abundance for our sacrifices; that is a pleasure we can no longer afford.

All this makes the plea for increased growth a hollow solution to our problems. Theoretically it is not impossible to imagine that if we continued to boost output continuously, we could overcome the blight of malnutrition and even poverty. But faced with an economy that already produces over one trillion dollars a year in goods and services, one wonders how long, and how much more output, would be needed to reach such a goal. Two trillion? Three trillion?

Moreover there are limits to reasonable growth. Growth can be accomplished, but if paid for by inflation, it is only an illusion of success. Wages rise, but so do prices, and the pressure of each on the other does not so much improve the quality of life for those who need it as it widens the already large gap between the haves and the have-nots. When inflationary growth is curbed by wage-price controls, the likelihood that the poor and deprived will benefit is dim indeed. Those countries which have already attempted wage-price controls find that such measures do little to alter existing inequities; indeed the measures often tend to harden the inequities into a firmer mold than before. Groups of earners are unwilling to sacrifice their rank in the income hierarchy by raising the wages of those below, not only because of status, but because the improvement of any group puts pressure on the overall price levels, pressure which adversely affects the others. Therefore all become only more stubborn in their resistance to changes which do not reward all equally.

Someone will inevitably point out that this criticism of growth is a criticism of uncontrolled, undirected growth, and that policies of selective growth could bring about desired changes. Economists are especially fond of this argument and see in it a reasonable compromise between the growth-oriented outlook of industry and the demands for social justice which conflict with it. In theory, the point is hard to refute. It is quite easy to envisage selective growth models that will benefit the poor and deprived; but realization of these models is quite another thing.

The plight of the American Negro is a case in point. In 1965, rioting in Watts took over thirty lives and initiated a series of "long hot summers" throughout the country that lasted for several years. Great efforts and great amounts of money were expended by the federal government and private industry to expand job opportunity, surely a major cause of the rioting. Major corporations opened plants in Watts, and encouragement, advice, and subsidization was given to black capitalism to generate jobs within the community. Yet five years later, the *Los Angeles Times* reported that unemployment had risen 61% since the summer of the riots. Recession had closed some plants and caused major cutbacks in others; a number of enterprises, such as a firm that was to manufacture baseball bats, had simply failed because of lack of foresight.[6] In short, the situation had not only not improved; it had gotten worse.

The same story can be seen in the figures for black income in the nation as a whole. In the mid-sixties, black incomes were less than three-fifths those of whites. During the inflationary prosperity fueled by the Vietnam War, this percentage rose to slightly over three-fifths, giving rise to optimism about the improved position of minority families. But more recently this rise has halted. This is made more discouraging by the awareness that the absolute difference in money terms between white and black families has actually *grown*. Furthermore, careful study of black incomes has shown that the black middle class, not the black poor, were the principal beneficiaries of what little improvement had taken place.

Hopes for selective growth are further diminished by the very nature of our competitive industrial economy. Whether one believes the market or the firm controls corporate decision, the motivation is private gain—and private gain, as should be quite obvious, is not always the best judge of the public good. Efficiency, not equality, is the criterion of performance. The corporation has a vested interest in the maintenance of inequality: the responsibility of the firm is to keep wages as low as reasonably possible so that profits will be maximized; simultaneously the salaries of corporate officers must be high to maintain competitive parity for talent, and profits must be optimized to ensure a steady flow of investment funds from outside. The result is obvious.

For those interested in changing the income and wealth structure there remains then only redistribution, a process accomplished in this country by taxation. When first introduced, the income tax had as its goal exactly that: redistribution. Although levels were kept quite low at first, during

WW II taxation on top incomes rose to 94%, an extreme that conservatives feared would mean the end of the rich in America. But the outcome was quite the contrary: the rich flourished, and it turned out that no one in fact ever paid such amounts. Lawyers, accountants, and loopholes ensured that the average income tax paid by the rich seldom exceeded 25%. In some cases, the rich paid no taxes at all.

The rather striking disparity between the rates stated and rates paid suggest the difficulties that progressive taxation encounters. The avowed aim of the income and inheritance taxes was originally redistribution. The income tax grew out of a long period of progressive agitation and public disapproval of the vast fortunes of the new industrial rich in the face of the poverty and deprivation of workers. But today one is more likely to hear tax specialists and economists talking of taxes in a Keynesian fashion—as stabilizers and regulators of aggregate demand. The old goal of redistribution has been lost in the mythologized world of the affluent middle class.

The negligible impact of taxation must be clearly understood. Throughout this book, pretax figures for income distribution have been used, and many economists feel these are misleading because they exclude the reallocations produced by taxation. In other words, they believe that maldistribution is diminished by the tax structure. But to put it bluntly, they are wrong.

The popular way of showing that taxation is progressive is to cite the stated rates. Thus income tax on very low incomes may be zero, while rising steadily to very high levels on high incomes. But stated rates, especially on high incomes, are seldom the rates actually paid. Congressman Henry S. Reuss reported, for example, that 301 individuals with incomes above $200,000 paid no tax whatsoever in 1969, and California's millionaire governor, Ronald Reagan, had not paid taxes for two consecutive years, although his official pay alone amounted to over $70,000.[7]

Reports such as these, although representing exceptions, are certainly not misleading. Joseph Pechman, the tax economist mentioned earlier, has noted that although before-tax income shares of the rich showed a slight tendency to decline in the postwar years, after-tax IRS figures actually showed a rise. Thus, the top 15% of tax units in 1952 held 30% of all personal income, but by 1967 had increased its share to 34% — a substantial rise.[8]

Even this understates the negative impact of taxation. Since World War II, innumerable tax benefits and payment forms have grown up which benefit only the rich. Pechman named tax-exempt interest and depletion allowances as outstanding examples, then added to the list deferred compensation and pension plans, stock-option arrangements, and direct payment of personal consumption expenditures through expense accounts. Gabriel Kolko estimated the size of these various benefits to the rich and concluded that the uncomputed income of the upper class would raise its total disposable income at least two or three percentage points above Pechman's own figures—again a substantial rise. To this he added the further observation that the effective tax rate on the top one percent of the population had dropped in the last twenty-five years from 33% to 26%.[9] John Gurley, a Stanford economist reviewing Pechman's work, argued that this figure fell even farther if certain unrealized capital gains were taken into account: "The average tax rate at the upper end, instead of being around 30 percent as Pechman calculates, is probably around 20 percent." He concluded, "The fact is that the rich are not being soaked; instead, they are soaking up wealth very rapidly in ever-increasing amounts."[10]

Indictment of the federal income tax, however, attacks the most virtuous element of the tax structure. Estate and gift taxes, Gurley claims, once designed to modify inheritance of wealth, have "been something of a joke among public finance experts." Pechman explains:

Estate and gift taxes are levied only on a small proportion of privately owned property in the United States. About 3 per cent of the estates of adult decedents and less than one-fourth of the wealth owned by the decendents in any one year are subject to estate or gift taxes. The relatively small size of the tax base is explained in part by the generous exemptions which exclude a large proportion of the wealth transfers, and also by defects in the taxes that permit substantial amounts of property free of tax.[11]

The same sort of indictment fits state and local taxes, which in the past several years have grown enormously. While federal taxes have hovered at a constant percentage of GNP, state and local taxes have grown from 7% to 12% of the GNP in less than twenty years. They are overtly regressive, placing their burden most heavily on the poor and the deprived. When combined with federal taxes, the overall burden of taxation becomes almost equally proportional at all levels, with those earning $3,000 paying just as much of their income as those earning five times as much.

It is sometimes argued that the overall regressiveness of the tax structure is offset, in part, by what are called transfer payments. These are payments made out of tax revenues to special groups, most importantly the poor, which actually constitute a return of money taken through taxation. In other words, the overall net effect of taxes and transfers combined is supposedly less unequal than the tax structure alone. On the surface this seems correct, but closer examination reveals serious flaws.

First, the poor themselves pay heavily for transfers. The *Economic Report of the President, 1969* showed that those with incomes under $2,000 paid an average 44% of their income in taxes, nearly twice as much as those earning $100,000 or more. Those earning between $2,000 and $4,000 paid 27%, or roughly the same as the average millionaire. Second, the money paid by the poor as a group is not transferred back to them as a group. Half of the poor are working poor, and therefore are either ineligible for transfers like public assistance, or receive their transfer payment only when they retire, as with Social Security.[12] In other words, we have created the cruelly anomalous position of making the poor pay for their unemployed, disabled and overaged brethren.

This is a disheartening situation. It is made more disheartening when one realizes the prospects for change. It is common nowadays to talk of eliminating poverty through increased transfer payments, such as President Nixon's guaranteed annual income program, without fully taking into account the costs of such programs. The estimates for the Nixon plan vary, depending on final form, between five and ten billion dollars. Five and ten billion dollars does not seem very much money in the present federal budget; but as we tried to show in Chapter Six, the Nixon program will do nothing more than maintain the existing sub-minimal definition of poverty. It will partially treat one problem, by making transfers to the working poor, but the very criterion of poverty it uses is so stark that its ultimate result will barely begin to touch the deep and widespread poverty that continues in America today.

For those who see the failure of the Nixon program, but argue that once instituted, its payment levels can be raised to adequate standards, the nemesis of costs remains. Raising the level to the Bureau of Labor Statistics' $6,960 for a family of four would cost nearly $30 billion, and raising it to the Bureau's intermediate $9,000 budget of "modest comfort" would cost $100 billion.[13] Critics such as Galbraith, and more recently the Urban Coalition, have suggested that increased welfare costs could be borne by reducing wasteful military and space expenditures, but anyone who imagines that even $30 billion can be so extracted indulges in fantasy. The situation demands a complete revolution in the tax structure, not reallocations within it.

But what are the prospects of a complete revolution in the

tax structure? On the federal level some headway has been made: exemptions have been increased, and the burden lightened for the low-income tax-payer; certain loopholes have been made smaller, such as for capital gains and oil depletion. But the headway is indeed small: the oil industry was able to maintain its depletion allowance at 22%, and has so far successfully defended the oil import quotas that cost the taxpayer $9 billion a year; new dodges for capital gains and stock-option programs have been created; and President Nixon's refusal to place profits under federal regulation with wages and prices, coupled with major tax breaks for business, suggest a new and firm intransigence about tougher taxation for the rich. And the proposals for the poor will result in some, but little, relief at the other end. As for state and local taxes, where regression is worst, the prospects for change are bleak. Even "revenue-sharing" with the federal government, the latest in a long list of proposed reforms, will barely scratch the surface.

Pechman, who is well acquainted with all these problems and whose own solutions are far from radical, has ably summarized what may be hoped for from tax reform. After listing what he thought were reasonable and practical alterations that could be made, he concluded:

> The long list of needed revision in our federal, state, and local tax system should convince anyone that the reforms now being contemplated will not make a significant change. . . . The influence of the groups arrayed against a significant redistribution of the tax burden is enormous, and there is no effective lobby for the poor and the near poor.

It may be that, at some distant future date, the well-to-do and the rich will have enough income to satisfy not only their own needs, but also to help relieve the tax burdens of those who are less fortunate. In the meantime, the tax system will continue to disgrace the most affluent nation in the world.[14]

3

Let us return to the myth of the middle class, as promulgated by the New Class.

We have seen that the myth of the middle class is not just a recent creation, but a stem of the classic American myth of egalitarian homogeneity, a myth that is over two hundred years old. Although this older myth itself never adequately described the contours of American life, it served an important purpose by diminishing class barriers and allowing upward mobility for the few and preventing psychic deprivation for the many. And, too, it was not a completely dishonest picture of America, because industrialization, for several reasons, did not create in the United States the vast gulfs between economic classes that it did in Europe.

After World War II, this older myth experienced a profound reinvigoration through the myth of the affluent middle class. Fueled in part by traditional optimism, in part by the striking contrast that the postwar world presented to the prewar depression, the country came more and more to see itself as embodying a new stage in western history, a stage in which the older preoccupations with production and the material needs of life were passing away, replaced by issues of aesthetics and the "quality of life."

But saying that the country came to see itself this way distorts the process of social perception. What happened was that the upper middle class who had access to the media and the other opinion-shaping instruments of American society measured their own postwar experiences, and then, through the older myth of homogeneity, interpreted that experience to mean a millennial change for all of America. Viewing their own lives as typical of American experience, they believed that they could validly interpret and predict the future of nearly two hundred million different individuals.

The hubris of this group received a monumental blow first

in the failure of the Kennedy era and then in the failure of the Vietnam War. Faith in technological rationality and planning was shaken, and the realities of poverty and racial discrimination began to reveal how untypical the lives of the New Class were. By the end of the sixties, the experiences of the Democratic Convention in Chicago, the Cambodian invasion, and the murder of students seemed to signal an end to the comfortable illusion that "affluent" America had reached "an end of ideology." To the contrary, the ideological issues raised seemed to overwhelm all of America's comfortable assumptions, leaving a country confused and badly divided in its wake.

The sudden reversal of nearly two decades of comfortable assumptions had its effect. David Riesman, for example, acknowledged in a 1969 preface to *The Lonely Crowd* that perhaps too much emphasis had been placed on "the upper-middle-class affluent American" as representative of the culture. Galbraith likewise has admitted that he underestimated the extent of poverty and deprivation, and now believes that the rich have been treated too lightly by the tax system.

But like their generation, neither of these men has gone beyond these slight revisions. Neither has proposed that their fundamental perceptions are at fault, or that before America can attempt to achieve a just society the mythology of America must be redesigned to accurately describe its realities. Nor is it likely that they will. Both Riesman and Galbraith are powerful and influential men, and they, like most members of the New Class, have worked long and hard to achieve their position. This does not mean that either is a venal or dishonest man, but that they, like all men, are governed by the dictates of self-interest and accumulated perceptions. They have spent years formulating, defending, and propagating their image of American society, and have behind them the support of their peers and their own experience.

But where does that leave those who see America differently, who see it as still fundamentally unequal and discriminatory, far from resolving the issues once thought forever settled by affluence? It leaves them responsible for formulating not only a more accurate picture of America than the New Class has provided, but also for formulating a picture of a new America that will deal with the inequalities of the present, as well as providing a means for reaching that end. It is not impossible to envision a country which uses industry and technology without being used by them. *Industry* and *technology* are broad catchwords that encompass an infinite variety of social systems, systems which enlightened men and women are free to choose. They may be highly concentrated, with division of labor carried to a logical extreme, where the majority is deprived of effective control over their lives, and decisions are increasingly the province of specialists. Or they may be decentralized, with labor integrated so that workers carry out an interesting variety of tasks, and feel themselves in control of their destinies, and decisions are made by the group, and not the individual.

The biologist René Dubos has said of our present environmental crisis that "trend is not destiny," and his words are applicable to our economic and political situation as well. But his words will be effective only if there is a massive reorientation of our social outlooks. The present trend is toward increasing centralization, increasing specialization, and increasing inequality. Even though the income shares of all groups have remained roughly the same, the distance between the incomes of each group has grown, and continues to grow. We face the prospect that the New Class will grow even more affluent, and even more sure of the success of the Affluent Society, while the majority of poor and deprived fall farther and farther behind, silenced by denial of access to higher education and the means of communication, and vainly awaiting their turn to be admitted to the great middle class which is supposedly the condition of us all.

This means that for those who would seek change, the changes must not be merely incremental and specific, but broad and aimed at the most popular conceptions of America. Another War on Poverty will not eliminate the poor any more than the present war has, unless it is done within a revolutionized understanding of America. Nor will expanded college admissions for minorities or revised study programs remove the inequality of opportunity unless the admissions are *vastly* expanded, and the lessons learned carried from the academy out into the world. What we need is a new set of social priorities, not merely adaptations within the old.

In short, the myth of the middle class must be demolished. But beyond that, a new myth is needed, a myth not like that of the middle class, an antithesis to reality, but a myth in the sense that Levi-Strauss uses the word: an organizer of reality, a framework for the perception of the world. Perhaps in this case the better term is "ideals" rather than myth, because the perception needed to confront our present world is already known as that.

The ideal is equality; many readers will be surprised that something so familiar should be considered so important, especially since it is an ideal honored in the traditional vocabulary of American society. But its honor and its reality, as this book has painstakingly described, are two very separate, very distinct matters. And not until we understand better why this is so can we hope to reassert the ideal so that it will contain practical force.

11 | Equality and Affluent America

Those who believe that complete equality can be established in a permanent way in the political world without introducing at the same time a certain equality in civil society, seem to me to commit a great error.

Alexis de Tocqueville,
Democracy in America

Equality has always figured prominently in our political rhetoric but insignificantly in our economic life. Thomas Jefferson claimed about the issue of economic equality that "legislators cannot invent too many devices for subdividing property," and other Founding Fathers made much stronger claims. But today, as we have seen, the issue of equality has been submerged into a myth of middle class affluence, and has lost the power it once had to arouse both passion and reform. What happened between the time of the American Revolution and now?

The epigraph at the beginning of this chapter is a suitable starting point for our investigation. It was written by Tocqueville while America was still only a half-century old and was meant as a high compliment to the young nation. To the Frenchman, America seemed the apotheosis of democratic dreams; he was effusive in his praise of American accomplishments and saw the country as a harbinger of the greatest era in man's history. Not least among the accomplishments he praised was equality; it seemed to him so impressive that he was moved to exclaim, "among the novel aspects that attracted my attention during my stay in the United States, nothing struck me more forcefully than the general equality of conditions."

Judged by European standards, American equality was no doubt astounding. Not only a political equality, but also a rough economic equality had been established among the citizenry of the country. As Jefferson put it, "the great mass of our population is of laborers; our rich, who can live without labor . . . [are] few, and of moderate wealth." The fact that Tocqueville did not even see fit to mention poverty as an American problem implies what an accomplishment the American world must have seemed to him in 1832.

Although we know now that conditions were not nearly as Elysian as the above gentlemen's comments would lead us to believe, they were impressive when measured against the Europe of the day. But consider how radically conditions had changed by the late nineteenth century, when another European commentator, Lord Bryce, visited America. Searching for the signs of equality which Tocqueville had so highly praised, he found himself disappointed. Pondering in 1889 in how many senses equality was still the defining characteristic of America, he concluded, "Clearly not as regards material conditions. Sixty years ago there were no great fortunes in America, few large fortunes, no poverty. Now there is some poverty (though only in a few places can it be called pauperism), many large fortunes, and a greater number of gigantic fortunes than in any other country of the world." So drastically, in fact, had conditions changed from the 1830s that Bryce was forced to retreat to the almost innocuous observation that at least Americans still retained their *respect* for equality. "It is in this that the real sense of equality comes out. In America men hold others to be at the bottom exactly like themselves." A man might be enormously wealthy or powerful, he continued, "but this is not a reason for bowing down to him, or addressing him in deferential terms, or treating him as if he were porcelain and yourself only earthernware." [1]

The fact that Bryce was able to find any consolation whatsoever in such a notion of equality says more about English than American values. The idea of "bowing down" is so alien to the American character that its absence is more in the nature of things, than an explicit victory for equality. To a hungry immigrant on New York's Lower East Side or an Illinois farmer fighting the railroad combines, Bryce's words would have been little solace indeed. Having overcome the English preoccupation with social deference, Americans were interested in equality in a more tangible sense.

Putting aside Bryce's digression, however, we can see why in discussing equality he was concerned to know about conditions of *economic* equality. For like Tocqueville, Bryce realized that political equality could be attained only if there were a "certain equality in civil society," an idea which, the Affluent Society notwithstanding, we would be hard pressed to refute today.

The fact that there is so little discussion today about equality—let alone the relation between political and economic equality—suggests how far we have come even from the days of Bryce. In accepting the myth of an affluent and homogeneous middle class, the New Class banished the idea of equality from political and economic discussion; yet now having seen how far we are from such an imagined world, it seems necessary to reopen the debate. But to do so requires us to examine equality as it was expounded by the Founding Fathers, and to see what role it played in their ideas of a just and humane world.

In order for us to accomplish even that preliminary task, however, it is necessary to go back and examine the thought of men like Rousseau, who, though not the direct inspiration of Americans, nonetheless served to summarize the spirit of equality in the eighteenth century which the American revolutionaries imbibed.

1

To Rousseau the idea of equality was as indispensable to the notion of democracy as liberty. He declared frequently that he could not imagine a democratic world in which there was no equality, and devoted himself on several occasions to attacks on the existing inequality of his age. Of these attacks perhaps none is more famous than his "Essay Upon the Origins of Inequality Among Men," written in 1754, and designed as a major critique of the social rationalizations of inequality, which though long under attack were only then beginning to crumble. The essay needs to be examined at some length in order to understand the feelings we shall see arising later in Americans like Jefferson.

The crux of the essay is Rousseau's attempt to establish what life in a state of nature was like before civilization asserted its "corrupting" influence. In doing so, he was not establishing any new convention, but relying on an older European fascination with man in his primitive state—a fascination, however, which until the time of Rousseau had been used to justify inequality.

Rousseau looks at man both in the state of nature and in existent civilization and finds, as have earlier conservative critics, inequality. But unlike earlier writers, Rousseau says that instead of confirming the necessity and desirability of inequality in civilization, the examination of inequality in the state of nature undermined any support for inequality in civilization. For instead of one kind of inequality in both states, Rousseau distinguishes two kinds, one of which he calls "natural" inequality, the other, "political" or "moral" inequality.

The former, seen most clearly in the state of nature, "consists in a difference of age, health, bodily strength, and the qualities of mind or of the soul." The latter, which is the essence of civilization, "depends on a kind of convention, and is established, or at least authorized by the consent of men." It consists of "the different privileges which some men enjoy to the prejudice of others; such as that of being more rich, more honoured, more powerful, or even in a position to exact obedience."

To look for the origins of natural inequality Rousseau thought a pointless effort "because that question is answered by the simple definition of the term." But to enquire into the origins, and hence the justifiability, of "political" inequality Rousseau believed to be one of the most important tasks an intelligent man could perform.

Thus after careful analysis of man "in the state of nature," and of what he believed was the evolution from this state to the present state of social inequality, Rousseau set about explaining the forms and interrelationships of inequality in present society: "These differences," he wrote, "are of several kinds; but riches, nobility or rank, power and personal merit [are] the principal distinctions by which men form an estimate of each other in society." And of these four chief categories of inequality, one is paramount. "I could show," he explained, "that among these four kinds of inequality, personal qualities being the origin of all the others, wealth is the one to which they are all reduced in the end; for, as riches tend most immediately to the prosperity of individuals, and are easiest to communicate, they are used to purchase every other distinction." [2] Here we need to dwell for a moment on what

Rousseau means: that "among these four kinds of inequality
. . . wealth is the one to which they are all reduced in the
end." Looking around him, Rousseau had seen that it was
wealth (wealth and income in modern terms) which bought
not only advantage, but also guaranteed privilege, that not
only sanctioned inequality, but was the chief rationale for its
existence. While one might want to modify the emphasis a
little for modern times, the general truth would seem to hold
nonetheless, and point out why economic inequality seemed
to Rousseau, as to Tocqueville and Bryce, inseparable from
any discussion of social and political equality.

Rousseau concludes his essay by proposing a further study
of the consequences of inequality. These concluding para-
graphs have become famous for their impact on subsequent
political thought, and deserve to be quoted at length in order
to understand why men like Jefferson and Paine could feel
equality to be one of the most critical social issues in the
young American republic.

Rousseau begins by conceding that inequality had not been
all for the bad but that the bad easily outweighed the good.
Rousseau then sets out to catalogue the true consequences of
inequality; he declares that the study he proposes would be
one "in which the advantages and disadvantages of every
kind of government might be weighed, as they are related to
man in the state of nature, and at the same time all the different aspects, under which inequality has up to the present appeared, or may appear in ages yet to come." He continues:

We should then see [in unequal societies] the multitude oppressed from within, in consequence of the very precautions
it had been taken to guard against foreign tyranny. We should
see oppression continually gain ground without its being possible
for the oppressed to know where it would stop, or what legitimate means was left them of checking its progress. We should see
the rights of citizens and the freedom of nations slowly extin-
guished, and the complaints, protests, and appeals of the weak

treated as seditious murmurings. We should see the honour of defending the common cause confined by statescraft to a mercenary part of the people. We should see taxes made necessary by such means, and the disheartened husbandman deserting his fields even in the midst of peace, and leaving the plough to gird on the sword. We should see fatal and capricious codes of honour established; and the champions of their country sooner or later becoming its enemies, and for ever holding their daggers to the breasts of their fellow-citizens. . . . It follows from this survey that, as there is hardly any inequality in the state of nature, all the inequality which now prevails owes its strength and growth to the development of our faculties and the advance of the human mind, and becomes at last permanent and legitimate by the establishment of property and laws. Secondly, it follows that moral inequality, authorized by positive right alone, clashes with natural right, whenever it is not proportionate to physical inequality—a distinction which sufficiently determines what we ought to think of that species of inequality which prevails in all civilized countries; since it is plainly contrary to the law of nature, however defined, that children should command old men, fools wise men, and that the privileged few should gorge themselves with superfluities, while the starving multitudes are in want of the bare necessities of life." [3]

2

Rousseau's thinking had an undeniable impact upon the American Revolution. Adding to the tradition of the English freeman and to the debates inspired by the English Revolution, his ideas fed the mainstream of American political thought at its source. Today, it is fashionable among political historians to dismiss the idea of equality as a relatively inessential part of the American Revolution, an idea much subordinate to that of liberty. While this may have been true of conservatives like Hamilton, it significantly distorts the thought of men like Jefferson and Paine who saw equality along with liberty as the foundation-stones of the new republic. And following Rousseau, these men were concerned lest equality be interpreted to mean merely political, as distinct from, economic equality.

In a particularly well known passage, written late in his life, Jefferson exemplified this concern for equality when he borrowed the natural/artificial distinction Rousseau popularized to set forth his own idea about the relation between two kinds of inequality:

> For I agree . . . that there is a natural aristocracy among men. The grounds of this are virtue and talents. Formerly, bodily powers gave place among the aristoi. But since the invention of gunpowder has armed the weak as well as the strong with missile death, bodily strength, like beauty, good humor, politeness and other accomplishments, has become but an auxiliary ground of distinction. There is also an artificial aristocracy, founded on wealth and birth, without either virtue or talents; for with these it would belong to the first class. The natural aristocracy I consider as the most precious gift of nature, for the instruction, the trusts, and government of society. . . . The artificial aristocracy is a mischievous ingredient in government and provision should be made to prevent its ascendancy.[4]

It is important to realize that Jefferson's faith in his so-called natural aristocracy of virtue and talent depended on prior conditions of general equality. In another famous passage, Jefferson expressed his hope for America:

> I have much confidence that we shall proceed successfully for ages to come, [he wrote to de Marbois] and that, contrary to the principle of Montesquieu, it will be seen that the larger the extent of the country, the more firm its republican structure, if founded not on conquest, but in principles of compact and equality.[5]

How important Jefferson considered equality to be can be inferred not only from these passages, but from his activities during the writing of the Declaration of Independence. Immediately after he wrote that "all men are created equal," he returned to Virginia determined to involve himself in abolishing economic privilege, no matter how small. "At the first session of our legislature after the Declaration of Independence, we passed a law abolishing entails. And this was followed by one abolishing the privilege of primogeniture, and dividing the lands of intestates equally among all their children. . . . These laws, drawn by myself, laid the ax to the foot of pseudo-aristocracy."

The fact that Jefferson did not make even more of economic equality as a prime condition of democracy cannot be imputed to its low priority in his concern, but rather to his conviction that equality was already an accomplished fact in America, and did not so much need to be established as protected. Thus in contrast to those European societies which Rousseau railed against, where the "privileged few gorged themselves with superfluities, while the starving multitudes are in want of the bare necessities of life," Jefferson was able to write:

Of twenty millions of people supposed to be in France, I am of the opinion there are nineteen millions more wretched, more accursed in every circumstance of human existence than the most conspicuously wretched individual of the whole United States.

One criticism levelled against both Jefferson and Rousseau is that despite all their talk of equality, both men used the term in an exceedingly ambiguous fashion, the point being presumably that neither man clearly understood exactly what he meant. In response, it needs to be first emphasized that usage of *equality* often *was* ambiguous. At one point, for example, Jefferson would insist that "all men were created equal" and thereby imply a much narrower sense of equality than he implied by his observation that "an aristocracy of wealth [is] of more harm and danger than benefit to society." At another point, he would adopt the widest possible usage of the term *equality* as when he wrote, "I am ready to say to every human being 'thou art my brother' and to offer him the hand of concord and amity."

But what Rousseau and Jefferson both seemed to realize, and what has escaped the critics of their ambiguity is that the ambiguity surrounding equality is not merely accidental or the consequence of inexact reasoning, but instead the product of the most precise reflection. By insisting that equality was a principle which covered not merely political but economic, educational, and even psychological relations in a democratic society, they were establishing a doctrine with profound social consequences. In essence they were declaring that equality, like liberty, was simultaneously a goal for individual and society alike, a rule for individual and social behavior, and a method for achieving a just society, and eventually a just world. To have specified equality as equal access to voting booths or equal opportunity to run for Congress made little sense to them; it presumed that some elements in the democratic community's life could be isolated and identified as subject to equality, while others could not. They could not predict the exact course which history would take, and to settle issues only for the present seemed to them to threaten the endurance of democracy. Better to establish a principle, however ambiguous, that could serve as a guidepost and a reminder, than a dry set of specific definitions ill-adapted to the vagaries of time.

3

In retrospect, what neither of them seemed to pay enough attention to the possibility that the ambiguity of equality's definition seriously jeopardized its role in American society. To be fair, both men probably realized the difficulty but, as leading theorists in an age of enormous ferment and optimism, hoped that the force of the ideal would overcome its weaknesses.

The first to outline the specific deficiencies of equality in the context of American democracy was Tocqueville. American conservatives had, from the outset of the American Revolution, been concerned with the threat that widespread equality on all fronts represented, but they had hesitated to make a direct assault upon it. Instead, as at the Constitutional Convention, they had stressed the dangers which they believed the "tyranny of the majority" represented to the young republic, and had fought to ensure that Hamilton's "rich and well-born" maintained their control over the key functions of the government and economy.

It may seem ironic that a man who had such high praise for America's egalitarianism should also fear it, but as we shall see, his fears are those peculiar to an earlier age and in need of substantial modification today.

Tocqueville, in contrast to the circumspect conservatives, sought to crystallize his fears in terms of a conflict between equality and liberty. This conflict was to his mind seminal because the two ideals, as Jefferson and Rousseau believed, formed the core of democratic thought; the danger to democracy existed, he felt, not because the ideals could *never* be reconciled (as conservatives thought) but because the one, equality, *threatened* to neglect and destroy the other. "Not that those nations whose social condition is democratic naturally despise liberty," he averred. "On the contrary, they have an instinctive love of it. But liberty is not the chief and constant object of their desires; equality is their idol: they make rapid and sudden efforts to obtain liberty, and, if they miss their aim, resign themselves to their disappointment; but nothing can satisfy them without equality, and they would rather perish than lose it." [6]

The danger of equality moreover was magnified not merely by America's consuming preoccupation with it, but by the very universality of its spirit which Jefferson and Rousseau had considered its greatest strength. The "fundamental fact" of equality, Tocqueville wrote, "extends far beyond the political character and the laws of the country, and that it has no less empire over civil society than over the Government; it creates opinions, engenders sentiments, suggests the ordinary practices of life, and modifies whatever it does not produce."

But curiously what disturbed Tocqueville about the imagined clash of equality and liberty did not include, as the conservatives had feared, a levelling of property and wealth; this
he took partly as an already accomplished fact in America,
partly as the continuous process of any democracy. What he
feared was the political levelling of widespread representation
which, if left unchecked, might lead to suppression of minorities. In other words, he was not so much creating a new argument about the place of equality in a democratic society as he
was reformulating the old aristocratic fear of the people in
terms of the conflict between two ideals which would most
benefit the majority. He was ultimately restating the Federal-
ist No. 10 in more direct language.

The obvious advantage which Tocqueville's formulation
brought to conservatives was the avoidance of an aristocratic
tone in the democratic debate. In place of harangues against
the "masses," the "mob," or the "rabble," whom they saw
threatening their stringently controlled democracy by elites,
conservatives could now use Tocqueville's dichotomy to
"prove" that democracy itself required opposition to equality. Whether or not Tocqueville intended his argument to be
used in this fashion remains unclear; late in his life he wrote
in his diary that "intellectually, I have an inclination for democratic institutions, but I am an aristocrat by instinct—that
is to say, I despise and fear the mob." But this point is moot;
it is enough to suggest how Tocqueville's formulation could
be put to use by those who recognized its implications.

The practical effect of Tocqueville's argument, coupled
with both the growth of industrialism and the spread of sec-
tionalism, was that the wide-ranging interpretation of equality
which Rousseau and Jefferson had sought began to be over-
taken by narrower and narrower interpretations. In general,
it was thought that America had already accomplished all of
the major preconditions for equality: it had representative
government; it possessed none of the shocking extremes of
wealth and poverty so prevalent in Europe; and land, the

source of life in any agrarian culture, was so abundant that the imagination literally could not encompass it. As a result, as "equality" declined as a critical term in democratic theory, "equality of opportunity" arose to take its place.

It would be wrong to argue that the idea of "equality of opportunity" was not in the minds of men like Jefferson and Rousseau long before Tocqueville wrote. Jefferson's phrase "all men are *created* equal" did not imply that all men were of equal talent, equal intelligence, or deserving of exactly equal rewards; nor did Rousseau's distinction between natural and moral inequality suggest preposterously that somehow all men were the same.

But it would be equally wrong to argue that equality of opportunity was *all* that these men had in mind. As suggested earlier, the deliberate ambiguity which the term equality possessed was not the product of slipshod or careless thought; to the contrary, the ambiguity of the term was supposed to provide an ideal flexible enough to adapt to changing social conditions. When Jefferson declared that "I am ready to say to every human being 'thou art my brother' and to offer him the hand of concord and amity," his words were not spoken as an indulgent homily, but out of the deepest sincerity and concern for mankind. His purpose was not merely to establish the procedural equality of legal rights or procedural equality for political representation, but to instill a spirit or tone in American life that would guarantee equality a permanent place in our thought and acts.

Karl Mannheim, in line with this idea that equality of opportunity represented a crucial modification of the original ideal of equality, argues that political necessity compelled conservatives to counter the driving force of liberty and equality by creating their own concept of liberty, a concept which he labels "qualitative liberty." Proponents of "qualitative liberty" wisely enough did not attempt to attack liberty head-on but rather sought to concentrate on the coordinate ideal of equality, emphasizing natural inequalities over social inequalities, and using the liberal notion of individualism against itself by arguing that the bulk of inequalities in society were in fact the result of natural characteristics, rather than social relations. This, according to Mannheim, allowed the conservatives to argue persuasively that "Freedom therefore can only consist in the ability of each man to develop without let or hindrance according to the law and principle of his own personality." [7]

Whether or not it was the conservatives who advanced this notion it is clear who it benefitted: combined with the sharp distinction which nineteenth-century conservatives and liberals alike drew between politics and economics, the doctrine was perfectly suited to protect existing interests and alignments of wealth and property. Even when the original form of equality was able to assert itself, as in the debate over slavery, all but the most radical polemicists shied away from egalitarian phraseology and substituted in its place arguments over freedom and liberty. Thus Lincoln, for example, made the appropriate obeisance to the proposition that "all men are created equal," but emphasized that the Civil War was fought because the nation could not exist "half-slave and half-free." And even men such as William Lloyd Garrison more often than not chose the same course, pledging undying devotion to the cause of Negro *freedom*, but rarely invoking the terminology of black and white *equality*.

Perhaps the issue of slavery, with the added complexity of racism and prejudice, is an unfair example to choose for a discussion of equality; more likely it is not. For it indicates, better than virtually any other issue, how far the idea of equality had been compromised only eighty years after the Revolution. One could propose to give the Blacks freedom, but one could not propose to give them equality in any broad, meaningful sense because already by the middle of the nineteenth century to have released the issue of equality into the American political mainstream would have laid bare too many other inequalities and unleashed too many volatile political debates. It would have meant examining the quickly stratifying income and wealth distribution generated by industrialism, and challenging the sanctity of property which Jefferson had seen as protecting the small farmer and laborer, but which was now rapidly becoming the chief tool of the aggressive entrepreneur against the small farmer and laborer.

The treatment of the Blacks after the Civil War indicates the extent of the failure of equality. Usurped by the idea of equal opportunity, equality played a pitiably small role in the Reconstruction. Congress willingly granted freedom to the Negro and promised the procedural equality of protection before the law via the Fourteenth and Fifteenth Amendments but callously ignored pleas for "forty acres and a mule." In the litany of American political ideals, the accomplishment of freedom and the guarantee of legal rights assured the full extent of equality of opportunity as it was then understood. To have granted more would have challenged the core of the conservatively defined canon and would have intruded upon the myth of the free individual, which was even then disappearing along with the small farm and the frontier.

Had it not been for the increasing misery and conflict created by industrialism, it is doubtful whether equality of opportunity could ever have been given anything but an extremely conservative cast. Certainly the growth of Social Darwinism even more firmly cemented the idea to a conservative mould, so much so that Lord Bryce himself was moved to speculate whether the original American notion of equality could withstand such association, little realizing how vitiated it then was. And the situation of black Americans clearly offered little reason for hope.

The pressures of industrialism, however, forced a reexamination of the concept of equal opportunity and a reassertion of some of the initial themes in the broader Jeffersonian ideal of equality. As it became apparent that the vastly unequal power of industrialists over laborers mocked the ideals of both liberty and equality and threatened the very base of democracy through its sheer size (as well as its specific corruptions), equality of opportunity, to borrow a distinction from Isaiah Berlin, shifted in its definition from negative to positive concerns. No longer was equal opportunity to be interpreted as covering merely those areas where individuals had *opportunity* to enrich themselves, no matter what the consequences, but now was to incorporate those areas where the society would actively intervene to protect the *equal* opportunity of its members.

In practical terms, this change in thinking led to increased emphasis on education; to increased attention to the corruption of government and the abuses of corporations and eventually to antitrust legislation and state and local political reforms; and to an increase in general "public spiritedness" that culminated in the Progressivism of the early twentieth century. Equality, for a brief time, seemed to be enjoying a covert resurgence through a broadened interpretation of the idea of "equality of opportunity."

4

Whatever one may think of it, the transition from the powerful but unspecific egalitarianism of Jefferson to the equality of opportunity which characterized American political thought from Jackson to Taft symbolizes a significant change in national ideals, a conservative retreat from the original notions of the American Revolution. Initially built on the widespread assumption that economic and political equality had been achieved and that the character of equality should henceforth reflect the opportunity offered by a young nation with ample room for growth, equality of opportunity came gradually to serve as an ideological underpinning of Social Darwinism and the principle of laissez-faire. Opportunity was seen as an objective quality inherent in the character of the social system, available to anyone willing to seize it. Those who failed did so not because of the defects of the social system but because of personal inadequacies against which equality of opportunity could not, and should not, offer protection.

This extremely conservative view of equality which served to protect the ambitious individual from social interference was slowly modified as it became obvious that society in general would have to be protected from the tremendous economic and political power small elites were able to accumulate.

Reform movements of one kind or another, acting out of a variety of motivations, reinterpreted the ideal of equal opportunity to justify attacks on corporate power and corruption, governmental corruption, and the inadequacies of a social system designed for an agrarian, rural world, attacks which culminated in the Progressive movement before World War I.[8]

With the end of Progressivism during the war came an end to the second phase of America's interpretation of equality. The "prosperity" of the twenties was especially responsible for removing the bite of arguments for economic equality raised before the war, and passage of the Nineteenth Amendment in theory removed the last major statutory impediment to political equality. The Depression tended to reintroduce the issue of economic inequality on a vast scale, but World War II, followed by postwar "affluence," eventually reasserted the attitude which initially had come to the fore in the twenties.

This third phase, which we seem to be experiencing at present, has been called by Peter Bachrach the age of "democratic elitism." The term is striking because it combines two words we usually consider antonyms, and points to a characteristic of modern life which too many New Class observers have come to accept as a necessity for the operation of America. It dates probably from the twenties, but functions in the present world explicitly as a postwar doctrine adapted to the changing postwar world. Insofar as one can say that the New Class shares an explicit ideology, it could be described best as the ideology of democratic elitism.

The novelty of democratic elitism is its indifference to the classical ideas of American democratic theory. To the extent that ideals such as liberty or equality play any explicit role, they do so as descriptive norms of community belief to be taken account of in social planning, but not to be considered the guiding norms for planners' behavior. Instead the norms which do guide behavior are rationality, efficiency, and economy—norms born in an economic, not a political, vocabulary.

Bachrach phrases this indifference to classical democratic ideas in a somewhat more hostile fashion: he argues that elitism—whether liberal, conservative, revolutionary, or reactionary—bears in common two assumptions totally incompatible with democracy as conceived by men like Jefferson: "all elite theories" he argues, accept "first, that the masses are inherently incompetent, and second, that they are, at best, pliable, inert stuff, or, at worst, aroused, unruly creatures possessing an insatiable proclivity to undermine both culture and liberty." [9] This clearly overstates the case in modern America; the assumption which can be seen as a common thread in New Class thought is remarkably more patronizing and more self-confident: the nature of American life is a technological world requiring a kind of decision-making that relies exclusively on specialists. It seeks to define and deal with America's problems, as President Kennedy put it, in terms of "technical problems, administrative problems . . . which do not lend themselves to the great sort of 'passionate movements.' "

One can see how perfectly compatible with the established role of the New Class this theory of democratic elitism is. By establishing that in fact most decision-making in any society is carried out by an elite minority, democratic elitism appeals to *realism* as a foundation for its role. Second, by asserting that American society can only successfully be described in the language of technology, complexity, and efficiency, the elitism invokes an appeal not only to the reality of the *present* but the necessity for maintenance and cultivation of that reality in the future. And third, by explicitly arguing that fundamental issues like economic inequality have been overcome or are no longer important, the elite shift attention away from their own unique position outside the mainstream of American life, and instead cast themselves in the role of authoritative spokesmen for the majority.

Bachrach illustrates his argument about democratic elitism by pointing to the writings of Robert Dahl. He shows that Dahl, as a prominent political scientist, finds himself in the perplexing position of affirming traditional democratic norms "personally" but publicly advocating that such norms as equality are impossible to attain and, hence, should not be espoused for fear of fostering further "cynicism toward democracy." He finds Dahl reaffirming all of the old myths: that America is fundamentally middle-class; that the complexity of modern, large industrial societies makes traditional notions of equality and liberty untenable; and that inequality, though more severe than might be imagined, is gradually being diminished and will diminish more in the future if we will only hew to our present course of domination by the elite. At best, Dahl concludes, if we are to include equality at all it will have to be narrowly defined as a political equality of opportunity which does not challenge the fundamental inequalities of our society, but provides merely for more equal access of the citizenry to the political process.

How complete the retreat this notion of democracy is from the Jeffersonian dream cannot possibly be overemphasized. In place of democracy, of liberty, of equality, as guiding values to both lead and judge the society in which we live, democracy has become *ipso facto* a description of the existing world, no matter how far short of democracy it falls, and a glorification of that reality in the name of reason, of progress, and of technology. Equality and liberty have been relegated to a museum of political concepts, and their barren descendants erected only where they do not clash with the existing world and do not threaten its stability.

There is something fearful in a nation which has lost sight of its ideals, and that, better than any other phrase, describes the situation of America today. Through New Class myths, it became commonplace to assume that the increased wealth and income which came with the postwar world were being distributed equally or so nearly equally that concern for economic equality could be raised to an icon, spoken of occasionally and regarded with awe, but no longer acted upon, because the idea represented by the icon had already been achieved.

But our investigations have shown clearly that equality in America is an illusion. A nation in which the richest seven or eight percent receive more income than the bottom half is not equal, nor is the nation in which the richest one or two percent own a third of the nation's wealth. It may be more equal than some other country; but this does not make America the home of equality that it so proudly claims to be.

Nor does the grinding poverty still so present in America speak well for the accomplishments of our middle-class world. We have left outside the convenient American myth of affluence half of our population and consigned nearly a third to substandard conditions that appear "affluent" only when compared with the misery of an Asian hovel or Latin American *barrio*. Surely this cannot be the nation to which so many man dedicated "their lives, their fortunes, and their sacred honor."

5

America at this moment is entering a critical stage in its history. In ferment over the Vietnam war, over racism, over pollution, over the crisis of our cities, it seems to be moving out of the mind-set that dominated it during the fifties and sixties. Students, blacks, browns, alienated women, and discontented workers all seem to be groping for some common cause around which to unite.

Most often they speak in terms of freedom and liberation, and mention equality only in passing as if it were already decided and incorporated into the notion of liberation, an analytically *a priori* concept contained in liberation itself. But equality is exactly *not* that: it is *not* a subordinate element in the idea of freedom or liberation but an autonomous, independent concept which stands complementary to the idea of freedom.

It would be comforting to think that as the issue of equality becomes more prominent, and more Americans become aware of the reality of their situation, the present inequalities could be dealt with by a properly guided Congress and president, whose concern was to reestablish the essence of American democracy. But life is not so simple. Advanced industrial capitalism is not unequal by accident but out of necessity. The striking differences in income and wealth which serve as a roadblock to egalitarian democracy cannot be obliterated merely by the passage of legislation. Workers must be paid in unequal scales in order to make them do unpleasant work, just as the owners of capital must be given huge rewards in order to make them invest. No amount of legislation in a private economy can change this economic fact of life.

Nor can these inequities even be significantly reduced, as moderates would have us believe. When the control of an economy rests in private hands, the government has at its disposal few tools with which to encourage equality. It can theoretically redistribute wealth and income through taxation, and it can induce faster growth, hoping thereby that the issue of inequality will disappear as everyone is made affluent. But by now one should realize exactly how limited these tools are. Gabriel Kolko's investigation of income distribution shows that inequalities of income have not changed in over half a century, despite an avowedly progressive tax system frequently "toughened" by Congress. Likewise Robert Lampman's survey of wealth inequalities show how ineffective the tax system has been in redistributing wealth. As for growth as a means of overcoming the sting of inequality, the sum of this book should suggest how ineffective it has been, despite our recent attainment of a trillion-dollar economy.

It would seem then that far from bringing about a resolution of the material scarcity which has plagued mankind throughout history, technology has instead only advanced the debate one step further. Instead of introducing a post-technological Affluent (or Opulent) Society in which problems would be merely a matter of administration and ideology would be brought to an end, technology has instead brought us to a point at which the ideology of equality and freedom must once again be introduced with the same force and power it held for Jefferson and the Founding Fathers.

There are numerous suggestions which an economist could bring to such a debate, but for the time being it seems better that they should be held in abeyance. For to propose them now would make them appear the province of specialists, above the realm of the common man, and so would repeat the original New Class fallacy. Instead it seems better to let the facts speak for themselves, let them enter the dialogue of all Americans, and rely upon the wisdom of Jefferson when he declared, "Whenever the people are well-informed, they can be trusted with their own government; whenever things get so far wrong as to attract their notice, they may be relied upon to set them to rights."

Then we can begin.

Appendix

I have added a few graphs which I thought the reader might find helpful.

Table 1

Share of Income for Each 5 Percent of Recipients, From Lowest to Highest, 1, 2, . . . , 20, and Top 1 Percent

	1–2	3rd	4th	5th	6th	7th	8th	9th	10th	11th	12th	13th	14th	15th	16th	17th	18th	19th	20th	Top 1%
CPS: Families + Unrelated Individuals: Money Income Before Tax																				
1944 CPS	0.84	1.04	1.45	1.86	2.27	2.68	3.10	3.53	3.96	4.41	4.86	5.33	5.82	6.32	6.91	7.62	8.63	10.46	18.90	6.80
1945 CPS	0.84	1.22	1.70	2.15	2.57	2.97	3.35	3.72	4.10	4.48	4.87	5.28	5.72	6.19	6.86	7.60	8.54	10.21	17.62	6.09
1947 CPS	0.72	1.11	1.57	2.01	2.43	2.83	3.22	3.61	4.00	4.39	4.80	5.22	5.66	6.14	6.81	7.58	8.59	10.42	18.91	6.83
1948 CPS	0.71	1.10	1.58	2.03	2.46	2.88	3.29	3.69	4.09	4.48	4.88	5.28	5.69	6.12	6.82	7.48	8.48	10.28	18.65	6.73
1949 CPS	0.64	1.05	1.52	1.97	2.41	2.84	3.25	3.67	4.08	4.49	4.91	5.32	5.75	6.19	6.94	7.65	8.63	10.39	18.32	6.45
1950 CPS	0.58	1.00	1.47	1.93	2.39	2.84	3.28	3.71	4.13	4.54	4.94	5.33	5.71	6.08	6.90	7.65	8.63	10.41	18.49	6.55
1951 CPS	0.61	1.09	1.60	2.08	2.54	2.98	3.40	3.82	4.22	4.61	4.99	5.37	5.74	6.23	6.87	7.50	8.45	10.15	17.77	6.22
1952 CPS	0.63	1.13	1.63	2.10	2.53	2.95	3.35	3.74	4.14	4.53	4.94	5.37	5.83	6.31	6.86	7.54	8.48	10.18	17.76	6.20
1954 CPS	0.54	0.97	1.44	1.90	2.35	2.80	3.24	3.68	4.12	4.56	5.00	5.45	5.90	6.36	6.94	7.79	8.73	10.42	17.81	6.11
1955 CPS	0.62	1.03	1.51	1.97	2.43	2.87	3.31	3.75	4.18	4.60	5.03	5.46	5.89	6.33	7.03	7.69	8.61	10.26	17.43	5.95
1956 CPS	0.63	1.07	1.56	2.03	2.48	2.92	3.35	3.78	4.20	4.62	5.05	5.48	5.92	6.37	6.99	7.65	8.56	10.18	17.18	5.83
1957 CPS	0.68	0.94	1.39	1.85	2.33	2.82	3.32	3.81	4.30	4.77	5.22	5.65	6.05	6.42	7.08	7.73	8.62	10.18	16.82	5.60
1958 CPS	0.66	1.06	1.52	1.99	2.44	2.88	3.33	3.76	4.20	4.63	5.06	5.49	5.93	6.36	7.03	7.84	8.72	10.28	16.83	5.57
1959 CPS	0.65	1.04	1.50	1.95	2.39	2.83	3.27	3.71	4.14	4.58	5.03	5.48	5.94	6.41	7.00	7.72	8.64	10.29	17.43	5.93
1960 CPS	0.64	1.04	1.50	1.95	2.40	2.84	3.27	3.70	4.13	4.57	5.00	5.44	5.89	6.35	7.04	7.67	8.61	10.29	17.66	6.08
1961 CPS	0.67	1.02	1.45	1.89	2.32	2.75	3.18	3.61	4.04	4.48	4.92	5.37	5.83	6.30	7.00	7.76	8.73	10.47	18.18	6.33
1962 CPS	0.71	1.08	1.53	1.97	2.40	2.82	3.24	3.66	4.08	4.52	4.97	5.45	5.95	6.48	7.05	7.81	8.73	10.34	17.21	5.77
1963 CPS	0.77	1.06	1.51	1.95	2.39	2.83	3.27	3.70	4.14	4.58	5.03	5.49	5.95	6.42	7.14	7.76	8.66	10.26	17.09	5.73
1964 CPS	0.77	1.08	1.52	1.95	2.38	2.82	3.25	3.68	4.12	4.56	5.01	5.46	5.93	6.40	7.12	7.81	8.71	10.31	17.13	5.74
1965 CPS	0.85	1.10	1.54	1.97	2.40	2.83	3.26	3.68	4.12	4.55	5.00	5.45	5.92	6.40	7.07	7.74	8.65	10.26	17.19	5.80
1966 CPS	0.94	1.12	1.56	1.99	2.42	2.85	3.28	3.71	4.14	4.58	5.01	5.45	5.90	6.35	7.09	7.71	8.61	10.21	17.08	5.76
1967 CPS	0.94	1.14	1.58	2.00	2.43	2.84	3.26	3.67	4.09	4.52	4.96	5.41	5.88	6.37	7.00	7.64	8.56	10.22	17.50	6.01
1968 CPS	1.03	1.20	1.64	2.07	2.49	2.91	3.33	3.74	4.16	4.58	5.00	5.44	5.89	6.49	6.94	7.54	8.44	10.06	17.05	5.81
OBE: Families + Unattached Individuals: Family Personal Income																				
1947 OBE	1.51	1.50	1.92	2.30	2.64	2.95	3.25	3.54	3.84	4.14	4.47	4.82	5.22	5.66	6.22	6.95	8.05	10.11	20.94	8.39
1950 OBE	1.40	1.43	1.84	2.22	2.57	2.90	3.21	3.52	3.83	4.15	4.49	4.87	5.27	5.71	6.12	6.85	7.97	10.09	21.55	8.83
1955 OBE	1.43	1.49	1.94	2.33	2.69	3.03	3.34	3.65	3.95	4.27	4.60	4.96	5.35	5.79	6.28	6.86	7.90	9.89	20.24	8.03
1960 OBE	1.28	1.40	1.84	2.23	2.59	2.93	3.26	3.57	3.90	4.24	4.60	4.99	5.43	5.92	6.46	7.17	8.28	10.21	19.69	7.46
1961 OBE	1.34	1.40	1.82	2.21	2.56	2.90	3.22	3.55	3.88	4.22	4.58	4.98	5.41	5.90	6.44	7.20	8.33	10.27	19.80	7.50
BLS: Spending Units: Money Income After Tax																				
1950 BLS	2.14	1.98	2.47	2.88	3.25	3.56	3.85	4.11	4.36	4.61	4.89	5.19	5.52	5.92	6.35	6.82	7.63	9.09	15.40	5.25
1960 BLS	2.10	1.84	2.29	2.69	3.06	3.40	3.73	4.04	4.35	4.66	4.99	5.35	5.74	6.18	6.66	7.03	7.79	9.17	14.92	4.90
IRS: All Tax Returns (All) & Joint Returns (JNT): Adjusted Gross Income																				
1948 ALL	1.27	1.36	1.78	2.18	2.54	2.89	3.22	3.54	3.86	4.18	4.52	4.87	5.25	5.65	6.09	6.45	7.54	9.77	23.06	10.15
1950 ALL	1.23	1.40	1.84	2.24	2.60	2.94	3.25	3.56	3.86	4.18	4.52	4.89	5.30	5.75	6.00	6.63	7.77	9.94	22.11	9.34
1955 ALL	1.02	1.18	1.59	1.99	2.38	2.76	3.14	3.51	3.90	4.29	4.70	5.13	5.58	6.03	6.43	7.15	8.25	10.28	20.68	8.10
1960 ALL	0.88	1.04	1.44	1.84	2.25	2.66	3.07	3.49	3.91	4.34	4.78	5.23	5.74	6.19	6.70	7.41	8.48	10.45	20.11	7.61
1964 ALL	0.66	0.90	1.29	1.68	2.09	2.50	2.92	3.36	3.80	4.27	4.74	5.24	5.85	6.26	6.79	7.52	8.63	10.68	20.85	7.98
1966 ALL	0.69	0.83	1.19	1.57	1.98	2.41	2.86	3.33	3.81	4.31	4.83	5.35	5.89	6.44	6.97	7.69	8.77	10.76	20.33	7.58
1967 ALL	0.76	0.83	1.17	1.55	1.95	2.38	2.82	3.29	3.77	4.27	4.77	5.29	5.81	6.33	6.90	7.63	8.75	10.80	20.92	7.95
1955 JNT	1.97	1.79	2.23	2.62	2.96	3.27	3.56	3.83	4.09	4.36	4.64	4.95	5.29	5.65	5.89	6.56	7.58	9.48	19.30	7.63
1960 JNT	1.79	1.70	2.15	2.55	2.91	3.25	3.55	3.85	4.14	4.43	4.74	5.06	5.41	5.80	6.15	6.69	7.68	9.51	18.61	7.13
1964 JNT		1.74	2.19	2.59	2.95	3.28	3.58	3.87	4.15	4.44	4.73	5.05	5.40	5.79	6.16	6.73	7.70	9.50	18.29	6.93
1966 JNT	2.15	1.87	2.29	2.66	2.98	3.27	3.53	3.79	4.05	4.32	4.62	4.95	5.32	5.76	6.26	6.84	7.49	9.07	18.79	7.53
1967 JNT	1.86	1.77	2.23	2.62	2.97	3.28	3.57	3.84	4.10	4.38	4.67	4.99	5.35	5.76	6.23	6.77	7.39	9.05	19.18	7.82

SOURCE: Edward C. Budd, "Postwar Changes in the Size Distribution of Income in the United States," *American Economic Review*, May 1970. This shows the marked stability overall of income distribution since the war, using all three of the government's separate estimates, the CPS (The Current Population Survey, or census), the OBE (Office of Business Economics, discontinued because of unreliability), and the IRS (Internal Revenue Service tax returns, showing after tax income). The seeming decline of the rich's holdings should be read in light of Chapter 10.

Table 2
Percentage of National Personal Income,
Before Taxes, Received by Each Income-Tenth

	Highest Tenth	*2nd*	*3rd*	*4th*	*5th*	*6th*	*7th*	*8th*	*9th*	*Lowest Tenth*
1910	33.9	12.3	10.2	8.8	8.0	7.0	6.0	5.5	4.9	3.4
1918	34.5	12.9	9.6	8.7	7.7	7.2	6.9	5.7	4.4	2.4
1921	38.2	12.8	10.5	8.9	7.4	6.5	5.9	4.6	3.2	2.0
1929	39.0	12.3	9.8	9.0	7.9	6.5	5.5	4.6	3.6	1.8
1934	33.6	13.1	11.0	9.4	8.2	7.3	6.2	5.3	3.8	2.1
1937	34.4	14.1	11.7	10.1	8.5	7.2	6.0	4.4	2.6	1.0
1941	34.0	16.0	12.0	10.0	9.0	7.0	5.0	4.0	2.0	1.0
1945	29.0	16.0	13.0	11.0	9.0	7.0	6.0	5.0	3.0	1.0
1946	32.0	15.0	12.0	10.0	9.0	7.0	6.0	5.0	3.0	1.0
1947	33.5	14.8	11.7	9.9	8.5	7.1	5.8	4.4	3.1	1.2
1948	30.9	14.7	11.9	10.1	8.8	7.5	6.3	5.0	3.3	1.4
1949	29.8	15.5	12.5	10.6	9.1	7.7	6.2	4.7	3.1	0.8
1950	28.7	15.4	12.7	10.8	9.3	7.8	6.3	4.9	3.2	0.9
1951	30.9	15.0	12.3	10.6	8.9	7.6	6.3	4.7	2.9	0.8
1952	29.5	15.3	12.4	10.6	9.1	7.7	6.4	4.9	3.1	1.0
1953	31.4	14.8	11.9	10.3	8.9	7.6	6.2	4.7	3.0	1.2
1954	29.3	15.3	12.4	10.7	9.1	7.7	6.4	4.8	3.1	1.2
1955	29.7	15.7	12.7	10.8	9.1	7.7	6.1	4.5	2.7	1.0
1956	30.6	15.3	12.3	10.5	9.0	7.6	6.1	4.5	2.8	1.3
1957	29.4	15.5	12.7	10.8	9.2	7.7	6.1	4.5	2.9	1.3
1958	27.1	16.3	13.2	11.0	9.4	7.8	6.2	4.6	3.1	1.3
1959	28.9	15.8	12.7	10.7	9.2	7.8	6.3	4.6	2.9	1.1

SOURCE: Gabriel Kolko, *Wealth and Power in America* (New York, 1962).
While over ten years old, this supplements Table I in showing the continuity
of maldistribution back to almost the beginning of this century.

Table 3

Distribution of Various Types of Personal Wealth, 1962

	Wealthiest 20%	Top 5%	Top 1%
Total wealth	76%	50%	31%
Corporate stock	96%	83%	61%
Businesses and Professions	89%	62%	39%
Homes	52%	19%	6%

SOURCE: Ackerman et al., *Income Distribution in the United States*. Assembled from various sources, this is an estimate of maldistribution of wealth.

Table 4
Median Earnings, 1969 and 1958, and Percent Change.
for Civilians 14 Years Old and Over Working Year Round Full
Time, by Occupation of Longest Job

	1969	
Occupation	Male	Female
All occupations	$8,455	$4,977
Professional, technical, and kindred workers	11,750	7,308
Self-employed	20,279	(B)
Salaried	11,427	7,312
Farmers and farm managers	4,108	(B)
Managers, officials, and propr's, exc. farm	11,015	5,847
Self-employed	7,830	3,617
Salaried	11,849	6,226
Clerical and kindred workers	7,942	5,161
Secretaries, stenographers, and typists	(B)	5,364
Other clerical workers	7,930	5,024
Sales workers	9,233	3,708
Retail trade	7,436	3,559
Other sales workers	10,372	4,925
Craftsmen, foremen, and kindred workers	8,741	4,957
Foremen	9,792	5,265
Craftsmen	8,507	4,495
Operatives and kindred workers	7,324	4,301
Durable goods manufacturing	7,520	4,996
Nondurable goods manufacturing	6,996	4,018
Other industries	7,252	3,739
Private household workers	(B)	1,706
Service workers, exc. private household	6,333	3,632
Farm laborers and foremen	3,051	(B)
Laborers, exc. farm and mine	6,024	(B)

B Base less than 75,000
SOURCE: U.S. Census, *Current Population Reports*, Series P—60, No. 75.
Although medians tend not to show the disparity between income groups
quite as clearly, I have included this to show a rough breakdown of income
by occupation. Note the incomes of the self-employed professional and
salaried versus the number of incomes that fall below the median. This was
a year when the Bureau of Labor Statistics considered $10,000 necessary
for "modest comfort" for the average family.

Table 5

Lifetime and Mean Income of Males 25 Years Old and
Over, by Years of School Completed: 1949 to 1968
[Prior to 1961, excludes Alaska and Hawaii. Includes members of the
Armed Forces living off post or with their families on post, but excludes
all other members of the Armed Forces. Figures for lifetime income
based on application of appropriate life tables to arithmetic mean income, by age, as obtained for a cross section of population in each year
shown]

Year	Elementary		High School		College	
	0–7 Years	8 Years	1–3 Years	4 Years	1–3 Years	4 Years or more
Lifetime income ($1,000):						
1949.	91	123	142	175	202	287
1956 [1].	122	166	189	228	268	359
1961 [1].	142	192	223	257	325	437
1967:						
Computed from grouped data [1].	183	246	283	338	401	558
Computed from ungrouped data [2].	177	240	275	325	383	529
1968, computed from ungrouped data [2].	196	258	294	350	411	586
Annual mean income:						
1949.	$2,062	$2,829	$3,226	$3,784	$4,423	$ 6,179
1956 [1].	2,574	3,631	4,367	5,183	5,997	7,877
1961 [1].	2,998	4,206	5,161	5,946	7,348	9,817
1967:						
Computed from grouped data [1].	3,715	5,280	6,529	7,907	9,229	12,532
Computed from ungrouped data [2].	3,606	5,189	6,335	7,629	8,843	11,924
1968, computed from ungrouped data [2].	3,981	5,467	6,769	8,148	9,397	12,938

[1] Estimates based on a series of estimated mean values for specific income
class intervals.
[2] Improved methodology introduced in 1967 permits the computation of
data based on actual reported amounts.
SOURCE: Bureau of the Census; *Current Population Reports*, Series P–60,
No. 66, and unpublished data.

Now notice the correlation between income and education, and
the fact that each year the absolute difference in incomes between the groups has been growing, not lessening. Then remember that only one in ten adults has graduated from college.

Table 6

Family Income in 1965	Percentage of 1966 High School Graduates Who Started College by February, 1967
Under $3,000	19.8%
$3,000–$4,000	32.3%
$4,000–$6,000	36.9%
$6,000–$7,000	41.1%
$7,500–$10,000	51.0%
$10,000–$15,000	61.3%
Over $15,000	86.7%
Total, all incomes	46.9%

SOURCE: *Current Population Reports*, Series P-20, No. 185, table 8.

Since education is becoming so critical for material security, try to recognize the disadvantage the poor and the deprived are under directly proportional to their lack of schooling. Also, just because the poor are so limited in means, when they are able to afford higher education, they enter junior colleges, or will not complete four-year courses. This explains the high entry rate, but low graduation rate, of colleges and universities overall.

Table 7

Father's Occupation When Son Was 16	Son's Occupation in March, 1962			
	Total	White Collar	Blue Collar	Farm
White-Collar	100.0%	71.0%	27.6%	1.5%
Blue-Collar	100.0%	36.9%	61.5%	1.6%
Farm	100.0%	23.2%	55.2%	21.6%
Total	100.0%	40.9%	51.4%	7.7%

SOURCE: Calculated from Peter M. Blau and Otis D. Duncan, *American Occupational Structure*, Table J2.1 p. 496. The data were obtained from a Census Bureau survey of 20,000 men.

If reports on educational opportunities were revealing, so too this study of continuity in occupation between generations should show that white-collar fathers beget white-collar sons, and blue-collar-fathers beget blue-collar sons. If upward mobility and equal opportunity are to be the way out of our present inequalities, these figures will have to change drastically.

Table 8

| Income Classes | 1965 Taxes | | |
	Federal	State and Local	Total
Under $2,000	19	25	44
$ 2,000– 4,000	16	11	27
4,000– 6,000	17	10	27
6,000– 8,000	17	9	26
8,000–10,000	18	9	27
10,000–15,000	19	9	27
15,000 and over	32	7	38
Total	22	9	31

As a final reminder to those who feel that government is combating inequality, this table is offered. Assume that the federal tax on the $15,000 and over group is not as high as stated, because of the numerous means available for concealing non-wage income unavailable to the lower classes.

SOURCE: Joseph Pechman, "The Rich, the Poor and the Taxes They Pay," *The Public Interest*, Fall 1969.

Notes

Chapter 1

1. Paul A. Samuelson, *Economics: An Introductory Analysis*, 7th ed. (New York, 1967), p. 112.

2. Jeremy Main, "Good Living Begins at $25,000 a Year," *Fortune*, May 1968.

3. "Income in 1969 of Families and Persons in the United States," U.S. Census Bureau, *Current Population Reports* (Series P-60, no. 75) and *Statistical Abstract of the United States, 1971* (Washington, D.C. 1972) p. 317, Table 504 and p. 332, Table 513.

4. *Statistical Abstract of the United States, 1970* (Washington, D.C., 1970), p. 321, Table 485.

5. Federal Reserve Board, *Survey of Financial Characteristics of Consumers* (Washington, D.C., 1966), Tables A2, p. 98 and A8, p. 110.

6. Arthur Shostak, *Blue Collar Life* (New York, 1969), p. 274.

7. Ibid., p. 275.

8. *Statistical Abstract 1970*, p. 111, Table 161.

9. *Survey of Financial Characteristics of Consumers*, p. 106, Table A6.

10. Bureau of Labor Statistics, "Three Budgets for an Urban Family of Four Persons: Final Spring 1970 Cost Estimates," (Washington, D.C., 1971).

11. Ibid.

Chapter 2

1. David Riesman, *The Lonely Crowd* (New York, 1955), p. 20.

2. S. M. Miller and Martin Rein, "Poverty and Social Change," in Louis A. Ferman et al., *Poverty in America* (Ann Arbor,' 1965), p. 497.

3. John Kenneth Galbraith, *The Affluent Society* (New York, 1958), p. 253; cf. Harold G. Vatter *The US Economy in the 1950s* (New York, 1963) for an objective presentation.

4. Zbigniew Brzezinski, quoted in James Carey and John Quirk, "The Mythos of the Electronics Revolution," *The American Scholar* Spring 1970, p. 221.

5. Galbraith, p. 342.

6. William H. Whyte, *The Organization Man* (New York, 1956), p. 7.

7. Ibid., p. 3.

8. Riesman, pp. 40–43.

9. Whyte, pp. 402–403.

10. Riesman, p. 349.

Chapter 3

1. Arthur Schlesinger, Jr., *A Thousand Days* (Boston, 1965), pp. 645–646.

2. Ibid., p. 931; see also James L. Sundquist, *Politics and Policy: The Eisenhower, Kennedy, and Johnson Years* (Washington, D.C., 1968).

3. Michael Harrington, *The Other America* (New York, 1962), p. 71.

4. Ibid., p. 15.

5. John C. Donovan, *The Politics of Poverty* (New York, 1967), pp. 37–38.

6. Daniel P. Moynihan, "The Professionalization of Reform," *The Public Interest*, Fall 1965, p. 8.

7. Daniel P. Moynihan, *Maximum Feasible Misunderstanding* (New York, 1969).

Chapter 4

1. John Kenneth Galbraith, *The Affluent Society* (New York, 1958), p. 323.

2. This and preceding quotation are from Sidney Lens, *Poverty: America's Enduring Paradox* (New York, 1969), ch. 3.

3. Ibid., p. 22.

4. Ibid., pp. 31–32.

5. Jesse Lemisch, "The American Revolution from the Bottom Up," in Barton J. Bernstein, ed., *Towards a New Past* (New York, 1968), pp. 7–8.

6. Lens, p. 60.

7. Ibid., pp. 65–66.

8. Alexander Hamilton, "Report on Manufactures," quoted in Lens, p. 81.

9. Harold V. Faulkner, *American Economic History*, 8th ed. (New York, 1960), p. 130.

10. Ibid., pp. 301–302.

11. Lens, ch. 7.

12. Stephen Thernstrom, *Poverty and Progress: Social Mobility in a Nineteenth-Century City* (Cambridge, Mass., 1964), p. 36.

13. Ibid., p. 37.

14. Ibid., p. 17.

15. Ibid., p. 43.

16. Ibid., p. 95.

17. Ibid., pp. 86–88.

Chapter 5

1. Sidney Lens, *Poverty: America's Enduring Paradox* (New York, 1969), pp. 232–233; also George Soule, *The Prosperity Decade* (New York, 1968), esp. chs. 10 and 13.

2. Richard Hofstader et al., *The American Republic* (Englewood Cliffs, N.J., 1959), vol. 2, p. 461.

3. Lens, ch. 16.

4. Gabriel Kolko, *Wealth and Power in America* (New York, 1962), pp. 13–14.

5. Joseph Pechman, "The Rich, the Poor and the Taxes They Pay," *The Public Interest*, Fall 1969, p. 22.

6. Robert Lampman, *The Share of the Top-Wealth-Holders in National Wealth 1922–56* (Princeton, 1962), p. 24, Table 6.

7. Ibid., p. 24.

8. Kolko, pp. 13–16.

9. *Statistical Abstract 1970*, p. 323, Table 490.

10. Robert and Helen Lynd, *Middletown* (New York, 1956), p. 5.

11. Herbert Gans, *The Levittowners* (New York, 1967), p. 419.

12. Lynd and Lynd, p. 253.

13. Ibid., p. 103. Other housing figures also from ch. 9.

14. John Kenneth Galbraith, *The Affluent Society* (New York, 1958), p. 201.

15. Lynd and Lynd, pp. 46–47.

16. Ibid., pp. 84–85.

17. Ibid., p. 87; cf. William Leuchtenburg, *The Perils of Prosperity, 1914–32* (Chicago, 1958) esp. ch. 6 for the comparison of the 20s and 50s.

Chapter 6

1. Linda Hall et al., "Nixon's Guaranteed Annual Poverty," *Ramparts*, December 1969, p. 64.

2. *Time*, July 27, 1970, p. 8.

3. Mollie Orshansky, "Counting the Poor: Another Look at the Poverty Profile," *Social Security Bulletin*, January 1965, p. 8.

4. U.S. Department of Agriculture, "Dietary Levels of Households in the U.S., Spring, 1965," p. 8.

5. Oscar Ornati, *Poverty Amid Affluence* (New York, 1966), p. 21.

6. "Fighting Inflation," *Life*, August 15, 1969.

7. *Report of the President's Commission on Income Maintenance Programs*, (Washington, D.C., 1969), p. 31.

8. Bureau of Labor Statistics, *Budget* and *Supplement*, 1972.

9. *I. F. Stone's Weekly*, September 9, 1969, p. 1.

10. *Report of the President's Commission*, p. 14.

11. Ibid., p. 32.

12. *Statistical Abstract 1970*, pp. 277, 301.

13. Nathan K. Kotz, *Let Them Eat Promises* (New York, 1969).

14. Ibid., pp. 51–52.

15. Ibid., p. 35.

16. On Hunter and Hollander, see H. M. Douty, "Poverty Programs: The View from 1914," *Monthly Labor Review*, April 1970, p. 70.

Chapter 7

1. John Kenneth Galbraith, *The Affluent Society* (New York, 1958), ch. 7.

2. *Income in 1969 of Families and Persons*, p. 19, Table 2 and p. 26, Table 11.

3. Federal Reserve Board, *Survey of Financial Characteristics of Consumers*, Table A8, p. 110.

4. Robert Lampman, *The Share of the Top-Wealth-Holders in National Wealth 1922–56* (Princeton, 1962), pp. 192–93, Table 90, p. 213, Table 99.

5. James Smith and Staunton Calvert, "Estimating the Wealth of the Top Wealth-Holders from Estate Tax Returns," *Proceedings of the American Statistical Association*, September 1965, p. 19.

6. Ferdinand Lundberg, *The Rich and the Super-Rich* (New York, 1968), p. 11.

7. U.S. Treasury, I.R.S., *Statistics of Income 1962*, Supp. Report, *Personal Wealth* (Washington, D.C., 1967) pp. 1–3.

8. Jeremy Main, "Good Living Begins at $25,000 a Year," *Fortune*, May 1968.

9. Ibid.

10. Gabriel Kolko, *Wealth and Power in America* (New York, 1962), p. 125.

11. Data on Executives from Robert Diamond, "A Self-Portrait of the Chief Executive," *Fortune*, May 1970.

12. "Good Living."

13. Lundberg, pp. 35–36.

14. Arthur Lewis "America's Centimillionaires," *Fortune*, May 1968.

Chapter 8

1. Jerome Rosow, "The Problem of the Blue-Collar Worker," (Washington, D.C., 1970), p. 1.

2. Ibid., p. 2.

3. Ibid., p. 3.

4. Ibid., p. 4.

5. "The Troubled American," *Newsweek*, October 6, 1969.

6. Arthur Shostak, *Blue Collar Life* (New York, 1969), p. 28; earning figures in *Statistical Abstract, 1970*, p. 230, Table 341.

7. Shostak, p. 29.

8. Rosow, p. 5.

9. *Economic Report of the President, 1969*, quoted in Joseph Pechman, "The Rich, the Poor and the Taxes They Pay," *The Public Interest*, Fall 1969, p. 33.

10. Shostak, pp. 235–236.

11. Dan Cordtz "Change Begins in the Doctor's Office," *Fortune*, January 1970.

12. Lee Hansen, "Income Distribution Effects on Higher Education," *American Economic Review*, May 1970, p. 337.

13. Bureau of Labor Statistics, *Employment and Earning Statistics for the U.S. 1909–68* (Washington, D.C., 1968).

14. National Industrial Conference Board, *Economic Almanac 1967–68* (New York, 1967), pp. 76–77.

15. "The Troubled American," *Newsweek*.

16. Leon Keyserling, *Progress or Poverty: The U.S. at the Crossroads* (Washington, D.C., Council on Economic Priorities, 1964).

Chapter 9

1. *The New York Times*, December 9, 1970, p. 34.

2. *Statistical Abstract 1970*, p. 327, Table 497.

3. Ibid., p. 686, Table 1096.

4. Ibid., p. 110, Table 159.

5. Ibid., p. 111, Table 161.

6. Hansen, p. 338.

7. Gabriel Kolko, *Wealth and Power in America* (New York, 1962), p. 116; Burton Clark, *Open-Door College: A Case Study* (New York, 1966), p. 128.

8. Robert Dahl, *Who Governs?* (New Haven, Conn., 1961), pp. 288 and 291.

Chapter 10

1. R. H. Titmuss, introduction to Richard H. Tawney, *Equality* (London, 1964), p. 19; see also R. H. Titmuss, *Income Distribution and Social Change* (London, 1962).

2. Lee Soltow, *Toward Income Equality in Norway* (Madison, Wisc., 1965), ch. 1.

3. John Kenneth Galbraith, *The New Industrial State* (New York, 1967), p. 399.

4. Ibid., p. 398.

5. Ezra J. Mishan, *The Costs of Economic Growth* (New York, 1967) for a popular handling of this subject.

6. "Watts Unemployment Rises 61%," *L. A. Times*, August 7, 1970.

7. Henry S. Reuss, quoted in the *Los Angeles Times*, May 9, 1971; see also the introduction by Reuss, in Joseph A. Ruskay and Richard Osserman, *Halfway to Tax Reform* (Bloomington, Ind., 1970).

8. Joseph Pechman, "The Rich, the Poor and the Taxes They Pay," *The Public Interest*, Fall 1969, p. 28, Table 4.

9. Gabriel Kolko, *Wealth and Power in America* (New York, 1962), chs. 3 and 4.

10. John Gurley, "Federal Tax Policy: a Review Article," *National Tax Journal* 20, no. 3 (September 1967), p. 321.

11. Joseph Pechman, *Federal Tax Policy* (Washington, D.C., 1966), p. 182.

12. *Economic Report of the President, 1969*, quoted in Pechman, "The Rich, the Poor and the Taxes They Pay," p. 33, Table 5.

13. These estimates are based on Donald Light, "Income Distribution: The First Stage in the Consideration of Poverty," *Occasional Papers of the Union for Radical Political Economics*, no. 1 (Cambridge, 1969), pp. 1–8.

14. Pechman, "The Rich, the Poor, and the Taxes They Pay," p. 43.

Chapter 11

1. James Bryce, *The American Commonwealth* (London, 1889), pp. 606–607.

2. Jean–Jacques Rousseau, *The Social Contract and Discourses*, trans. G. D. H. Cole (New York, 1941), pp. 232–233.

3. Ibid., pp. 234–235.

4. *Democracy: by Jefferson*, ed. Saul K. Padover (New York, 1939), p. 126.

5. Ibid., p. 45.

6. Alexis de Tocqueville, *Democracy in America* (New York, 1955), p. 54.

7. Karl Mannheim, "Conservative Thought," *Essays on Sociology and Social Psychology* (London, 1953), p. 106.

8. Grant McConnell, *Private Power and American Democracy* (New York, 1967) for a careful analysis of the failure of Progressivism.

9. Peter Bachrach, *Theory of Democratic Elitism* (Boston, 1967), p. 2.

In addition there are a number of works not cited in the text which I believe may be of use or interest to the reader, and which I have listed below:

Frank Ackerman et al., *Income Distribution in the United States* (mimeo., 1970). Available from URPE, Box 287, Cambridge, Mass. An excellent summary of the present state of distribution, plus arguments about its necessity.

Edward C. Budd ed. *Inequality and Poverty* (New York, 1967). A very good introduction to the issues through a selection of readings by well-known economists and social critics.

George Katona and John B. Lansing, "The Wealth of the Wealthy." *Review of Economics and Statistics*, February 1964.

Miller, Herman. *Income Distribution in the United States* (Washington, D.C., U.S. Census Bureau, 1966). Detailed coverage of the subject, plus technical problems of reporting and analysis. His *Rich Man, Poor Man* (New York, 1971) is a nontechnical version of the same subject.

Miller, Herman. *Trends in the Income of Families and Persons in the United States: 1947 to 1960* (Washington, D.C., U.S. Census Bureau, 1963).

Miller, S. M. and Pamela Roby. *The Future of Inequality* (New York, 1971).

Patricia C. Sexton, *Education and Income: Inequalities of Opportunity in our Public Schools* (New York, 1966).

Richard H. Tawney, *Equality* (London, 1931). The book that first made me think the issue was important. Without equal.

Lester Thurow et al., "The American Distribution of Income: A Structural Problem," a study for the Joint Economic Committee, U.S. Congress (Washington, D.C., 1972). This appeared too late to be used, but is the best concise summary of the problem available to date.

Lloyd Ulman and Robert J. Flanagan, *Wage Restraint* (Berkeley and Los Angeles, 1971). Not so much on income distribution per se, but an excellent refutation of those who think wage and price controls will help.

Sheldon S. Wolin, *Politics and Vision* (Boston, 1960). This helped shape much in the final chapter on equality.

Index

Abolition of Poverty, The (Hollander), 112, 113
Adams, John, 59
Affluence, 119
 signs of, 84-85, 146
Affluent Society, xv, xvi, xviii, 3, 4, 5, 15, 20, 29, 37, 47, 52, 76, 77, 119, 123, 151, 152, 154, 184, 188, 207
Affluent Society, The (Galbraith), 29, 33, 38, 86, 118, 172
Aid to Dependent Children (ADC), 105
Agriculture, 74
 subsidies for, 107
Alienation, 139, 141
Alliance for Labor Action, 142
Alliance for Progress, 39
America:
 colonial, 55-60
 concepts of, xvi, xvii, 3-6, 15-17, 21-22, 50, 185, 187, 188, 194, 196, 197, 204, 205, 206
 nineteenth-century, 63-67, 78
American Economic History (Faulkner), 64

American Economics Association, 112
American Economic Review, 160
American Revolution, 58-59, 186, 192, 195, 201
Antipoverty programs, 43, 46, 47, 94, 100, 105
Atomic energy, 23-24, 33
Automation, xv, 3, 9, 10, 20, 135, 140, 148, 150
Automobile, the significance of, 84-85, 88, 155

Bachrach, Peter, 202, 203, 204
Bacon's Rebellion, 58
Bank of the United States, 117
Benson, Ezra Taft, 107
Berle, Adolph, 27
Black poor, 44
Blue-Collar Life (Shostak), 10, 12
"Blue-Collar Worker, The Problem of the," 134
Blue-collar workers, 9-12, 16, 23, 135-40, 145, 147, 148, 161
Brook, Eugene, 134
Brookings Institution, 78-79, 80

Bryce, Lord, 187-88, 191, 200
Brzezinski, Zbigniew, 24-25
Budgets, xvi
  estimated moderate, 14-15
  BLS, 99-100, 104, 141, 151, 180
  food, 95-97, 100, 109
  OEO, 100
  poverty, 95, 96-97, 99
  See also Living standards
Bundy, McGeorge, 40
Bureau of Labor Statistics (BLS)
  budgets set by, 14-15, 79, 99-100,
  104, 180
Burnham, James, 27
Burns, Arthur, 23, 118

Cambodia, 183
Capitalism, 61, 118, 131, 136
"Case" poor, 21-22
Children, Aid to Dependent
  (ADC), 105
Children, deprived, 110-11
Citizen's Crusade Against Poverty,
  46
Civil rights, 36, 41-42, 141-42
Civil War, 58, 168, 199, 200
Clark, Burton, 161
Clark, Joseph, 106
Cold War, the, 36
College graduates, 13, 26, 27, 158-
  59, 160
Colonies, American, 56-57
Commodity Distribution Program,
  106-7
Comsat, 43
Communism, xvi, 37
Consumer price index, 98, 112
Cooldige, Calvin, 74
Cooper, John Sherman, 107
Cost of living, 95, 98
  in Middletown, 87
  See also Budgets; Living stan-
  dards
Council of Economic Advisors, 144
Cuba, 36, 39, 42

Dahl, Robert, 162-65, 204
Debt purchasing, 9, 10
  See also indebtedness
Decision-making, 47, 162, 203
Declaration of Independence, 58,
  60, 63, 193, 194

Democracy, 204-5, 206
Depression, the, xvi, 9, 11, 33, 36,
  51-53, 90, 116, 118, 135, 202
Deprivation, xvi, 79, 110, 113, 133,
  151
Djilas, Milovan, 170
Dillon, Douglas, 40
Domestic help, 125
Dubos, René, 184

Economic Opportunity Act, 45,
  46, 47, 48
Economic Report of the President
  (1969), 179
Education, xv, xvii, 14, 25, 32, 34,
  39, 48, 50, 75, 103, 104, 147-48,
  158, 160, 201
Eisenhower Administration, 18, 23,
  36, 37, 42, 76
Elite planning, 46-48
Elitism, 62, 162
  democratic, 202-4
English, Dr. Joseph, 111
Equality, xvi, xvii, xviii-xix, 16, 162,
  163, 185, 186-207
  economic, xviii, 8, 61, 91, 186,
  187, 188, 194, 202, 205
  of income, ix
  middle class, 84
  political, 187, 188, 201, 202, 204
  social, 91
  of wealth, ix
"Estimate of The Income of the
  Very Rich, An" (Smith), x

Farmers, 63, 65, 77, 78
  benefits for, 107-8
Faulkner, Harold, 64, 66
Federal Employment Relief Agen-
  cy, 106
Fifties, the, 18-34, 36, 37, 39, 52,
  53, 54, 63, 76, 77, 80, 86, 87,
  118, 119, 158, 206
  America before, 51-73
Food budgets. See budgets, food
Food for Peace program, 107
Food Stamp Program, 106, 108-10
Ford, Edsel, 79
Ford, Henry, 43, 79
"Forgotten American, the," 139-40
Fortune magazine, 7, 120, 123-26,
  131-32, 156

Founding Fathers, xviii, 16, 58, 186, 189, 207
Franklin, Benjamin, 58
Freeman, Orville, 108
Frost, Robert, 38
Future Shock (Toffler), 5

Galbraith, John Kenneth, xvi, 13, 20-22, 27, 28, 29, 31, 32, 33, 34, 37, 38, 40, 43, 52, 72, 86, 118-20, 133, 154, 162, 171, 172, 173, 180, 183
Gans, Herbert, 83-84
Great Society, 49-50
Green Berets, 39, 42
Greening of America, The (Reich), 5
Garrison, William Lloyd, 199
Gross National Product (GNP), xvi, 3, 22, 123, 179
Growth, xvii, 174, 207
  economic, 22
  selective, 175, 176
"Guaranteed annual income," 113, 180
Gurley, John, 178

Hamilton, Alexander, 61-62, 192, 196
Harrington, Michael, 43, 44, 45, 52, 79, 94, 105, 112, 113
Health, Education and Welfare, Department of (HEW), 95, 96, 103, 104, 111
Heller, Walter, 40
Henrietta, James, 57
High school graduates, 13, 26, 159
Hofstadter, Richard, 78
Hollander, Jacob, 112-13
Hollingshead and Redlich, 105
Home ownership, 9, 11, 85-86, 127, 157
Hoover, Herbert, 74
House Banking Committee, 145, 156, 157
Housing problems, 145, 156-57
Hunger, 93, 106, 108, 111
  See also malnutrition
Hunter, Robert, 112-13

Income
  annual, 6, 23, 125, 126, 127, 143, 146, 149, 151, 153, 157, 165, 179

Black, 176
  concentration of, 117, 118, 120
  equality in, ix
  guaranteed annual, 113, 180
  inequality of, 8
  maximum, 117
  median, 88, 89
  minimum, 88, 117
  of the poor, 9
  per capita, 3, 22
  of the wealthy, x
Income distribution, xi, xii, xiii, xvi, xvii, xix, xx, 6, 8, 22-23, 53, 54, 78, 79-81, 99, 118, 159, 173, 176-77, 205, 207
Income Maintenance Programs, President's Commission on, 99
Income tax. *See* Tax, income
Income vs. need, 123, 136
Indebtedness, 13-14, 86
Industrialism, 53, 62, 71, 76, 167, 170, 171, 197, 200
Industrialization, 62-63, 182
Industrial systems, 172-73
Inequality, 162-63, 165, 170, 189-92, 198, 207
  economic, 169, 171, 191, 204
  four kinds of, 190-91
  in wealth, 118, 120
Infant mortality, 104, 105
Inflation, 10, 89, 98, 104, 114, 140, 174-75, 176
Investment, 78

Jackson, Andrew, 117, 201
Jacobs, Paul, 143
Jefferson, Thomas, xviii, 58, 60, 186, 187, 189, 191, 192-95, 196, 197, 198, 200, 201, 203, 204, 207
Johnson, Lyndon, 35-36, 47, 49, 50, 94

Katona, George, x
Katzenbach, Nicholas, 50
Kennedy, John F., 35-43, 47, 50, 108, 183, 203
Kennedy, Robert, 36, 106
Keyserling, Leon, 151
Khrushchev, Nikita, 36, 39
King, Martin Luther, 36, 41
Kolke, Gabriel, 79-80, 81, 84, 125, 161, 170, 207
Kuznet, Simon, 22, 118, 170

Labor Action, Alliance for, 142
Lampman, Robert, 80-81, 84, 121-22, 170, 207
Land distribution, in colonial America, 56-58, 59-60
Land Ordinance of 1785, 60
Lansing, John B., x
Leisure, xv, 20, 29, 31
Lekachman, Robert, 164
Lens, Sidney, 60
Levi-Strauss, Claude, 168, 185
Levittowners, The (Gans), 83-84
Liberty, 192, 196, 198, 199, 200, 203, 204-5
Lichtman, Richard, 145
Lincoln, Abraham, 199
Linowitz, Sol, 43
Lipset, Seymour M., xii
Living standards, 6, 14, 89, 137, 169
Locke, John, 58
Lonely Crowd, The (Riesman), 19
Lowe, Dr. Charles, 111
Lundberg, Ferdinand, 122, 131
Lynd, Helen and Robert, 82-83, 85, 86, 87, 88

McCarthy, Joseph, 37, 77
McGovern, George, 101
McNamara, Robert, 40, 42, 50
McRea family, study of the, 153, 154, 156, 157, 158, 164, 165
Main, Jackson Turner, 57, 62
Malnutrition, xv, xviii, 5, 93, 96, 105-6, 108, 110, 111, 174
Managerial Revolution, The (Burnham), 27
Managers, 12-13, 16, 17, 27, 28, 29, 40, 43, 75
Mannheim, Karl, 198, 199
Marx, Karl, 63
"Maximum feasible participation," 48-49, 100, 114
Means, Gardiner, 27
Meany, George, 142
Mechanics Union of Trade Associations, 65
Medical care, 104, 145-46
Michigan, University of, Survey Research Center, 81
Middle Class, x, xi, xv, xx, 15-16, 164, 168-69

Black, 176
definition of, xvii, xviii, 163
lower, 7, 8, 9, 34, 53, 54, 77, 88, 89, 91, 134-52, 143, 169
meaning of, 6-7
upper, xvii, xviii, 7, 8, 12, 34, 53, 54, 64, 66, 81, 83, 91, 153-66, 182, 183
Middletown (Lynd), 82
Middletown, 82-88
Miller, Herman, 139, 141
Miller, S. M., 20
Millionaires, 126, 130-32, 179
Mills, C. Wright, 37, 161
Mitchell, William C., xi-xii
Modern Corporation and Private Property, The (Berle and Means), 27
Moonlighting, 137
Mortgages, 86, 88, 156, 157
Moynihan, Daniel P., 47
Muncie, Indiana, case study of, 82-88

NASA, 43
National Defense Educational Act (NDEA), 25-26
National Food Consumption Survey, 108
National Industrial Conference Board, 149
National Institutes of Health, 111
National School Lunch Program, 106
National Welfare Rights Organization, 114
Need vs. income, 123, 136
Negroes, 44, 175, 200
in colonial America, 57, 62
freedom for, 199, 200
problems of the, 175
See also Slavery
New Beginnings, 93, 111-12, 113, 114, 154
Newburyport, Mass., community study of, 68-72, 82, 85
New Class (American), xvi, xviii, 13, 17, 27-29, 32-34, 36-50, 64, 66, 75, 118, 119, 120, 132-33, 135, 148, 152, 153, 154, 162, 164, 165, 171, 172-73, 182-84, 202-3, 205, 207

New Class (Communist or social-ist), 71
New Deal, xi, 117, 118, 135
New Frontier, 36, 38, 42, 49, 50
New Industrial State, The (Gal-braith), 162, 171
"New money," 131, 132
Newsweek, 139, 142, 150
New World
  emigration to the, 55
  wealth and poverty in the, 57-58
Nineteenth Amendment, 202
Nixon, Richard, 36, 98, 113, 114, 134, 139, 142, 143, 180, 181
Norris, George, 78

Office of Economic Opportunity (OEO), 45, 46, 48, 49, 98, 114
  budgets set by, 95, 98, 100
"Old money," 132
Open Door College, The (Clark), 161
Opportunity, equal, xviii, 200, 201, 202
Opulence, 153, 158, 165
Opulent Society, xviii, 153, 207
Organization Man, The (Whyte), 12, 28
Organization Man, 29, 31, 40
Ornati, Oscar, 96-97
Orshansky formula, 95
Other America, The (Harring-ton), 43, 94, 112

Paine, Thomas, xviii, 58, 191, 192
Palmer Raids, 77
Pauperism, Society for the Pre-vention of, 67
Peace Corps, 36, 39
Peckman, Joseph, 80, 84, 178, 181
Politics, American, 45, 46
  poverty and, 100-1
Pollution, 75, 174, 206
Poor, the, ix, 7, 8, 9, 15, 44, 46, 48, 49, 53, 77, 91, 92-114, 133, 179-80
  Black, 176
  in Newburyport, 71-72
Poverty (Hunter), 112
Poverty, x, xv-xviii, 4, 5, 7, 21-22, 34, 43, 44, 49, 52, 174, 205
  American Colonial, 57

Citizen's Crusade Against, 40
  decline in, 101, 111
  definitions of, 113, 180
  European, 53
  government definition of, 7, 15, 79, 94, 95, 98, 101
  majority, 90
  modern, 84
  in the twenties, 78, 79
  nineteenth-century, 67-72, 182
  urban, 67
  war on, 42, 43, 45, 46, 93-94, 112, 151, 185
Poverty Amid Affluence (Ornati), 96-97
Poverty and Progress: Social Mo-bility in a Nineteenth-Century City (Thernstrom), 68-70
Poverty level, 98, 99, 102, 114
Power, xi-xiii
Power elite, xi, xii, 34
Professionals, 12-13, 16, 17, 40, 43, 75
Progressivism, 201, 202
Prosperity Decade, The (Soule), 77
Public Interest, The, 80

"Quality of life," 75, 76, 182

Racism, 5, 37, 43, 44, 141, 199
  See also Slavery
Rauh, Joseph, 41
Reagan, Ronald, 177
Recession, 36, 175
Redistribution, 174
  income, 23, 81, 117, 118, 206
  land, 59, 116, 117
  wealth, 117, 176-77, 206, 207
Redlich, Hollingshead and, 105
Reed, John, 57
Reich, Charles, 5
Rein, Martin, 20
Report on Manufactures (Hamil-ton), 62
Reuss, Henry S., 177
Routher, Walter, 142
Revenue-sharing, 181
Rich, the, 7, 8, 15, 53, 54, 78, 81, 91, 115-33, 177, 178
Riesman, David, 19, 30, 31, 32, 33, 37, 52, 183

Rockefeller, John D., Jr., 79
Roosevelt, Franklin D., xi, 52, 106
Rosow, Jerome, 134-37, 139, 140, 143, 144
Rousseau, Jean-Jacques, 189-95, 196, 197, 198
Rusk, Dean, 40, 50

Samuelson, Paul, 6, 23, 121
Savings, xvi, 8, 78, 97, 100, 125-26, 147
Schlesinger Jr., Arthur, 40, 41
School Lunch Program, National, 106, 110
Science, 24, 38, 48, 50, 75, 83, 140
Segregation of the wealthy, 127-29
Service industries, 9, 10, 149
Seventies, the, 167-85
"Shape of Political Theory to Come, The," (Mitchell), xii
Share of the Top Wealth-Holders in National Wealth (Lampman), 121
Shares of Upper Income Groups in Income and Savings (Kugnet), 22
Shostak, Arthur, 10-12, 141
Shriver, Sargent, 45
Sixties, the, 34, 35-50, 52, 75, 76, 80, 96, 100, 102-3, 151, 154, 176, 183, 206
Skilled labor, 65, 66, 70, 78
Slavery, 57, 67, 199
Smith, Adam, 61
Smith, James D., x, xiii
Social Class and Mental Illness (Hollingshead and Redlich), 105
Social Darwinism, xviii, 58, 200, 201
Social Structure of Revolutionary American, The (Main), 57
socialization, 31
Social Security, 103-4, 114, 135, 180
Society for the Prevention of Pauperism, 67
Soule, George, 77
Southern Rural Research Project, 93
Special Milk Program, 106
Speculation, 78
Sputnik, 24, 25, 26

Stevenson, Adlai, 40
Subsidies, agricultural, 107
Suburban life, 31
Survey Research Center, University of Michigan, 81

Taft, William Howard, 201
Tawney, R. H., 119
Tayler, Maxwell, 42
Taxation, xvii, 176-79, 181, 206
Taxes, ix, 143-44
  estate, 178, 179
  federal, 179, 181
  gift, 178, 179
  income, 79, 117, 176-77
  inheritance, 177
  local, 179, 181
  state, 179, 181
Tax Reform Act of 1969, 143
Tax system, x, 144, 207
Technology, xv, 23, 28, 29, 32, 33, 34, 37, 38, 39, 48, 50, 75, 76, 83, 135, 140, 148, 150, 184, 204, 205, 207
Thernstrom, Stephen, 68-70, 82, 85
Thirties, the, 52, 53, 90, 117
Thurow, Lester, 167
Time magazine, 93-94, 95, 146
Times, Los Angeles, 175
Times, New York, 23, 153-54, 155, 156, 164, 165
Titmuss, R. H., 170
Tocqueville, Alexis de, 63, 83, 116, 128, 186, 187, 188, 191, 195, 196, 197, 198
Toffler, Alvin, 5, 6
Transfer payments, 179-80
Travel, 125, 129, 130
Trickle-down theory, 23, 118, 170
Truman, Harry, 156
Tugwell, Rexford, 78, 79
Turner, Frederick Jackson, 66
Twenties, the, 76, 77, 78, 79, 80, 82, 85, 86, 87, 89, 202

Unemployment, 36, 51, 103, 117, 175
Unions, 135, 139, 140, 142
Upward mobility, 159-60, 182
Urban Coalition, 43, 180
Urbanization, 83

Values, changing, 142-43

Veblen, Thorstein, 161
Veterans programs, 104
Vietnam War, 5, 36, 42, 43, 50, 94,
  100, 103, 110, 138, 142, 176, 183,
  206

Wage-price controls, 175
Wages, 10, 13, 16, 51, 66, 67, 77,
  102, 149, 174, 176
  minimums, 102, 113, 117
Warner, Lloyd, 68
Wealth
  American, 116
  concentration of, 117, 118, 120-23
  equality in, ix
  European, 116
  measure of, 120
Wealth and Power in America
  (Kolko)
Wealth distribution, x-xiii, xvi,
  xvii, xix, xx, 6, 9, 22, 53, 54, 80,
  173, 205
Wealth of Nations, The (Smith),
  61

"Wealth of the Wealthy, The"
  (Katona and Lansing), x
Welfare, xx, 113, 144
  expenditures, 103, 104, 105
  in Newburyport, 71
White-collar workers, 9, 16, 135,
  136, 145, 149-50
Who Governs? (Dahl), 162
Whyte, William H., 28, 29, 31-32,
  33, 37
Williams, Colonel Israel, 57
Work, attitudes toward, 28, 29, 89
Working class, xx, 63, 65-66, 85,
  88, 135, 149, 168
Working wives, 10, 89, 137, 138,
  149
World War I, 76, 77
  period preceding, 202
World War II, 51-52, 77
  period following, xvi, xviii, 13,
  53, 75, 117-18, 169, 202

Yankeetown (Warner), 68